Formalising Natural Languages with NooJ 2013

Formalising Natural Languages with NooJ 2013: Selected papers from the NooJ 2013 International Conference

Edited by

Svetla Koeva, Slim Mesfar
and Max Silberztein

CAMBRIDGE
SCHOLARS
PUBLISHING

Formalising Natural Languages with NooJ 2013:
Selected papers from the NooJ 2013 International Conference,
Edited by Svetla Koeva, Slim Mesfar and Max Silberztein

This book first published 2014

Cambridge Scholars Publishing

12 Back Chapman Street, Newcastle upon Tyne, NE6 2XX, UK

British Library Cataloguing in Publication Data
A catalogue record for this book is available from the British Library

ISBN (10): 1-4438-5824-2, ISBN (13): 978-1-4438-5824-3

TABLE OF CONTENTS

EDITORS' PREFACE[1]

NooJ is a linguistic development environment that provides tools for linguists enabling them to construct linguistic resources for formalising a large gamut of linguistic phenomena: typography, orthography, lexicons for simple words, multiword units and discontinuous expressions, inflectional and derivational morphology, local, structural and transformational syntax, and semantics.

For each resource that linguists create, NooJ provides parsers that can apply it to any corpus of texts in order to extract examples or counter-examples, to annotate matching sequences, to perform statistical analyses, etc. NooJ also contains generators which can produce the texts described by these linguistic resources, as well as a rich toolbox allowing linguists to construct, maintain, test, debug, accumulate and reuse linguistic resources.

For each elementary linguistic phenomenon to be described, NooJ proposes a set of computational formalisms, the power of which ranges from very efficient finite-state automata to very powerful Turing machines. This distinguishes NooJ's approach from most of the other computational linguistic tools, which typically offer a single formalism to their users.

Since its release in 2002, NooJ has been enhanced with new features every year. Linguists, researchers in Social Sciences and more generally, professionals who analyse texts have contributed to its development and participated in the annual NooJ conference. In 2013 the European project META-NET CESAR brought a new version of NooJ, based on the Java technology and available to all as an open source AfferoGPL project. Moreover, several companies are now using NooJ to construct business applications in various domains, from Business Intelligence to Opinion Analysis. Silberztein's article "NooJ v4" presents the latest version of the NooJ software, designed to satisfy both the needs of the academic world (through the open source Java version) and the needs of private companies (through the enhanced engineering functionalities).

The present volume contains 18 articles selected among the 43 papers presented at the NooJ 2013 International Conference held on June 3-5, at

[1] We would like to thank Ivelina Stoyanova for her help in ensuring that the texts of all articles are in correct English and Dhekra Najar for her help with the formatting of the final document.

the Deutsches Forschungszentrum für Künstliche Intelligenz GmbH (DFKI, German Research Centre for Artificial Intelligence) in Saarbrücken. These articles are organised in three parts: "Vocabulary and Morphology" contains six articles; "Syntax and Semantics" contains six articles; and "NooJ Applications" contains five articles.

The articles in the first part are focused on the construction of dictionaries for simple words and multiword units, as well as the development of morphological grammars:

— Farida Aoughlis, Kamal Nait-Serrad, Annouz Hamid, Aït-Kaci Ferroudja and Habet Mohammed Said's article "A New Tamazight Module for NooJ" describes the formalisation of the conjugation of a class of Tamazight (Berber) Verbs.
— Kaja Dobrovolic's article "Introduction to Slovene Language Resources for NooJ" presents the first Slovene module for NooJ that contains a large-coverage dictionary of over 100,000 lemmas.
— Maximiliano Duran's article "Formalising Quechua Verb Inflections" presents the inflectional grammar that describes the morphology of verbs in Quechua.
— Sandrine Fuentes and Anubhav Gupta's article "Updated Spanish Module for NooJ" presents the latest version of the Spanish electronic dictionary that has been adapted to NooJ.
— Zoe Gavriilidou and Lena Papdopoulou's article "Derivation of Multiply Complex Negative Adjectives from Verbal Stems in Greek" describes a set of morphological grammars that handles the productive derivation of Greek verbs into adjectives.
— Mario Monteleone and Simonetta Vietri's article "The NooJ English Dictionary" shows how the authors have mined the WIKI English dictionary to construct an electronic dictionary that can be used by NooJ to parse English texts.

The articles in the second part discuss the construction of syntactic and semantic grammars:

— Pilar León-Araúz's article "Semantic Relations and Local Grammars for the Environment" presents the EcoLexicon terminological knowledge database that uses NooJ local grammars to automatically extract from texts hyponymic and meronymic semantic patterns, and can even disambiguate polysemic patterns in certain cases.
— Yury Hetsevich, Sviatlana Hetsevich, Alena Skopinava, Boris

Lobanov, Yauheniya Yakubovich and Yury Kim's article "Describing Set and Free Word Combinations in Belarusian and Russian with NooJ" presents a set of local grammars designed to recognise set and free word combinations such as quantitative expressions in Belarusian and Russian.

— Dehkra Najar and Slim Mesfar's article "Political Monitoring and Opinion Mining for Standard Arabic Texts" presents a set of local grammars used to identify references to political actors and organisations in journalistic texts in the context of opinion expressions, and to produce annotations to mark the opinion holder, the opinion target and the polarity of the opinion (positive or negative).
— Héla Fehri, Kais Haddar and Abdelmajid Ben Hamadou's article "Co-reference Resolution Using NooJ Recognition Process of Arabic Named Entities" presents a system based on local grammars capable of recognising referring expressions and linking them to the named entities (sportive place names) they refer to.
— Valérie Collec-Clerc's article "Adapting Existing Japanese Linguistic Resources to Build a NooJ Dictionary to Recognise Honorific Forms" presents the set of dictionaries and local grammars that the author has created in order to extract from a corpus of Japanese texts sentences that contain honorific expressions.
— Hajer Cheikhrouhou's article "Recognition of Communication Verbs with NooJ" presents the semantic class of communication verbs extracted from the LVF dictionary, and shows how to formalise it with NooJ, adding the Arabic translation for each lexical entry.

The articles in the third part describe applications that use NooJ:

— Sahbi Sidhom and Philippe Lambert's article "Project Management in Economic Intelligence: NooJ as Diagnostic Tool for Nanometrology Cluster" shows how NooJ's morpho-syntactic parser can be associated with a domain-specific knowledge organisation to construct an automatic cluster capable of managing large collections of texts and to extract interactions between actors in the domain.
— Edoardo Salza's article "Using NooJ as a System for (Shallow) Ontology Population from Italian Texts" shows how the author used NooJ capabilities to construct an information extraction

application capable of building an ontology that contains both the concepts in the text and their relations.

— Ralph Müller's article "NooJ as a Concordancer in Computer-Assisted Textual Analysis. The case of the German module" shows how NooJ can be used in literature studies and how a better set of lexical resources would improve NooJ's usefulness dramatically for corpus analyses.
— Kristina Kocijan, Sara Librenjak and Zdravko Dovedan Han's article "Introducing Music to NooJ" presents a system built with NooJ capable of parsing sheet music. The authors have developed a set of "lexical" resources to recognise musical objects such as notes and pauses written using the LilyPond notation, and a set of syntactic grammars to recognise more complex musical objects such as chords and slurs.
— Rania Soussi, Slim Mesfar and Mathieu Faget's article "STORM Project: Towards a NooJ Module within Armadillo Database to Manage Museum Collection" presents a software application that allows users to retrieve information from a corpus of museum text collection, using queries in Arabic, English or French.

This volume should be of interest to all users of the NooJ software because it presents the latest development of the software as well as its latest linguistic resources, which are now free and distributed as open source thanks to the endorsement of the European META-SHARE CESAR project. As of now, NooJ is used as the main research and educational tool at over 30 research centres and universities across Europe and in the world; there are NooJ modules available for over 50 languages; more than 3,000 copies of NooJ are downloaded each year.

Linguists as well as Computational Linguists who work on Arabic, Belarusian, Bulgarian, English, French, German, Greek, Italian, Japanese, Quechua, Russian, Slovene and Spanish, will find in this volume state-of-the-art linguistic studies for these languages.

We think that the reader will appreciate the importance of this volume, both in view of the intrinsic value of each linguistic formalisation and the underlying methodology, as well as the potential for new applications of a linguistic-based corpus processor in the field of Social Sciences.

—The Editors

NooJ V4

Max Silberztein

Abstract

This paper presents the latest version of the NooJ software. We show the need for a major overhaul of the software: the CESAR META-SHARE project as well as the use of NooJ in an industrial environment. From a technical point of view, the fact that there are now three implementations of NooJ, including one in open source, has posed several problems of compatibility and protection of the resources. We present the various technical solutions that we have adopted.

Introduction

From its very beginning, NooJ was designed to become a "total" linguistic development environment, capable of formalising a large gamut of linguistic phenomena: Typography, Spelling, Inflectional and Derivational Morphology, Local and Structural Syntax as well as Transformational Syntax, and Semantics. For each of these levels of linguistic phenomena, NooJ provides users with one or more formalisation tools such as simple dictionaries, finite-state graphs and regular grammars, recursive graphs and context-free grammars, contextual and unrestricted grammars[1].

From the development point of view, NooJ provides linguists with a set of tools that allow them to construct, edit, test, maintain and share elementary pieces of linguistic description, which can be accumulated into consistent packages called NooJ modules. In order to apply the linguistic resources to texts, NooJ also includes a set of parsers that process these modules and access any property they contain — at any level of linguistic phenomena, from Typography to Semantics. NooJ is indeed used for applying linguistic modules to large texts for the purposes of automatic text annotation or information extraction.

---

[1] See (Silberztein 2005) and (Silberztein 2013).

Large linguistic modules for processing potentially large corpora of texts have been used in Social Sciences, e.g. in Psychological and in Literature studies[2], as well as in business-type applications[3]. Finally, the European Community got word of NooJ and the EU Competitiveness and Innovation Framework Programme Project CESAR, led by Prof. Tamas Varadi, decided to use NooJ to develop linguistic resources for several languages[4].

In the framework of the CESAR project, a team of computer scientists at the Mihajlo Pupin Institute (Belgrade) implemented Mono and Java versions of NooJ[5]. In particular, the Java version is now available as an open source package and is freely distributed under a GPL license by the CESAR project (http://www.meta-net.eu/projects/cesar).

Three Implementations for NooJ

NooJ was initially developed in the C# programming language on the .NET virtual machine, developed by Microsoft. The .NET virtual machine runs on all versions of Windows (from Windows XP to Windows 8), therefore NooJ can run on any Windows PC.

Mono-NooJ

Because .NET is proprietary technology, a group of developers decided to create an open source version of it: this initiative became the Mono project[6]. Mono is an open source implementation of Microsoft's .NET Framework based on the standard specifications of the C# programming language and the Common Language Runtime standard (used by .NET's virtual machine). Mono is largely compatible with .NET and can run most software developed with/for .NET. The Mono virtual machine is available for Mac OSX, Linux[7] and Solaris UNIX; therefore, Mono-NooJ can be used on these operating systems as well.

---

[2] See for instance (Ehmann 2012) and (Pignot, Lardy 2012).

[3] See (Sidhom, Lambert 2014). Also: in the framework of the STORM French national research project, Armadillo is constructing a search engine capable of performing queries in Arabic, English and French in a large corpus of Arabic texts that describe Archeological items and Architectural monuments, see (Soussi et alii 2014).

[4] Cf. http://www.meta-net.eu/projects/cesar.

[5] Cf. (Spasic et alii. 2013).

[6] See www.mono-project.com.

[7] Versions 3.X of Mono support the openSUSE desktop interface for Linux.

Note, however, that the Mono and .NET versions of NooJ are not perfectly identical: for instance, the .NET version of NooJ contains a few functionalities that are specific to the Windows operating system (such as DLLs that originated from the Windows or Microsoft Office platforms). Because these functionalities are not available on Linux, UNIX or Mac OSX, the Mono version of NooJ does not contain them: for instance, Mono-NooJ running on Linux would not be able to access neither a Microsoft Office Outlook database, nor a FrameMaker document[8].

The biggest limitation of Mono-NooJ is that it cannot process languages with non-European alphabets such as Arabic (which is written from right to left) and Khmer (in which vowels can be placed above or below consonants). This limitation was impossible to overcome, as the version of Mono available until April 2013 did not process RTF files in these languages correctly. However, the focus of the CESAR project was on European languages, so it was not considered a serious limitation. Despite these limitations, Mono-NooJ has been used by a fairly large number of Linux users.

Java-NooJ

In parallel to the effort to port NooJ on Mono, a second team at the Pupin Institute decided to translate the complete NooJ software source from C# to Java. Although the two languages have a very similar syntax, the amount of work involved proved to be challenging[9].

The two technical problems to be solved were the consequences of the differences between the C# and Java programming languages, and the differences between the .NET and Java graphical user interfaces (GUI). In particular, C# allows various methods to obtain references of parameters (via the "ref" or "out" keywords), whereas Java's methods only accept copies of parameters. To rewrite NooJ methods in Java, the team at the Pupin Institute had to encapsulate all objects that needed to be modified by a C# method, inside new, temporary objects that were then passed to the corresponding Java method. Before each method call, the temporary objects had to be created; after each method call, their content had to be copied back to the initial objects. When the method in question is called recursively, potentially millions of times (for instance, when NooJ's syntactic parser processes a large corpus of texts), this overhead becomes significant.

---

8 These capabilities are added to any Windows system as soon as Microsoft Office is installed. The Mono version of NooJ does have the capability to read .DOC files though. It would be possible to add support to Open Office file formats.

9 Cf. (Spasic et alii 2013).

Another solution would have been to redesign NooJ's data architecture, but that was not possible given this limited resource and time frame.

The second problem was to reconstruct NooJ's GUI, because the API support to construct a GUI in Java is very different than the API support in .NET. The team at the Pupin Institute could not reuse any of the .NET GUI resources. Therefore, they had to redesign a whole new GUI from the ground up. Because of the limited resources available for this project, the Java version of NooJ has a much simpler GUI than its .NET version. However, it is perfectly suitable for educational purposes and Java-NooJ has been used successfully by a large number of students in NooJ tutorials.

In conclusion: we now have three versions of NooJ: the original .NET version that runs on Windows, the Mono version that also runs on openSUSE Linux, Mac OSX and Solaris UNIX (provided Mono is installed), and the Java version that runs on any PC (provided Java is installed).

Compatibility Issues

All "open" NooJ linguistic resources can be read by any of the three versions of NooJ. These resources are comprised of:

— Dictionaries (.dic format);
— Dictionary property definition files (.def format);
— Character Equivalence Tables (charvariants.txt files);
— Textual grammars (.nof, .nom and .nog formats);
— Any text file;

Moreover, the Mono and .NET versions of NooJ can share the following binary files:

— graphical grammars (.nof, .nom and .nog formats)
— compiled dictionaries (.nod format)
— texts and corpora (.not and .noc formats)
— projects (.nop formats).

However, the Java version of NooJ cannot directly process binary files compiled in a .NET or Mono version of NooJ, and uses its own set of binary files.

Protecting the NooJ community

Although the Java version of NooJ is now open source, it was not possible to simply open access to all linguistic resources, including those posted on www.nooj4nlp.net (at the "resources" page) without their authors' permission. Indeed, several linguistic modules available for download do not contain the source file for the dictionaries, or they contain grammars that have been locked (i.e. protected).

Of course, it would not be acceptable to just publish the Java methods used to access these protected and locked files without giving away the resources. That is why the Java version of NooJ does not access binary and locked files constructed or compiled with .NET-NooJ.

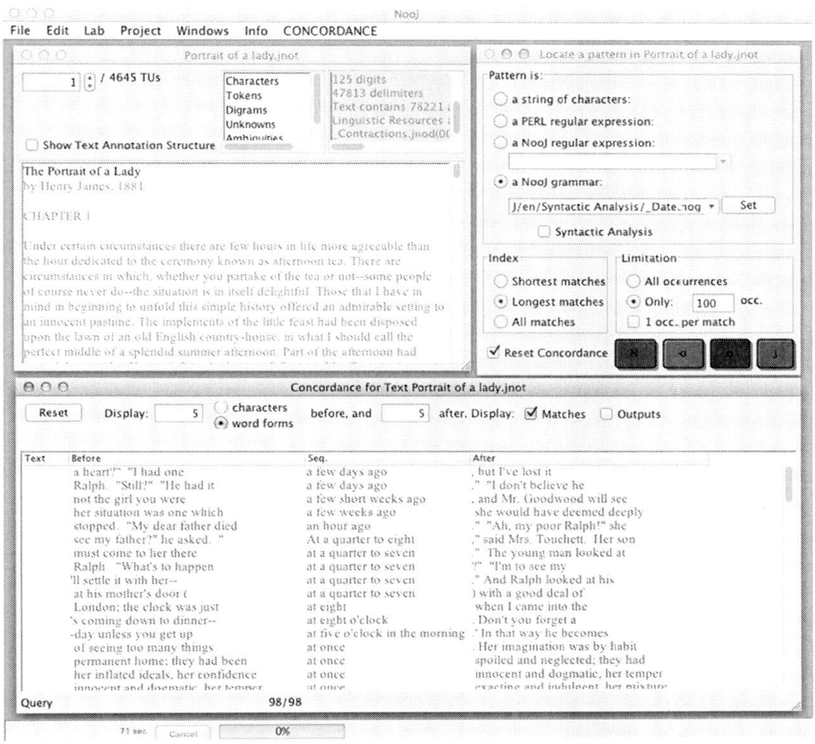

The Java version of NooJ

For dictionaries, texts and corpora the situation is the following: users of Java-NooJ must compile NooJ dictionaries, texts and corpora from their source origins. The resulting files will have extensions .jnod (dictionaries), .jnot (annotated texts) and .jnoc (annotated corpora).

For grammars the situation is the following: the latest version of .NET-NooJ (v4) allows any unlocked graphical grammar (.nof, .nom or .nog format) to be exported into the Java-NooJ open file format; reciprocally, .NET-NooJ can now read any grammar that was created using Java-NooJ. The double compatibility allows users to create, edit and exchange grammars that were developed on both .NET (v4) and Java versions of NooJ.

However, in order to protect copyright, grammars that were created with .NET-NooJ and locked by their author cannot be read by Java-NooJ.

In conclusion:

— Mono and .NET versions of NooJ can create, read and share any NooJ files.

— all .dic, .def, .txt, unlocked .nof, .nom and .nog files are compatible with the new, open source Java version of NooJ;

— locked grammars, and .noc, .nod and .not compiled files cannot be accessed by Java-NooJ;

— Java-NooJ has three new binary file formats: .jnoc, .jnod and .jnot to store compiled corpora, dictionaries and texts.

The open source version of NooJ

The Java version of NooJ is available under the Affero-GPL license[10]. That means that anyone can download it and use it in any way they wish, including for commercial applications. However, there are two legal constraints:

— any software application that uses part of NooJ sources becomes automatically available under the same Affero-GPL license;

— the previous constraint includes any web service or web application that runs on a server.

The latter constraint would force any entity which uses NooJ's technology to offer services via a web server to publish the source of the application offering these services.

We believe these two constraints offer good protection for the NooJ community: there is no possibility that NooJ can "fork out", i.e. that two or more incompatible versions of NooJ get developed independently from different actors or competitors because any modification or enhancement of NooJ will instantly be available to the whole community and thus can be imported back to the NooJ "main" version.

Note, however, that the Affero-GPL license only applies to the NooJ software and it does not concern any of the many linguistic resources developed with NooJ. In other terms, NooJ users are free to develop their

[10] See http://www.gnu.org/licenses/agpl-3.0.html.

resources as they wish, using any of the three versions of NooJ, including Java-NooJ. They will still be able to decide for themselves how they wish to distribute their own resources.

NooJ v4 new functionalities

Since Java-NooJ was released by the Mihajlo Pupin Institute, Héla Fehri has taken control of the Java source and, during a "bug hunting" 3-month mission, has done an excellent job of making Java-NooJ more robust. She has already fixed a dozen simple and complex problems. The latest version of Java-NooJ has been used in several tutorial sessions without any major problems.

In parallel to the work on the Java version, I have updated NooJ to make its technology converge with Java-NooJ, and at the same time, make it more useful for industrial needs[11]. Version v4 brings the following set of new functionalities:

— The definition of multiword units has been extended to enable the processing of sequences of delimiters (such as "$" or "…"), as well as terms starting with a delimiter (such as ".NET"). In particular, these objects are now processed as ALUs and are accepted as valid NooJ lexical entries:

```
.NET,TERM+OS
$,DOLLAR,TERM+Currency
…,PUNCTUATION+EndOfSentence
```

— One consequence of the generalised multiword unit definition is that a grammar now can produce an output containing delimiters. For instance, if a grammar's output is the following:

```
<E>/$BRACKET
```

and the value of variable $BRACKET is "<", NooJ now clearly distinguishes the "<" character produced in the output from the meta-character "<" used to insert new annotations in the TAS. Similarly, all output keywords used by NooJ's syntactic parser to trigger some special behavior (e.g. EXCLUDE, <ONCE>), now have been unified and regarded as first-order features (e.g. +EXCLUDE, +ONCE).

---

[11] Many thanks to Stéphanie Brizard and her team at Invoxis for their rigorous testing and their suggestions on how to improve the NooJ experience.

— The fact that any character or sequence of characters can now constitute a valid lexical entry has pushed us to implement a robust management of special characters. Indeed, we now need to be able to process strings such as "," as bona fide lexical entries… We have introduced a double mechanism of character protection. Consider the following lexical entries:

```
\,,PUNCTUATION+Type=comma
",",PUNCTUATION+Type=comma
"abc",PUNCTUATION+Type=comma
"a\"b",PUNCTUATION+Type=quote
```

The backslash \ (escape) character is used to protect the character following it: the first lexical entry from the above examples is a comma. Double quote characters are used to protect a sequence of characters: the second entry is also a comma and both lexical entries are equivalent. In the same manner, the third lexical entry represents the exact word form "abc", i.e. the two strings "ABC" and "Abc" are not recognized by this entry. The last lexical entry contains the sequence "a"b", i.e. the lowercase letter "a", followed by a double quote character, followed by a single letter "b".

— The complex inheritance system that allowed linguists to link different lexical entries has been reviewed. It was inefficient because it potentially doubled the number of dictionary lookups that had to be performed for each token of a text, and could not represent differences between variants and their standard form, such as when a standard form has a property that it does not share with its variants. For instance, the dm dictionary[12]contains the following two lexical entries:

```
combatif,combattif,A+Opt
combattif,A+Rec
```

The first entry indicates that *combatif* is an optional (+Opt) spelling variant of *combattif*; the second lexical entry indicates that *combattif* is the recommended (+Rec) spelling for this term. Obviously, we don't want the optional variant *combatif* to inherit the feature +Rec from the lexical entry *combattif*. In the new system, NooJ simply links the *combatif* variant to its lemma *combattif*, without copying the lexical properties of the *combattif* lexical entry. It is now even possible to have only the first lexical entry without the second one. One drawback of the new system, compared to the old system, is that any potential property for the standard form *combattif*

[12]Cf. (Trouilleux 2012).

(as for example: +Hum, +Emotion +Aggressive) that we want to associate with its variants, such as *combatif,* now would need to be copied explicitly into every lexical entry for each of its variants.

— A number of tools and functionalities have been added to facilitate the development of large resources in an industrial environment. For instance, it is now possible to edit project (.nop) files: add, remove and/or compile new resources inside a project that has already been created. The interface in Info > Preferences has been enhanced so that resources can be picked from any source folder (it is no longer limited to a specific folder in My Documents), etc.

Perspectives

Java-NooJ is still in its infancy, but it already has been proved useful in teaching NooJ and linguistics thanks to its simplified user experience. Because its source is available to anyone for studying, it has been used as an educational tool to teach Computational Linguistics techniques to students in Computer Science. Moreover, the very fact that its source is publicly available has opened up new possibilities for cooperation with groups of scientists who have been working on specific NLP tools that can now be interfaced with NooJ's development environment and specific functionalities.

NooJ v4 is now evolving rapidly to become a powerful industrial development tool that can process new types of linguistic objects (e.g. non-alphabetical terms) in a more robust way (e.g. special treatment of special characters) and offers new tools (e.g. the new project editor) critical to an engineering approach. However, NooJ v4 is more complex to use than Java-NooJ.

At this point nobody really knows precisely how the two versions will evolve, but the Affero-GPL policy should guarantee that the two versions will always be compatible, and that any new functionality in one version can be made available in the other.

References

Ehmann B., Balazs L., Shved D., Bénet V., Gushin V., 2012. The Russian Linguistic Resources in Space Psychological Research. In *Formalising Natural Languages with NooJ.* A. Donabédian, V. Khaskarian, M. Silberztein Eds. Cambridge Scholars Publishing: Cambridge.

Soussi R., Mesfar S., Faget M., 2014 (in this volume). Towards a NooJ module within Armadillo database to manage museum collection. In

Formalizing Natural Languages with NooJ: Selected papers of the NooJ2013 International Conference. S. Koeva, S. Mesfar, M. Silberztein Eds. Cambridge Scholars Publishing: Cambridge.

Pignot H., Lardy M, 2013. Formalising a dictionary of 17th Century English with NooJ. In *Formalising Natural Languages with NooJ.* A. Donabédian, V. Khaskarian, M. Silberztein Eds. Cambridge Scholars Publishing: Cambridge.

Sidhom S., Lambert P., 2014 (in this volume). Project Management within Economic Intelligence: using NooJ as a Diagnostic Tool for nanometrology clustering. In *Formalizing Natural Languages with NooJ: Selected papers of the NooJ 2013 International Conference.* S. Koeva, S. Mesfar, M. Silberztein Eds. Cambridge Scholars Publishing: Cambridge.

Silberztein M., 2003. *NooJ Manual.* Available at: www.nooj4nlp.net.

Silberztein, M., 2005, NooJ's Dictionaries. In Actes de la *2nd Language and Technology Conference*, Poznan.

Silberztein, M., 2013, NooJ Computational Devices. In *Formalising Natural Languages with NooJ.* A. Donabédian, V. Khaskarian, M. Silberztein Eds. Cambridge Scholars Publishing: Cambridge.

Spacic M., Milosevic U., Kovacevic N., Stanojevic M., 2013. Porting NooJ to Multiple Platforms. In *Formalising Natural Languages with NooJ.* A. Donabédian, V. Khaskarian, M. Silberztein Eds. Cambridge Scholars Publishing: Cambridge.

Trouilleux F., 2012. Le DM, a French Dictionary for NooJ. In Automatic Processing of Various Levels of Linguistic Phenomena: Selected Papers from the NooJ 2011 International Conference. K. Vuckovic, B. Bekavac, M. Silberztein Eds. Cambridge Scholars Publishing: Cambridge.

PART I:

DICTIONARIES AND MORPHOLOGICAL GRAMMARS

A New Tamazight Module for NooJ

Farida Aoughlis, Kamal Naït-zerrad, Hamid Annouz, Ferroudja Kaci and Mohammed Said Habet

Abstract

In this paper we present the Tamazight linguistic module and describe its main components. The NooJ linguistic resources are the electronic dictionaries (verbs, nouns), the rules which formalize Tamazight inflectional and derivational descriptions, and the morphological grammars. We show the application of these linguistic resources, dictionaries and grammars to text.

Introduction

Tamazight (Berber) is a branch of the Hamito-Semitic linguistic family which consists of Berber, Semitic, Cushitic (East Africa), ancient Egyptian and, with a degree of more distant relatives, the "Chadic" group (Hausa). Tamazight is spoken in an area ranging from Morocco, where it is spoken by 50% of the population according to (Boukous, 1995), to Egypt, moving from Algeria, where it is used by 25 % of the inhabitants. Our study will focus on a variety of Tamazight (Kabyle), spoken in Kabylia, in northern Algeria. Tamazight language presents particular morphological phenomena mainly related to its inflectional and agglutinative morphology.

In this work, we focus on the description of dictionaries as well as the construction of morphological grammars for verbs and nouns It should be stated that categories in the Amazigh language are related (Chaker, 1991). Berber syntactic units are organised into four large sets:verbs, nouns, connectors or relationals (prepositions, conjunctions and coordination), and various determinants.

As is the case with Semitic languages, the Berber verb (or noun) is composed of a root and a scheme. The root consists of one or more meaningful consonants (Naït-Zerrad, 1995b). The scheme provides the nouns and the verbs, for instance:

- In mmesgallen ("*they swore*"):
  The root is GL, G is the first and L the second radical consonant; since it is formed of two consonants, it is called biconsonant (Mammeri, 1990).

- Root ZDM ($C_1C_2C_3$) provides the following words:
  No Scheme: $C_1C_2C_3$[1] →zdem, (verb = "*to collect wood*").
  Scheme *an* +C_1C_2 + *a* + C_3: anC_1C_2aC_3 →anezdam (agent name = "*who collects wood*").
  Scheme *a* + C_1C_2+*a*+ C_3: C_1C_2aC_3 → azdam (verbal action name = "*collecting wood*"), (Naït-Zerrad, 1995b).

Verb

Verb stems incorporate theme, aspect and person indices. The verb is conjugated according to gender, number and person (Naït-Zerrad, 1995a).

Following André Basset works (Chaker, 1991), the majority of Berber scholars adopt a common Berber ternary system with three basic themes (intensive, aorist and preterit) marked by a set of vowel and / or consonant alternations. There are two other themes: negative preterite and intensive negative aorist.

A verb can be decomposed as follows :

Verbal form = radical or theme + affix(es).

The radical is composed of a root and a vocalic scheme, so we have:

Verbal form = lexical root + vocalic scheme + affix(es)

The scheme consists of one or more vowels that indicate the tense or the aspect of the verb. Affixes (prefixes and / or suffixes) serve as person or aspect marks. For example, for the verb aru[2] "*write*":

- turamt = t-u-r-a-mt, "*you wrote*"
  Root: *r*

---

[1] C1: 1st consonant, C2: 2nd consonant, etc…

[2] In "aru", the voyel "u", represents a weak radical consonant "w" (tirawt).

Scheme: *u-a* (preterit or past)
Radical or theme: *ura*
Affixes or person indices: t + *mt,* 2nd person, feminine, plural.

Verbal Themes

We describe the verbal themes (aorist, intensive and preterit):

Aorist

We found out:

- Imperative aorist (anaḍ urmir): aorist simple form corresponds to 2nd person of singular imperative,
  Krez, "*Plow!*"

- ad + aorist (ad + urmir):
  Used in particular to shape the future,
  Ad kerzeɣ, "*I will plow*"

- Negative optative : a wer + aorist
  a wer yekrez ! *"May he not plow!"*

Intensive

We found out:

- Intensive aorist (urmir ussid): This theme has an imperfective meaning,
- Itett *"he usually eats "* / *"he actually eats "*,
  Kerrzeɣ, "*I usually plow*",
- Negative intensive aorist: Ur kerrzeɣ ara, "*I don't usually plow*",
- Intensive imperative (anaḍ ussid): Kerrez, "*plow usually!*"

Preterite (or Past)

- Preterite (izri):
  This theme corresponds to perfective; it expresses achieved action in the past.
  Iwala, "*he saw*",
  Kerzeɣ, "*I plowed*".
- Negative preterit (izri ibaw):

Ur kr**i**zeɣ ara, "*I have not Plowed*",
Ur yur**i** ara, "*He didn't write*".

Participle

The participle does not contain person indices and is invariable in gender and number. It is found in the preterite, the aorist and in the intensive aorist. Its form is of 3rd masculine person:

- Preterite: yeččа**n**, "(*those*) *who has/have eaten*",
- Negative preterite: (ur) **ne**čči (ara), "(*those*) *who has/have not eaten*",
- Intensive aorist : **i**tette**n,** "(*he*) *who eat(s)*",
- Intensive negative aorist: (ur) **n**tett, "(*those*) *who do not eat*",

Aorist: (ara) **yeččen**, "(*those*) *who will eat*".

Aspect

In Tamazight the verb has an aspectual character-André Basset was the first scholarspecialising in Berber, who mentioned it. Aspect is a quantification of the process, not a temporal location.

Depending on the language, the aspect category (Chaker, 1991) can express very different semantic content:

- Momentary / durative,
- Perfective / imperfective,
- Single / repetitive, etc...

For instance, we have :

- Yečča, "*he ate*", perfective action.
- Ad yečč, "*he will eat*", imperfective action.

Person Indices

For the ordinary verbs conjugation, person indices (Table 1) are the same for all themes:

	Singular	Plural
1st P m f	---(e)ɣ	n(e)---
2nd P m	t(e)---(e)ḍ	t(e)---(e)m
2nd P f	t(e)---(e)ḍ	t(e)---(e)mt
3rd P m	i/y(e)---	---(e)n
3rd P f	t(e)---	---(e)nt

Table.1: Person indexes[3]

Noun

The noun paradigm includes forms for gender (feminine, masculine), number (singular, plural) and state (Naït-Zerrad, 2001).

Gender

- Generally, the masculine begins with the vowels a, *i* or *u* :
  axxam, "*house* ",
  imi, "*mouth*",
  uzzal, "*iron*".

- The feminine form is derived from the masculine by prefixation and suffixation using ***t***:
  aqcic, "*boy*" → **t**aqcic**t,**"*girl*".

- A masculine noun ending with *d* or *ḍ* ends with *ṭ* in the feminine:
  Aɣeggad, "*leather*" → taɣeggaṭ, "*belt*",
  Ayazid, "*chicken*" → tayaziṭ, "*hen*".

Number

- The singular form often begins with a vowel;
- The plural can be designated by:
  (1) Changing an initial vowel and adding a suffix (external plural):
  Axxam, "*house*" → **i**xxame**n,** "*houses*"
  T**a**xxamt, "*room*"→ t**i**xxam**in,** "*rooms*".

[3] P: person, f: feminine, m: masculine.

(2) Vocalic changes (internal plural):
ayaziḍ, “*cock*” → **iyuzaḍ**, “*cocks*”

(3) Suffix+ vocalic changes (mixed plural):
Izi, “*fly*” → **izan** “*flies*”

State

The state is a characteristic of the noun in Berber. The two types of state are free state and constructed state.

Free State

The free state is used when an initial vowel is not subjected to modification.

(1) The noun is in isolation from any syntactic context :
Axxam, “*a house*”.

(2) The Noun can be the direct object of a verb :
Yečča aɣrum.
SUJ3ms.eat.PRET bread
“He ate the bread”.

(3) It can be a lexical subject before the verb:
Argaz yeffeɣ.
man.EL[4] SUJ3ms.go out.PRET
“The man went out”.

(4) It can be a theme indicator :
Imensi, yečča.
Dinner.EL SUJ3ms.eat.PRET.
“Regarding the dinner, he ate”.

Constructed State

The constructed state is shown through a formal variation of the first syllable in a specific syntactic context, as follows:

---

[4] EL: free state, EA: constructive state.

(1) A noun following a preposition (d, n, ɣer, ɣef...), exception s "*towards*" and ar "*untill*":
Yečča d weqcic.
SUJ3ms.eat.PRET with boy.EA
"*He ate with the boy*".

(2) A lexical subject following a verb:
Yečča weqcic.
SUJ3ms.eat.PRET boy.EA
"*The boy ate*".

(3) A noun which is an indirect object of the verb:
Yesla i teqcict mi tcennu.
SUJ3ms.listen.PRET RELI girl.EA when SUJ3FS.sing.AORI
"*He heard the girl singing*".

Morphological modifications consist in either keeping or suppressing an initial vowel, and adding a *w* or *u*:

(1) Masculine nouns with vowel a:
a → wa : ass.EL "*day*" → wass.EA
a → we : aqcic.EL "*boy*" → weqcic.EA
a → u : ameksa.EL "*shepherd*" → umeksa.EA

(2) Feminine nouns with vowel a:
ta → ta (no change) : tala, "*fountain*".
ta → te : tasraft.*EL*, "*trap*" → tesraft.*EA*
ta → t : tafunast.*EL*, "*cow*" → tfunast.*EA*

(3) Masculine nouns with initial i:
i → yi : iḍ.*El*, "*night*" → yiḍ.*EA*
i → i : igenni.*EL*, "*sky*" → igenni.*EA*
i → y(e) : ixxamen.*EL*, "*houses*" → yexxamen.*EA*

(4) Feminine nouns with initial *ti*:
ti → ti : tili "*shadow*".
ti → te : tixxamin.*EL*, "*rooms*" → texxamin.*EA*
ti → t( ) : timura.*EL*, "*countries*" → tmura.*EA*

(5) Masculine nouns with initial u:
u → wu : uccen.EL, "*jackal*" → wuccen.EA

(6) Feminine nouns beginning with *tu* :
tu → *tu :* tuɣmest, *"tooth"* → tuɣmest.

Tamazight NooJ Module Dictionaries

The Noun Dictionary

The noun dictionary "nom.EL+EA" contains 504 entries (Kaci, 2013). Below, the example presents some entries from the noun dictionary:

udi,N+FLX=UDI
ugel,N+FLX=UGEL
ul,N+FLX=UL
urrif,N+FLX=URRIF
uqbel,ADV+FLX=UQBEL
ulac,ADV+FLX=UQBEL
uday,N+FLX=UDAY
ucbiḥ,N+FLX=UDAY
usu,N+FLX=UDI
ucmit,N+FLX=UDAY
uḥdiq,N+FLX=UDAY
uzzal,N+FLX=UZZAL

The entry udi, "*butter*", is represented by "Udi,N+FLX=UDI", where Udi is a noun (N), and UDI is the inflectional paradigm of the noun "*udi*".

The inflectional paradigms are described in the inflectional file "nom,EL+EA.nof". Eight inflectional models have been defined:

- Two for the gender (masculine, feminine)
- Two for the number (singular, plural)
- Four models for the constructed state.

Below, we give an extract of the inflectional file:

UDI = <E>/EL+m+s|<LW>w/EA+m+s |
<B>awen/EL+m+p | <B>awen<LW>w/EA+m+p;
UGEL = <E>/EL+m+s | <LW>w/EA+m+s |
<L><B><RW>an/EL+m+p | <L><B><RW>an<LW>w/EA+m+p;
UL = <E>/EL+m+s|<LW>w/EA+m+s |
<RW>awen/EL+m+p | <RW>awen<LW>w/EA+m+p;
URRIF = <E>/EL+m+s|<LW>w/EA+m+s |
<RW>en/EL+m+p | <RW>en<LW>w/EA+m+p;
UQBEL = <E>/EL | <LW>w/EA;
UDAY = <E>/EL+m+s | <LW>w/EA+m+s |
<LW>t<RW>t/EL+f+s | <LW>t<RW>t/EA+f+s|

<RW>en/EL+m+p | <RW>en<LW>w/EA+m+p |
<LW>t<RW>in/EL+f+p | <LW>t<RW>in/EA+f+p;
UZZAL = <E>/EL+s|<LW>w/EA+s;

For instance, the inflectional paradigm UDI for the noun "*udi*" gives the following inflectional forms:

udi,udi,N+FLX=UDI+EL+m+s
udawen,udi,N+FLX=UDI+EL+m+p
wudawen,udi,N+FLX=UDI+EA+m+p
wudi,udi,N+FLX=UDI+EA+m+s

The Verb Dictionary

The verb dictionary "taseftit.dic" contains 3434 entries. The aorist verb form is used as the dictionary entry because it is the simplest verb form. The example below shows some entries taken from the verb dictionary (Annouz, 2013):

#use taseftit.nof
kreḍ,V+FLX=LMED
kref,V+FLX=BREK
kreh,V+FLX=LMED
krem,V+FLX=LMED
kres,V+FLX=BREK
krez,V+FLX=BREK
kri,V+FLX=XSI
krireḍ,V+FLX=BLILEḤ
kru,V+FLX=BDU
krunti,V+FLX=KRUNTI
kseb,V+FLX=BREK

The entry" krez" is defined by "krez,N+FLX=BREK", where krez is a verb (V), and BREK is the inflectional paradigm of the verb "krez".

The grammar "taseftit.nof " contains the inflectional paradigms for the conjugation (Annouz, 2013). We have 89 models for the root, 9 models for the imperative, 161 for the intensive imperative, 80 for the preterite, 84 for the negative preterite, 161 for the intensive aorist, 26 for the aorist, 66 for the participle of positive preterite, 43 for the participle of negative preterite, 19 for the aorist participle, 164 for the participle of positive intensive aorist, 145 for the participle of negative intensive aorist.

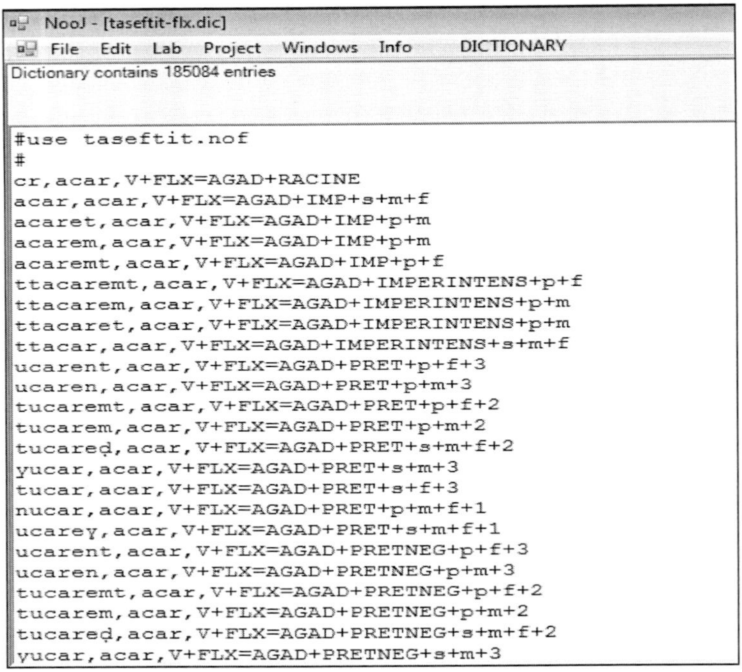

Fig.1: An extract of the "taseftit-flx.dic" dictionary

An extract of the inflectional file for the paradigm BREK is given below:

BREK= :RACINE6 |:IMPERATIF4 |:IMPERINTENS10
|:IMPERINTENS51 |:PRETERIT6
|:PRETERITNEGATIF6 |:AORISTEINTENSIF8
|:AORISTEINTENSIF19 |:AORISTE7
|:PARTICIPPPRET10 |:PARTICIPNEGPRET10 |:PARTICIPAOR8
|:PARTICIPAOINPO18
|:PARTICIPAOINPO60 |:PARTICIPAORINE16 |:PARTICIPAORINE18;
PARTICIPAORINE16= <LW>n<R>e<R><D>/PARTICIPAOINTNEG;
PARTICIPAORINE18= <L2><S>a<LW>nette/PARTICIPAOINTNEG;
PARTICIPAOINPO60= en<L4><S>a<LW>yette/PARTICIPAOINTPO;
IMPERATIF4 = <E>/IMP+s+m+f
| <L3>e<R><S><RW>et/IMP+p+m
| <L3>e<R><S><RW>em/IMP+p+m
| <L3>e<R><S><RW>emt/IMP+p+f;
IMPERINTENS10= <L3>e<R><D>/IMPERINTENS+s+m+f

| <L3>e<R><D><S><R>et/IMPERINTENS+p+m
| <L3>e<R><D><S><R>em/IMPERINTENS+p+m
| <L3>e<R><D><S><R>emt/IMPERINTENS+p+f;

We generated the inflectional dictionary “taseftit-flx.dic” (Figure 1) from “ taseftit.dic” dictionary. It gives 185084 conjugated verb forms which can be recognized in the texts.

The Grammatical Words Dictionary

The grammatical words dictionary entries (Kaci, 2013) contain all direct or indirect object affixes of the verb, which can be located between the preposition “d” and the verb, the “d” homonyms (“d” proximal particle and “d” predicative particle). We have 66 entries. We give below, an extract from the grammatical words dictionary:

d,PP;
d,PREP ;
d,PROX ;
iyi,CLIT+IND+1+s+m+f
yi,CLIT+IND+1+s+m+f
yak,CLIT+IND+2+s+m
ak,CLIT+IND+2+s+m
k,CLIT+IND+2+s+m
yam,CLIT+IND+2+s+f
am,CLIT+IND+2+s+f
m,CLIT+IND+2+s+f
yas,CLIT+IND+3+s+m+f
as,CLIT+IND+3+s+m+f
s,CLIT+IND+3+s+m+f
yaɣ,CLIT+IND+1+p+m+f

Linguistic analysis

The linguistic analysis of the text “belaid.not” gives 2459 unambiguous linguistic units. The annotations show the analysed entries, a sample is given in Figure 2.

The concordance (Figure 3) for “<V>+<N+EL>+<N+EA>” in “belaid.not” gives 38966 forms.

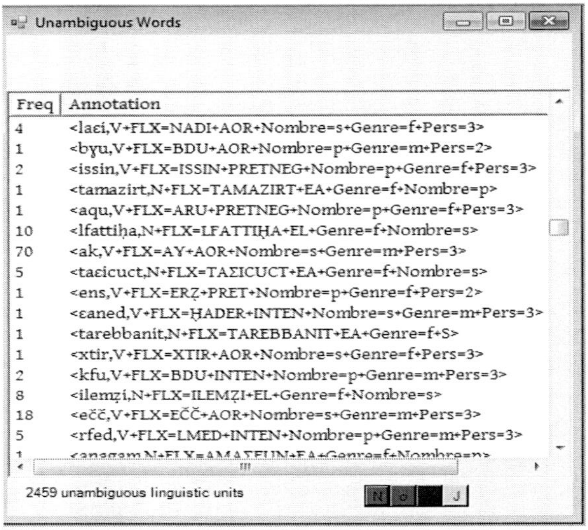

Fig.2: A sample of annotations and text analysis for "belaid.not"

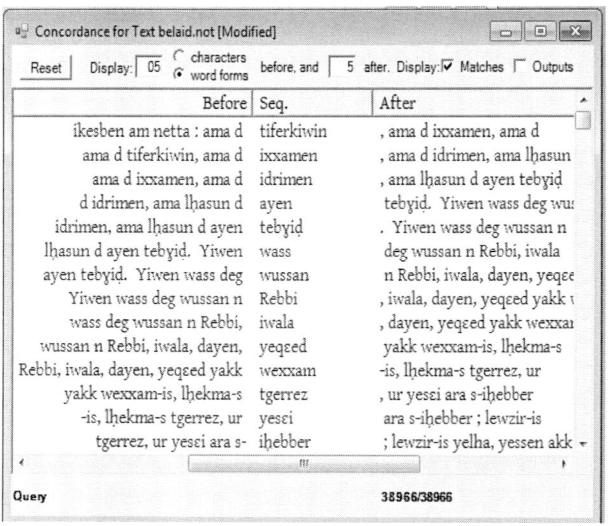

Fig.3: An extract from the results of the concordance query "<V>+<N+EL>+<N+EA>"

Conclusions

The verb dictionary is limited to primary verbs, as derived verbs are not studied. Verbs are extracted from J. M. Dallet dictionary (Dallet, 1982).

Our future work would focus on derived verbs, inflectional grammars for passive and factitive verbs, and the expansion of the noun dictionary with new entries. Nouns and adjectives derived from verbs would also be considered, and disambiguation grammars would be added.

Acknowledgements

The authors would like to thank Dr. Med Sadek Fodil for proofreading the English version of the paper.

References

Kaci, F. 2013, *La grammaire de la préposition d avec le logiciel NOOJ,* mémoire de Master 2, INALCO, Paris.

Annouz, H. 2013, *Construction d'un dictionnaire électronique des flexions verbales du kabyle à l'aide du logiciel NOOJ (Verbes primaires),* mémoire de Master 2, INALCO, Paris.

Boukous, A. 1995, *Sociétés, langues et cultures au Maroc: Enjeux Symboliques*, Ed: Najah El Djadida, Casablanca.

Chaker, S. 1991, *Manuel de linguistique berbère,* Bouchène Ed. : Alger.

Dallet, J.M. 1982, *Dictionnaire Kabyle-Français,* Ed: SELAF, Paris.

Mammeri, M. 1990, *Précis de la grammaire berbère*, Bouchène Ed. : Alger.

Naït-Zerrad, K. 1995a, *Manuel de conjugaison kabyle, 6000 verbes, 176 conjugaisons (le verbe en berbere)*, Enag Ed. : Alger.

—. 1995b, *Grammaire du berbère contemporain (kabyle) , I-Morphologie* , Enag Ed. : Alger.

—. 2001, *Grammaire moderne du kabyle, tajerrumt tatrart n teqbaylit*, Ed: Karthala, Paris.

Silberztein, M. 2003, *NooJ Manual*. Available at: www.nooj4nlp.net.

Introduction to Slovene Language Resources for NooJ

Kaja Dobrovoljc

Abstract

The aim of this paper is to present the content of the first version of the Slovene module for NooJ that includes a novel-based corpus of approx. 78,000 word forms, a large-coverage dictionary of approx. 100,000 lemmas and a set of basic inflectional, morphological and syntactic grammars. In order to facilitate and encourage further linguistic research in this development environment, special emphasis was put on rendering these resources fully compatible with other freely available state-of-the-art NLP resources and tools for the Slovene language.

Introduction

Slovene is a South Slavic language spoken or understood by around 2.5 million people around the world, the majority living in the Republic of Slovenia. Two of its most distinctive characteristics that also affect natural language processing applications are its complex morphology (e.g. the existence of the dual grammatical number in the inflection of nouns, verbs, adjectives, pronouns and numerals) and a free word order contingent upon the intended emphasis in the sentence.

From the mid-1990s onwards, several nationally and EU funded projects have encouraged the construction of fundamental infrastructure for the Slovene language engineering research and development. Among the most significant projects dealing with written language resource construction and annotation are the MULTEXT-East (MTE[1]) project, in which first language resources with a standardised markup and annotation were developed; the Linguistic annotation of Slovene (JOS[2]) project, in which morphosyntactic specifications were extended by syntactic and

[1] http://nl.ijs.si/ME/

[2] http://nl.ijs.si/jos/

semantic annotation systems; and projects dealing with construction of large corpora of written texts (FIDA/FidaPLUS[3]). The results of this work have also been used in the recently completed Communication in Slovene (SSJ[4]) project that has produced some fundamental language technology applications and resources, as well as a series of new and upgraded reference corpora, including the 1 billion word Gigafida reference corpus. For more details about the current state in the field of language technologies for Slovene see META-NET White Paper (Krek, 2012).

The advances in the development of freely available language resources inherently also led to an increase in corpus-based linguistic research of Slovene. Although the aforementioned resources are freely available for browsing through user-friendly web concordancers and advanced corpus querying systems, such as noSketchEngine[5] or CUWI[6], there is currently a lack of tools which impedes the complex automatic processing of linguistic phenomena at various level. As a powerful and user-friendly development environment that enables the construction of large coverage formalised descriptions of natural languages, NooJ has now also been localised for the Slovene language.

The following sections thus describe the content of the current version of the NooJ module for Slovene. The paper starts with a short presentation of the corpus, followed by a detailed description of the morphological dictionary and its conversion into a NooJ-compatible format. The remaining sections focus on the second stage of NooJ localisation for Slovene by describing the initial set of inflectional, morphological and syntactic grammars that represent different linguistic phenomena. All presented resources and tools are freely available for download from the NooJ website[7].

Corpus

The corpus included in the online version of the module consists of a novel by the prominent contemporary Slovene author Miha Mazzini published under the title of *Telesni čuvaj* (Mazzini, 2000). In addition to being reprinted in 2004 and published online, this humorous thriller has also been published in English (under the title of *Guarding Hanna* in 2002 and 2008), Polish (*Pies*, 2008), Serbian (*Hanin telohranitelj*, 2008) and

---

[3] http://www.fidaplus.net/
[4] http://www.slovenscina.eu/
[5] http://nl.ijs.si/noske/
[6] http://nl.ijs.si/cuwi/
[7] http://www.nooj4nlp.net/pages/slovene.html

Italian (*Mi chiamavano il cane*, 2011). It therefore presents a convenient starting point for further contrastive and translation studies.

Due to copyright protection, the novel's paragraphs were randomised before being imported into NooJ. Although this prevents from reading the novel as an integral narrative and from potential discourse analysis, it does not affect linguistic processing at morphological and syntactic level, as the chosen text delimiter is newline (\n), hence each paragraph is processed separately. The initial corpus analysis using the default linguistic resources in NooJ shows that the novel includes 2,871 text units (paragraphs) and 97,975 tokens, of which 78,367 are categorised as word forms, i.e. sequences of letters between two delimiters.

Dictionary

Despite the considerable progress in developing lexical resources for efficient morphological processing of the Slovene language in recent years (Arhar Holdt & Holozan, 2009; Arhar Holdt, 2009; Erjavec, Fišer, Krek, & Ledinek, 2010; Erjavec, 2010; Rojc, Verdonik, & Kačič, 2007), there is currently no freely available repository of inflectional patterns for the Slovene language that would enable a relatively effortless extension of existing morphological lexicons or the compilation of new ones. Similarly to the approach used for the compilation of the Croatian dictionary for NooJ (Vučković, Tadić, & Bekavac, 2010), a list of patterns could be extracted from the existing open-source morphological lexicons for Slovene developed in the scope of the SSJ and MTE projects, however, initial attempts at such work (see section Inflectional grammar) have revealed time-consuming inconsistencies and mistakes. Moreover, the actual formation of inflectional patterns used for the compilation of these lexicons has unfortunately not been publicly documented, so it is difficult to evaluate their reliability in terms of methodological consistency and reflection of actual language use.

Instead of (re)constructing a morphological dictionary from scratch by linking a list of lemmas with their corresponding inflectional patterns that have yet to be systematically formalised, we decided to simply convert an extensive dictionary of inflected forms into a NooJ-compatible dictionary format. For this purpose, we chose the largest freely available morphological dictionary to date, the Slovene lexicon of inflected forms Sloleks that includes over 100,000 lemmas and their corresponding inflectional paradigms, amounting to a total of almost 2,800,000 word forms and their variants.[8]

The lexicon is encoded in the standard Lexical Markup Framework (LMF) XML format, structured so as to conform to the rich inflectional properties of Slovene and Slavic languages in general (Krek & Erjavec, 2009). Its fundamental unit, the lexical entry, consists of a lemma and all its inflected forms, together with the corresponding linguistic meta-information, such as grammatical features, variant spellings, accordance with the orthography codification, reference corpus frequency, derivationally related lexical entries, etc.

The lexicon's set of grammatical attributes, values and codes follows the MTE-JOS morphosyntactic specifications that are available in source XML and derived HTML, both in Slovene and English[9] (Erjavec et al., 2010). As such, the lexicon is compatible with the morphosyntactic specifications developed for all other languages included in the MULTEXT-East project, many of which are also part of the NooJ community (Stankovic, Utvic, Vitas, Krstev, & Obradovic, 2012).

Although the dictionary included in the Slovene module for NooJ is principally based on the original Sloleks dictionary, the two versions are not completely identical. To avoid confusion, we named the version included in the module as *Sloleks4NooJ*. Below we give a short overview of the differences between the two versions in terms of lexica, grammatical information and the dictionary format.

In relation to lexical entries, the Sloleks4NooJ includes all lemmas and their inflectional paradigms from the original dictionary, except for decimal numbers (which normally in Slovene use comma as decimal mark), since the comma character already has a special function in NooJ as the delimiter between a word form, its (optional) lemma and the corresponding category code (e.g. `cars, car, N`). In addition, Sloleks4NooJ also includes the lexical entries from the corpus that were not covered by the original Sloleks dictionary but appeared at least ten times in the one billion word reference corpus.

As shown in Table 1, the final version of Sloleks4NooJcomprises 100,689 lemmas and their corresponding inflectional paradigms, adding up to a total of 2,793,692 lexical entries, i.e. word forms and their formalised grammatical descriptions. The lexicon includes all lexical entries belonging to closed word classes (prepositions, conjunctions, pronouns

[8] The Sloleks dictionary was compiled as part of the SSJ project. The LMF version of the lexicon is freely available for download under the Creative Commons license at http://eng.slovenscina.eu/sloleks/prenos.

[9] http://nl.ijs.si/jos/msd/html-en/index.html

and particles), while the remaining majority of the lexicon covers the most frequent lemmas within other part-of-speech (POS) categories as distributed in the referential corpus of Slovene.

POS	Code	Lemmas	Word Forms	WFs per Lemma	MSDs
Noun	N	54,332	925,655	17.0	104
Adjective	A	26,665	1,571,899	58.9	279
Verb	V	10,275	261,470	25.4	165
Adverb	R	6,922	9,947	1.4	4
Numeral	M	1,952	18,160	9.3	215
Pronoun	PRO	169	6,182	36.6	1,122
Preposition	S	97	102	1.1	6
Interjection	I	85	85	1.0	1
Abbreviation	Y	70	70	1.0	1
Particle	Q	68	68	1.0	1
Conjunction	C	54	54	1.0	2
Total		100,689	2,793,692	27.7	1,900

Table.1: Sloleks4NooJ dictionary in numbers

In terms of the formalised grammatical description of its lexical entries, Sloleks4NooJ includes all stipulated information from the MTE-JOS specifications, as well as information on the (potential) incompliance of the spelling with standard orthography. All other meta-information, such as corpus frequency, derivational relations or semantic information, has not been transferred from the original Sloleks dictionary.

As for the Sloleks4NooJ dictionary format, compatibility was given priority over convenience. While MTE-JOS compact morphosyntactic description tags (MSDs) are position-dependant (e.g. for the Ncnsn tag, code *n* denotes neuter gender in position 2 and nominative case in position 4), NooJ information codes are not. We therefore decided to keep the attribute-value pairs instead of replacing them with new randomly chosen codes. Furthermore, clarity was given priority over brevity, so the attribute-value pairs have not been abbreviated in any way, although this causes longer resulting annotations. The only exception to this rule were the part of speech categories, as the processing time shortened considerably when the categories (written in full) were instead replaced by the category codes. The codes chosen are the same as those specified in the MTE tagset, with the exception of pronouns, for which the three letter PRO code has been used instead of P, since the latter already functions as a special symbol for delimiters.

Three prototypical examples of Sloleks4NooJ dictionary entries are given below, in which the specific word form (*ptico, modrega, prizadane*) is followed by its lemma (*ptica, moder, prizadeti*), the category code (*N* for noun, *A* for adjective, *V* for verb) and a string of morphosyntactic attribute-value pairs. The last example includes an additional non-MTE attribute-value pair signalising that the word form does not comply with the current orthographic standard.

```
ptico,ptica,N+Type=common+Gender=feminine+Number=singular+Case=accusative
modrega,moder,A+Type=general+Degree=positive+Gender=masculine+Number=singular+Case=genitive
prizadane,prizadeti,V+Type=main+Aspect=perfective+VForm=present+Person=third+Number=singular+Orthography=nonstandard
```

All grammatical properties are also listed in the properties definition file. Properties that are not part of the dictionary and only occur in morphological grammars (see the following section) have also been added and marked accordingly.

The initial lexical analysis of the corpus using the Sloleks4NooJ dictionary results in 228,232 annotations (47,379 different), 11,034 types of ambiguities, 4419 unambiguous linguistic units and 169 unknown entries. The latter include rare interjections (*aaaa, bomf*), foreign word forms (*bella, hard*) or word forms that have not reached the minimum frequency threshold of 10 occurrences in the reference corpus (*černjoha, zabrbrala*).

Lexical Analysis

Despite the eventual decision of importing a pre-existing morphological dictionary with unabridged inflectional paradigms, a sample inflectional grammar describing the declension patterns for feminine nouns has been created as a demonstration example for further schematic descriptions of inflectional and derivational paradigms in Slovene.

On the first level, the grammar (DeclensionsF.nof) is divided into the three different declension groups for feminine nouns that differentiate by noun endings in the singular genitive, i.e. the ending-*e* for the first group (e.g. *lipa-lipe*), the ending-*i* for the second (e.g. *perut-peruti*) and the zero ending-ø for the third group (e.g. *Karmen-Karmen*).

All three groups are then further divided into prototypical patterns, each representing a specific inflectional paradigm, which amounts to 20 different inflectional patterns altogether (13 for the first, 6 for the second and 1 for the third declension group). These patterns are described as a combination of subgraphs for singular, dual and plural, some of which are embedded in more than one inflectional pattern. The example in Figure 1 shows that singular forms in the LADJA pattern are formed in the same way as those in the LIPA pattern.

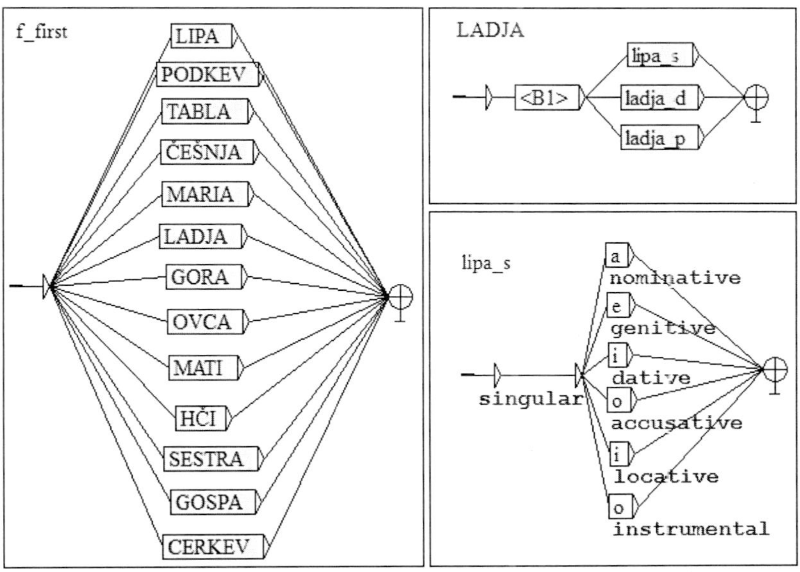

Fig.1: DeclensionF.nof (74 graphs): inflectional patterns within the first declension group (left); graph for the LADJA pattern (upper right); grammar for inflection of singular forms within the LIPA pattern (lower right)

Note that these inflectional patterns were extracted from the list of feminine nouns in the Sloleks dictionary. As such, they do not bring any new inflectional information in comparison to the original dictionary, and have yet to be systematically evaluated. Furthermore, this inflectional grammar only describes the inflectional patterns that are compliant with the current normative standards and do not include nonstandard word forms.

The first of the two morphological grammars (RomanNumerals.nom) is based on the example given in the NooJ manual (Silberztein, 2003: 105). It identifies Roman numerals, determines their type and converts them to their equivalent in Arabic numerals (see Figure 2). An example of such annotation output for the numeral XXI is given below:

```
XXI,M+Form=roman+Conversion=21+Type=cardinal
```

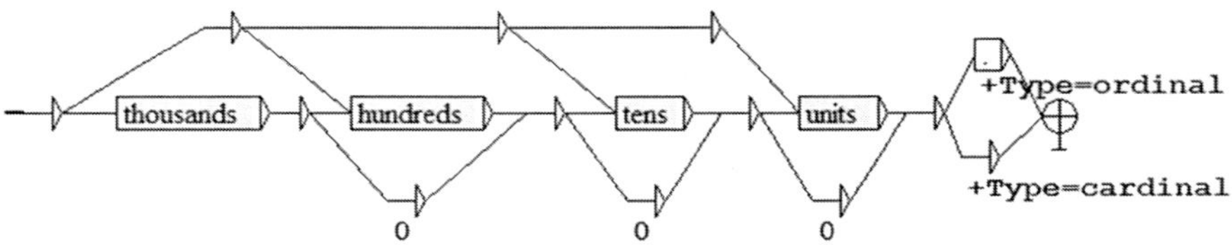

Fig.2: RomanNumerals.nom (5 graphs): the first subgraph

The second morphological grammar recognises gerunds (gerundial nouns), determines their type and identifies the verb they derive from. At the first level, the grammar is divided into three subgrammars (one for each type), depending on the ending of the gerund. As can be seen in Figure 3, these embedded graphs extract the root of the noun, add the corresponding verbal ending and check if this newly formed verb is a valid verb in the dictionary, as well as if the original word form is actually a noun (to prevent inclusion of other word forms with the same endings). If both constraints are met, the gerund inherits the lemma and the corresponding grammatical information from the dictionary and receives two additional attribute-value pairs: the gerund group (value of attribute Gerund) and the lemma of the verb it derives from (value of attribute Gerund_Verb). An example of such output for the noun *razkazovanje* is given below:

```
razkazovanje,N+Type=common+Gender=neuter+Number=si
ngular+Case=accusative+Gerund=nje+Gerund_Verb=razk
azovati
```

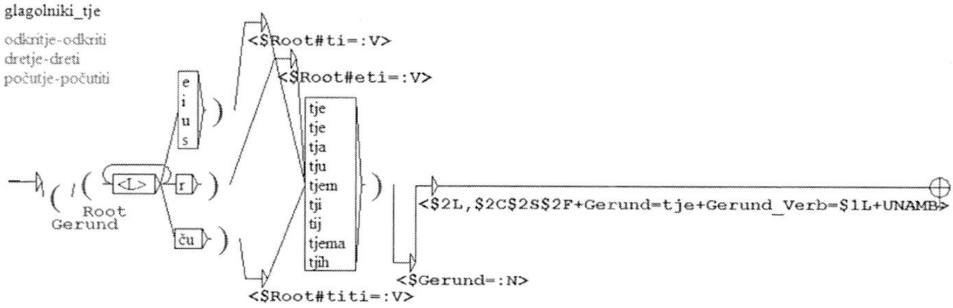

Fig.3: Gerunds.nom (27 graphs): the graph for detection of gerunds ending with-*tje*

This grammar represents an important addition to the existing morphosyntactic annotation system as gerunds currently do not integrate any special attribute that would imply their specific nature in comparison to other nouns. Thus, a grammar that identifies such nouns and establishes the derivational connection with their original verb enables the potential transfer of important verbal characteristics, such as valence information. Furthermore, omission of one of the two constraints could also be used for identifying new potential gerunds that are not yet in the dictionary but their original verb is, or vice versa.

Syntactic grammars

The four syntactic grammars recognise different types of named entities and shallow syntactic structures. As can be seen in Figure 4, grammar ProperNames.nog annotates words or word strings written in capital letters, or words written in upper letters, as potential proper nouns if they are preceded by a word in lower case or words at the beginning of a sentence. In the module corpus, this grammar identifies entities, such as *Italija, Bach, Hana Woyczik, Che Guevara, BMW* etc.

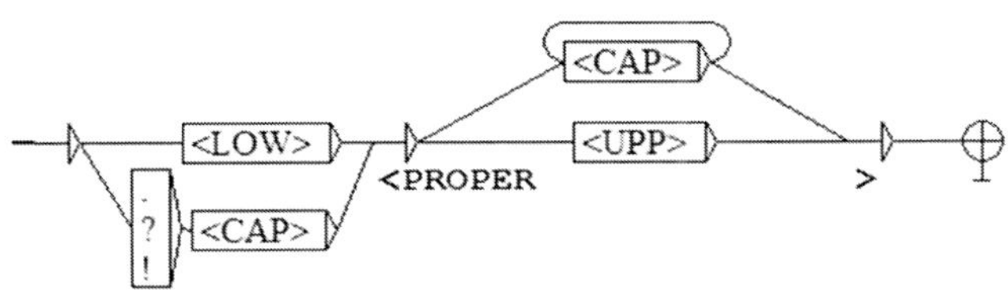

Fig.4: ProperNames.nog (1 graph)

The second syntactic grammar (Figure 5) recognises adverbial expressions that indicate a certain point in time. Similarly to the English version of the grammar (Silberztein, 2003: 149), these expressions span from simple descriptions of time and date to complex adverbial phrases that also include deictic expressions, days of the week, temporal adverbs, time zones etc. (e.g. the expression *jutri, v četrtek, 26. decembra 2013, natanko ob 10. uri dopoldne po srednjeevropskem času*).

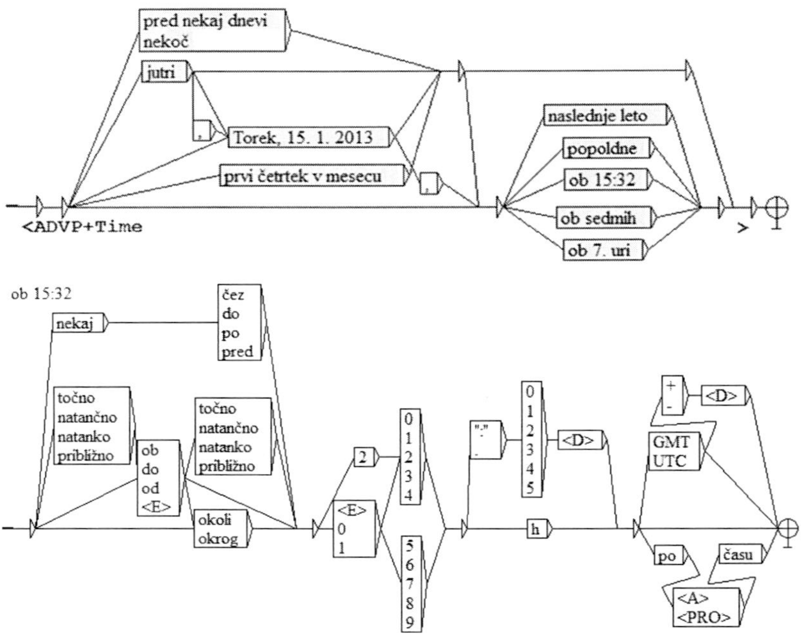

Fig.5: AdvP_time.nog (16 graphs): the main graph (above) and the subgraph for time in digits (below)

The third grammar in the series of rule-based named entity recognition (Figure 6) extracts numerals written in words and converts them to their equivalent in digit form. In Slovene numerals in letter form can either be written as one complex word or as a sequence of words, which would ideally require a combination of a morphological (for processing individual word forms) and syntactic grammar (for processing strings of word forms).

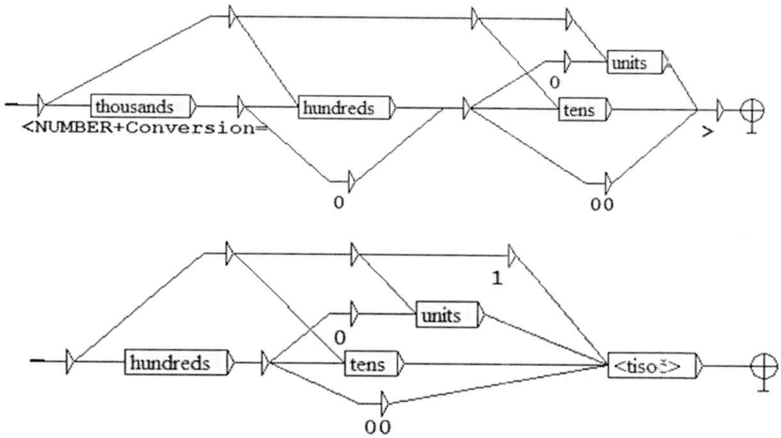

Fig.6: Numerals.nog (14 graphs): the main graph (above) and the *thousands* subgraph (below)

The last syntactic grammar (Figure 7) is an example of a rule-based parser for the recognition of shallow syntactic structures (chunks) that extracts single or coordinate nominal phrases attributing them the corresponding case. If such a nominal phrase is preceded by a preposition in the same case, it is marked as a prepositional phrase (PP).

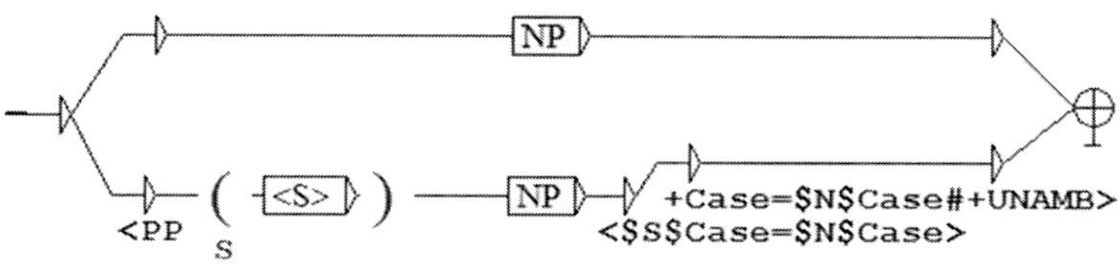

Fig.7: NP_PP.nog (8 graphs): the main graph

Graphs at the bottom-most level (see Figure 8) describe the internal structure of simple noun phrases, i.e. nouns that can be preceded by one occurrence of a limited set of quantity modifying adverbs (*nekaj, malo, veliko*) or by an unlimited number of occurrences of either numerals, written in digits, or adjectives, pronouns or numerals in letter form that agree with the head noun in case, gender and number. Any premodifier from the last group (marked with the variable PreM) can also be modified itself by an adverb or by adjectives in the neuter nominative singular form (e.g. *slovensko* in *slovensko-francoski odnosi*).

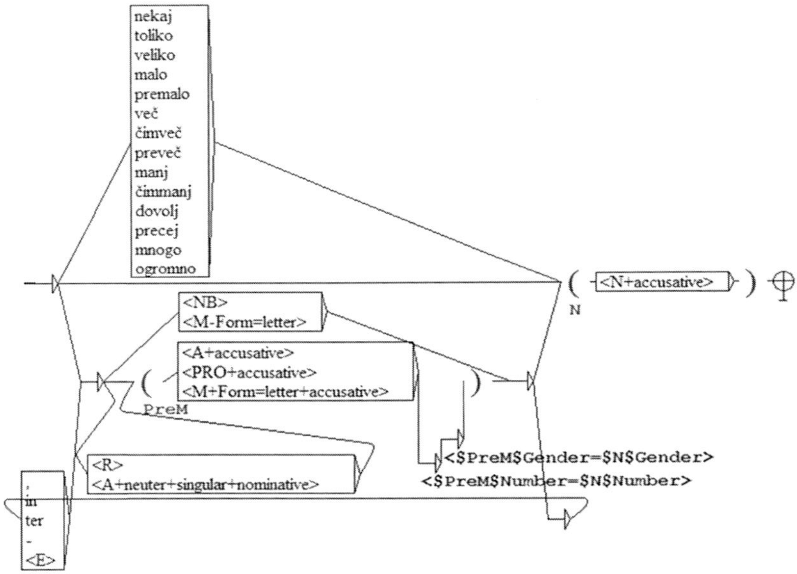

Fig.8: NP_PP.nog: subgraph for nominal phrase in accusative case

Conclusion and future work

We have presented the first set of resources and tools for processing the Slovene language in NooJ: a medium-sized corpus of contemporary Slovene, a large-coverage morphological dictionary and a few basic inflectional, morphological and syntactic grammars. These resources serve as demonstration examples for linguistic research in NooJ and represent an important contribution to the popularisation of this development environment among the growing community of Slovene researchers in the fields of natural language processing and corpus linguistics.

For this purpose, we intend to further expand the module by including other freely available language resources for Slovene, as well as developing new grammars for their linguistic analysis. As we have already pointed out in the previous sections, we believe a well-documented systematic description of Slovene inflectional and derivational paradigms should be of utmost priority.

References

Arhar Holdt, Š., 2009. Učni korpus SSJ in leksikon besednih oblik za slovenščino. *Jezik in slovstvo*, *54*(3/4), 43–56.

Arhar Holdt, Š., & Holozan, P., 2009. Leksikalna podatkovna zbirka ASES (Amebisov skupni elektronski slovar). In V. Mikolič (Ed.), *Jezikovni korpusi v medkulturni komunikaciji* (pp. 30–51).

Erjavec, T., 2010. MULTEXT-East version 4: multilingual morphosyntactic specifications, lexicons and corpora. In N. Calzolari (Ed.), *Proceedings of the 7th International Conference on Language Resources and Evaluations, 19-21 May 2010, Valletta, Malta* (pp. 2544–2547).

Erjavec, T., Fišer, D., Krek, S., & Ledinek, N., 2010. The JOS linguistically tagged corpus of Slovene. In *Proceedings of the 7th International Conference on Language Resources and Evaluations, 19-21 May 2010, Valletta, Malta* (pp. 1806–1809).

Krek, S., 2012. *The Slovene Language in the Digital Age*. (G. Rehm & H. Uszkoreit, Eds.) (p. 79). Berlin, Heidelberg: Springer Berlin Heidelberg.

Krek, S., & Erjavec, T., 2009. Standardised encoding of morphological lexica for Slavic languages. In V. A. Shyrokov & L. Dimitrova (Eds.), *Organization and development of digital lexical resources / MONDILEX Second Open Workshop, Kyiv, Ukraine, 2-4 February, 2009* (pp. 24–29).

Mazzini, M., 2000. *Telesni čuvaj : verzija 1.72*. Ljubljana: Študentska založba.

Rojc, M., Verdonik, D., & Kačič, Z. (2009). A framework for efficient development of Slovenian written language resources used in speech processing applications. *International Journal of Speech Technology*, *10*(2-3), 121–141.

Silberztein, M., 2003. NooJ Manual. Available for download at: www.nooj4nlp.net

Stanković, R., Utvić, M., Vitas, D., Krstev, C., & Obradović, I., 2012. On the Compatibility of Lexical Resources for NooJ. In K. Vučković, B. Bekavac, & M. Silberztein (Eds.), *Automatic Processing of Various Levels of Linguistic Phenomena: Selected Papers from the 2011 International NooJ Conference* (pp. 96–109). Cambridge Scholars Publishing.

Vučković, K., Tadić, M., & Bekavac, B., 2010. Croatian language resources for NooJ. *Journal of Computing and Information Technology*, *18*(4), 295–301.

FORMALIZING QUECHUA VERB INFLECTIONS

MAXIMILIANO DURAN

Abstract

A conjugated Quechua verbal form may be inflected by a particular subset of suffixes in postposition or interposition. Combinations of up to ten suffixes are possible and their order is not arbitrary. Using a matrix approach, we introduce the grammar constraints that must be respected to make these combinations valid and obtain a complete catalog of paradigms. NooJ grammars generate near three million inflected Quechua verbal forms, IQVF, out of 2,000 verbs. Tests on our corpus show good results.

Key words: *Quechua, Quechua verbs inflectional descriptions, conjugated Quechua verbal form, postposition and interposition suffixes, suffix matrix, Quechua verb paradigms.*

Motivation and generalities about Quechua

The Quechua language was the official language of the Inca civilisation. It originated in the Central Andes of Peru around the first half of the first millennium of the present era.

According to the first chronicles (XVI century), it was spoken across the whole territory of the Inca Empire, which covered the area between the province of Pasto in south Colombia, all the territory of Equator and Peru, part of Bolivia and the north of Argentina and Chile.

Some years after the Spanish colonisation, the Quechua-speaking population started to decline. From a nearly 100% penetration of the Inca language in the region (estimated at around 12 million), nowadays only 6,280,000 people understand the language (census 2010), which is to say 13% of the population of the region.

If the tendency shown in the following statistics is maintained in the next decades, we should fear the worst concerning the survival of the Quechua language. This is one of the reasons why UNESCO has declared it in danger of extinction in its World Languages Atlas published in 2009 in Paris.

1 1947 52 % (intro. of the radio)
2- 1970 30 % (intro. of the TV)
3- 1990 20 % (intro. of internet)
4- 2010 13 %
5- 2020 ?

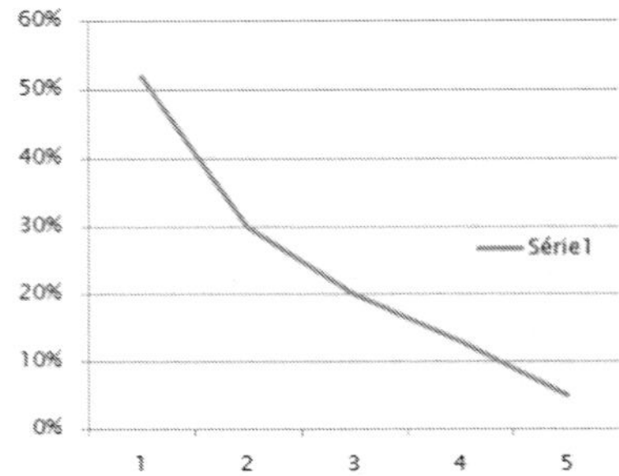

Fig.1: Changes in the Quechua-speaking population in Peru

How can we save this endangered language? In this context, I think that any effort to save this "linguistic species" in danger of **extinction** should be welcomed. It is evident that the most significant effort has to come from the government which can enforce in the Quechua-speaking regions compulsory education in Quechua language from an early age.

Quechua speakers in the Andes region according to the census of the past eight years	
Country	Quechua speakers
Perú	3,360,000
Bolivia	2,100,000
Ecuador	500,000
Argentina	300,000
Colombia	20,000
Chile	unknown
	Total 6,280,000

The publication of various dictionaries (of words, etymological dictionaries, toponyms, proper nouns, metaphors, sayings, synonyms, etc.) will also contribute to this purpose, as well as radio and TV broadcasting in Quechua in these regions.

Computer science may also help: using current advanced computing technology, it might be possible to develop electronic dictionaries and tools for automatic translation from Spanish, French or other languages into Quechua and vice versa.

A dictionary of Quechua verb inflections. The present work contributes to this rescue movement.

Matrix of suffixes and inflections

This article presents the process of compiling a dictionary of inflected Quechua verbs (IQV), indispensable for NLP and any text analysis.

As a preamble I first demonstrate the use of the matrix approach to obtain a dictionary of inflected nouns. My corpus contains 1,500 Quechua nouns.

The morphology of Quechua is very much dominated by the agglutination of suffixes. Based on the Quechua grammar, I isolated 71 nominal suffixes[1] and then built a matrix of binary grammatically compatible combinations of these suffixes.

TR	CHUCH	CHUI	CHUS	MAA	MAN	MMI	ÑA
MMI	0	0	0	0	0	0	0
ÑA	1	1	1	1	0	1	0
PAS	0	0	0	0	0	0	0
PUNI	1	1	1	1	0	1	1
QA	0	0	0	0	0	0	0
RAQ	1	1	1	1	0	1	0

Fig.2: A portion of the Boolean matrix of compatible combinations between nominal suffixes.

The entire matrix contains 906 "1"s. A "1" in this table means that the combination of suffixes in the left-right order is possible. Example: the combinations *ña-chu, raq-mi, puni-chus, raq-chus, raq-chu*, etc. Agglutinated to a noun these give us new inflected nouns. Example: *wasi-ñachu* (is it already home?); *wasi-raqmi* (the house is before all), *wasi-punichu* (is it precisely the house?).

Then we built a ternary matrix with the 906 valid entries as the column header and the original 71 nominal suffixes as the row header. From the total of 809,826 possible ternary entries less than 5,500 combinations were grammatically compatible and acceptable, like *n-kama-raq, lla-paq-mi, paq-raq-chá, kama-ña-chu,* which give us: *wasi-nkamaraq* (just up to his house), *wasi-llapaqmi* (it is exclusively for the house), *wasi-paqraqchá* (it is for the house in priority). We proceeded in this way to combine up to six suffixes.

---

[1] vecteur_N_V = (-ch , chá, -cha , -chiki , -chu , -chus , -chu? , -kama , -kaqlla, -kuna, -lla , -má , -man , -manta , -masi , -m, -mpa , -ña , -naq , -nta , -ntin, -niraq, -nta, -niq (-ñiq), -p -pa, -paq , -pas , -pi, -poss(7v), -puni, pura, -qa , -hina , -raiku, -raq , -ri , -ri?, -sapa , -s, -si , -su, -ta, -taq, -wan, -y!, -ya!, -yá, -yupa , -yuq) is the set of nominal suffixes for the nouns ending in a vowel.

In order to generate all possible inflections of a Quechua noun, we built the corresponding paradigms using NooJ. The parsing of these grammars has allowed us to compile our first automatically generated dictionary of inflected nouns. We have obtained 5,710,221 inflected nominal forms out of the 1,500 nouns, as we can see in Fig. 3.

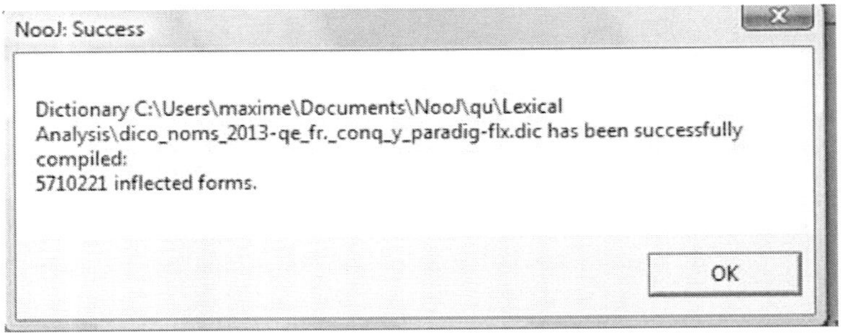

Fig.3: Inflected forms generated by 1,500 Quechua nouns

Matrix approach to verbal suffixes

The fundamental set of the verbal endings for present, future and subjunctive mode corresponding to all persons is represented by the three vectors:

PRE = *(NI, NKI, N, NCHIK, NIKU, NKICHIK)*
FUT = *(SAQ, NQA, SUNCHIK, SAQKU, NQAKU, NKU)*
SUB = *(I, IKI, IKU, IKICHIK)*

What we call the present tense is in fact an indefinite present. On the one hand, it places the statement at the moment in which this action takes place, but on the other hand it may also place it in a moment in which the action has just taken place and is still not completed.

The conjugation for the three singular persons has the following structure:

ñoqa (I) root +***NI***
qam (you) root + ***NKI***
pay (he, she) root +***N***

Its complete NooJ paradigm looks as follows:

PRESENT = <B>(*ni*/PR+s+1 |*nki*/PR+s+2 |*n*/PR+s+3 |*nchik*/PR+pin+1|*nkichik*/PR+p+2|*nku*/PR+p+3|*niku*/PR+pex+1);

For the future we have the scheme:

ñoqa (I) root +***SAQ***
qam (you) root + ***NKI***
pay, (he, she) root +***NQA***

Its NooJ complete paradigm looks as follows:
FUT = <B>(*saq*/F+s+1 |*nki*/F+s+2 |*nqa*/F+s+3 |su*nchik*/F+pin+1 |*nkichik*/F+p+2 |*nqaku*/F+p+3 |*saqku*/PR+pex+1);

The present form plays a crucial role in the conjugated Quechua verbal form for the other tenses. It serves as a fixed point around which all the inflectional topology based on the combinations of suffixes is constructed (tenses, modes, aspects, etc.).

For instance, the past preterite is obtained by taking the present form and interposing the suffix *-rqa-* between the verbal root and the ending for marking the person. We then have:

Present			Past preterite	
taki-ni	I sing	→	*taki-**rqa**-ni*	I sang
taki-nki	you sing	→	*taki- **rqa**-nki*	you sang
taki-n	he sings	→	*taki- **rqa**-n*	he sang

Its NooJ paradigm looks as follows:
PAST = <B>(rqani/PIDF+s+1 |rqanki/PIDF+s+2 | rqan/PIDF+s+3 |
rqanchik/PIDF+pin+1 |
rqaniku/PIDF+pex+1|rqankichik/PIDF+p+2|rqanku/PIDF+p+3);
(PIDF: Past preterite).

Quechua disposes of two sets of verbal suffixes: the interposition suffixes **SVIP1**[2] and the postposition suffixes, **SVPP1**[3]. **SVIP1** contain 30 elements, including –rqa, placed between the root and the personal endings. As in the case of nouns, we can build combinations of 2, 3, or 4 of these suffixes resulting in grammatically compatible agglutinations.

Fig. 4 shows part of the matrix of compatible binary combinations of interposition suffixes. For example, the value "1" for the position (chi, chka) in this matrix means that the combination chichka is compatible and so may be merged to the root of the verb takiy (to sing, taki-) and the

---

2 **SVIP1** = (chi, chka , ikacha , ikari , iku , isi, kacha , kapu , ku , lav , mu , nav , nakamu , naku , naya , paya , pu , ra , raya , ri , riku , rpari , rqa , pti , rqu , ru , spav , sqa , tamu , wa)

3 **SVPP1** = *(CH, CHA, CHAA, CHIKI, CHUI, CHUN, CHUS, CHUSINA, MAA, MAN, MM, MMI, ÑA, PAS,PUNI,QA,RAQ,SSI,SIS, TAQ,YAA)*

ending of the second person singular (-nki) and obtain the verbal form taki-chichka-ni (I am making him sing). Another example of compatibility occurs for kacha, ku, which also has value "1" in this matrix, giving in this case taki-kachaku-nki (you keep singing once and over again), etc. We found a total of 315 "1"s.

	CHI	CHKA	IKACHA	IKARI	IKU	ISI	KACHA	KAPU	KU	LLAV	MU	NAV
CHI	0	1	0	0	1	1	0	0	1	1	1	1
CHKA	0	0	0	0	0	1	0	0	0	0	0	0
IKACHA	1	1	0	0	0	1	0	0	1	1	1	0
IKARI	1	1	0	0	1	1	0	0	1	1	1	0
IKU	1	1	0	0	0	1	0	1	1	1	0	0
ISI	1	1	0	0	1	0	0	1	0	1	1	0
KACHA	1	1	0	0	1	0	0	1	1	1	1	1
KAPU	1	1	1	0	1	0	0	0	0	1	1	1
KU	0	1	0	0	1	0	0	1	0	1	0	1
LLAV	1	1	1	0	1	1	0	0	0	0	1	1
MU	0	1	0	0	0	0	0	0	0	1	0	1

Fig.4: Compatibility binary matrix of interposition suffixes

The Quechua grammar allows us to find the ternary combinations of compatible interposition suffixes. We have obtained near 3,000 compatible and attested ternary agglutinations. Here are some examples:

RIVISIRA, RIVISIRAYA, RIVISIRQA, RIVISISQA, RIVKUCHKA, RIVKUIKU, RIVKUISI, RIVKUKAPU, RIVKULLAV, RIVKUPA, RIVKUPU, RIVKURA, RIVKURQA, RIVKURQU, RIVKURU,

Postposition suffixes

As mentioned above, there is also a set of postposition suffixes, **SVPP1,** containing 21 elements. They appear after the verbal ending, as in the following examples, where we have between one and four agglutinated suffixes.

rima-nki *-man* you should talk
rima-nki *-man-pas* besides, you should talk
rima-nki *-man-pas-cha* you should perhaps talk
rima-n *-lla-man-ña-taq* I fear that he speak up

The binary combination matrix contains 56 compatible agglutinations as shown in Fig 5.

	CHUN	CHUS	CHUSINA	MAA	MAN	MMI	ÑA	PAS	PUNI	QA	RAQ
CHUN	0	0	0	0	0	0	0	0	0	0	0
CHUS	0	0	0	0	0	0	0	0	0	0	0
CHUSINA	0	0	0	0	0	0	0	0	0	0	0
MAA	0	0	0	0	0	0	0	0	0	0	0
MAN	2	2	2	0	0	2	2	2	0	0	2
MMI	0	0	0	0	0	0	0	0	0	0	0
ÑA	1	1	1	1	0	1	0	1	0	0	0
PAS	1	0	0	0	0	0	0	0	0	0	0
PUNI	1	1	1	1	0	1	1	1	0	1	1
QA	0	0	0	0	0	0	0	0	0	0	0
RAQ	1	1	1	1	0	1	0	1	1	0	0
SSI	0	0	0	0	0	0	0	0	0	0	0
TAQ	0	0	0	0	0	0	0	0	0	0	0

Fig.5: Binary compatibility matrix of postposition suffixes

Here, too, the "1" corresponding to the vector (*ÑA, MMI*) indicates that the combination *ÑAMMI= ñam* is grammatically compatible and we can form *rima-nchik-ña-m*, which we have already mentioned.

Similarly, we have also obtained the matrix of ternary combinations with the 56 compatible binary combinations as the column header and the vector SVPP1 as the row header. The result contains only 80 non-null elements, as shown in Fig.6.

Following the same method, we obtain the matrix $MSVPP_{3x1}$ of compatible combinations of four postposition suffixes. Some of its entries are listed below:

MANÑAPASCHAA, PUNIRAQPASCHAA, PUNIRAQPASCHIKI, PUNIRAQPASCHUN RAQPUNIÑACHUN, RAQPUNIÑACHUS RAQPUNIÑACHUSINA,MANÑAPASCHIKI, MANÑAPASCHUN

Créer Matrice	CH	CHAA	CHIKI	CHUI	CHUN	CHUS	CHUSINA	MAA	MAN	MMI
MANCHAA	0	0	0	0	0	0	0	0	0	0
MANMMI	0	0	0	0	0	0	0	0	0	0
MANÑA	ANÑAC	ANÑACH	ANÑACH	ANÑACH	ANÑACH	ANÑACH	ÑACHUS	ANÑAM	0	ANÑAMI
MANPAS	0	NPASCH	NPASCH	0	NPASCH	0	0	0	0	0
MANRAQ	0	NRAQCH	NRAQCH	NRAQC	NRAQCH	NRAQCH	RAQCHU	NRAQM	0	NRAQM
MANTAQ	0	0	0	0	0	0	0	0	0	0
ÑAMMI	0	0	0	0	0	0	0	0	0	0
ÑAPAS	0	APASCH	APASCHI	0	APASCHI	0	0	0	0	0
ÑASSI	0	0	0	0	0	0	0	0	0	0
PUNIMMI	0	0	0	0	0	0	0	0	0	0
PUNIÑA	UNIÑAC	NIÑACH	NIÑACH	NIÑACH	NIÑACH	NIÑACH	IÑACHUS	NIÑAM	0	NIÑAMI
PUNIPAS	0	NIPASCH	NIPASCH	0	NIPASCH	0	0	0	0	0
PUNIQA	0	0	0	0	0	0	0	0	0	0
PUNIRAQ	0	NIRAQCH	NIRAQCH	NIRAQC	NIRAQCH	NIRAQCH	RAQCHU	NIRAQM	0	NIRAQM

Fig.6: Partial view of the compatibility ternary combinations of postposition suffixes.

Similarly, the matrix of combinations of five suffixes can be derived, as in the following list:

MANRAQPUNIÑACH, MANRAQPUNIÑACHAA,
MANRAQPUNIÑACHIKI, MANRAQPUNIÑACHUI,
MANRAQPUNIÑACHUN, MANRAQPUNIÑACHUS,
MANRAQPUNIÑAMAA, MANRAQPUNIÑAMMI,
MANRAQPUNIÑATAQ, MANRAQPUNIÑAYAA

The agglutination of inter- and postpositioned suffixes

The Quechua grammar allows combinations of both inter- and postpositioned suffixes, as in these examples:

*rima-ri-**nki**-man* what about if you talk
*rima-r-llai-**nki**-man-raq* I think that before you should, etc.

We used all their matrices to program the corresponding paradigms in NooJ. For example:

conjugVERBES = <E>/INF|:CHU |:progCHU |:pasCHU |:futCHU |:impeCHU |:iptiiCHU |:imanCHU |:nominITA|:GSTA;
VERBEAY = <E>/INF|:CHU |:PRESENT |:FUT |:RQA |:PREASS |:CHKAASS |:IMP |:COND |:PPL |:PTIC |:presenCHU |:progCHU|:impeCHU |:FUTCHU |:iptiiCHU |:imanCHU |:sqaCHU |:ptiiqaCHU | … |:GDYN |:STINCHU |:TA|:SQAIKI |:TRTS1 |:WANCHU |:TRDE1 |:DE1PCHU |:TRDE3 |:DE3PCHU |:TRTA2 |:accustfTA |:yay |:chiy |:riy |:kuy |:puy |:muy |:rjuy |:WANKICHU) |:TRDE1CHU|:TRTS1CHU |:PIDF2|:PIDF2CHU |:PIDF2 |:PICTR |:PICTRAC |:SPA |:GSPA |:IPI;

Below is a sample of the 44 conjugated forms generated for the verb *takiy* (to sing).

takiychu,takiy,V+FR="chanter"+FLX=conjugVERBES+NEG
takichkanikuchu,takiy,V+FR="chanter"+FLX=conjugVERBES+pex+1+NEG
takichkankuchu,takiy,V+FR="chanter"+FLX=conjugVERBES+p+3+NEG
takirqanikuchu,takiy,V+FR="chanter"+FLX=conjugVERBES+PP+pex+1+NEG

We have added to these more than 50 other paradigms, some of which are very complex, and we applied them to a set of 2,000 Quechua verbs and generated a dictionary of 2,750,000 conjugated forms.

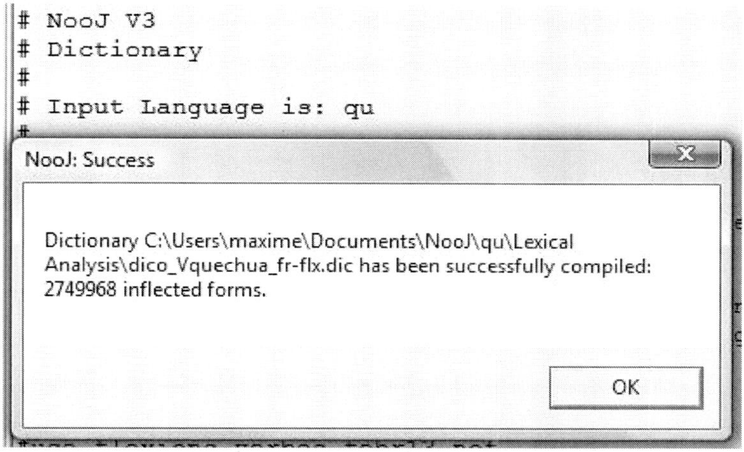

Color matching

We have applied the function 'Color matching sequences in text' from NooJ's Linguistic Analysis on a corpus consisting of a short Quechua tale[4] using our inflected dictionaries, and we obtained good matching results (bold text for the nouns and red for the verbal forms):

Chaytam kunan willasqayki masiiman qina. Uyariwayyari: Ñoqaqa **tutallapim** kausani; **tutallapim** takini llakisqapas, kusisqapas. Manam **pitapas** llakichiita, manchachiita munanichu. Takiillam takikuni, takiita munaspa. **Runakunataq**, imanasqachá, "kay **pakpakup** takinqa **atim**", ninku. Wañuisi qamun **ñoqa** takiptii, manataqmi ñoqá yachanichu ima chai wañuikasqanta. Kausaillatam ñoqaqa yachani. Chaymi llapan **runakuna**, **chai iskay chakipi puriq**, chai puñuysiki **runakuna**, cheqniwan. Ñoqa takikuni **tutakunapi**, paykunataq nin: " Taytallay! , piraq wañunqa, **pakpakum** , **sachapi** waqachkan" nispa. Chaymi cheqniwanku; chaimi warmakunapas rikuwaspa **rumiwan** choqawan, **sacha kallmapi punchau** puñukuptii. Chaymi ripusaq, **chaiñacha**.

- Manam chaiqa allinchu, nispa, **chaiñacha** kutichin. Imanasqataq mana quk takiiman **takiikita** tikrankichu? Jinallata takiptikiqa, mayta riptikipas, maypi kaptikipas, qinallataqmi **runaqa** cheqnisunki.

---

[4] Guardia Mayorga (1973). *Pakpaku chayñachawan rimanakun* The owl's dialog with the goldfinch.

The non-colored lexemes, showing the absence of matches, correspond to adjectives, adverbs or their inflections, which we will process in the future.

References

Duran, M. 2009, *Diccionario Quechua-Castellano*. Editions HC. Paris.

Guardia M., C. 1973, *Gramatica Kechwa*, Ediciones los Andes, Lima. Peru.

Itier, C.. 1997, *Parlons Quechua, La langue de Cuzco*, L'harmatan.

Perroud, P. C. 1972, *Gramatica Quechwa Dialecto de Ayacucho*. Lima. 3[a] Edicio.

Duran P., German. A. 1980, *Uchuk Runasimi (Jechua – Quechua). Conversación y vocabulario Castellano-Quechua* Ocopa, Concepción Perú.

Silberztein, M. 2003, *NooJ Manual*. htpp://www.nooj4nlp.net (220 pages updated regularly).

—. 2005, *NooJ's Dictionnaries*, Proceedings of the 2nd Language and Technology Conference, Poznan.

UPDATED SPANISH MODULE FOR NOOJ

SANDRINE FUENTES AND ANUBHAV GUPTA

Abstract

This paper presents an updated version of Spanish module derived from the module developed for the INTEX platform by the UAB under the supervision of Xavier Blanco. Additionally, some of the dictionaries compiled by fLexSem group are touched upon. Finally, certain morphological and syntactic grammars to tackle linguistic phenomena specific to Spanish viz. clitics, diminutives and superlatives are discussed.

Introduction

The Spanish dictionary was developed during the 90's at the Department of French and Romance Philology, Autonomous University of Barcelona. This database, developed under the supervision of Xavier Blanco, included, on the one hand, a lexicon of simple words, DELAS (with 85,000 entries, of which 50% were nouns, 25% verbs, 20% adverbs and the remaining 5% other parts of speech) and, on the other hand, a lexicon of compound nouns, DELAC (with 300,000 entries). These resources, that constituted the Spanish dictionary (DELAs), were implemented in the INTEX platform (Blanco, 2000). The present work reports on the adaptation of this Spanish module to NooJ.

In the following section we present the dictionary along with some examples of the inflection rules employed. The ensuing section deals with the morphological grammar used to describe the diminutives and the superlatives of Spanish. Finally, the grammars to tackle other linguistic phenomena specific to Spanish, such as clitics, are discussed.

Dictionary

The dictionary compiled as part of the current module contains approximately 12,000 adjectives, 31,000 nouns and 11,000 verbs (Table 1 lists the distribution of the parts of speech). The nouns are further divided into 9 semantic classes, i.e. abstract, animal, animal collective, concrete, human, human collective, location, temporal, plant.

Part of Speech	Count
Adjective	12494
Adverb	1494
Conjunction	48
Determinant	205
Interjection	195
Common Noun	30851
Proper Noun	167
Preposition	51
Pronoun	141
Verb	11118

Table 1

The dictionary takes into account the 57 inflection types that the nouns and the adjectives can belong to. Various general rules and exceptions are used to describe the inflection related to both the gender and the number as presented by Ambadiang (1999):

> Concerning vocal termination, the nouns ending in-i an-u are masculine in general, with exception of forms such as *metrópoli*, *palmacristi* and *tribu*.
> …
> some nouns are used in the masculine as well as feminine form ({*el/la*} *acné*, {*el/la*} *cochambre*, {*el/la*} *pelambre*, {*el/la*} *pringue*, {*el/la*} *tilde*, {*el/la*} *tizne*), while in other cases there are two nouns formally identical which receive two distinct genders (*el frente ~ la frente*, *el parte ~ la parte*)
> …
> The adjectives ending in-a,-í,-e,-ar,-z,-l (with exception of those terminating in-ol) are invariable with respect to gender *alerta*, *iraní*, *dulce*, *bacilar*, *ágil*, *cruel*, *papal*, *audaz*, *veloz*, *feliz*, *falaz*)
> …
> a. The plural of the nouns terminating in a non-accented vowel is formed by adding-s to its singular form (*libros*, *coches*, *tribus*).

b. The plural of the nouns ending in any consonant as long as it is not /s/ is formed by adding-es to the singular (*paredes*, *pieles*, *rehenes*, *reyes*, *relojes*). The said addition sometimes entails a change in accent (*régimen/regímenes*, *espécimen/especímenes*).

...

(i) the nouns ending in-é that admit only-s in plural (*bebés*, *cafés*), (ii) those ending in a non-accented vowel followed by-s and those that don't change, with the article being the only indicator of their number (*ángelus*, *atlas*, *bíceps*, *cosmos*, *crisis*, *dosis*, *glotis*, *lunes*, *tórax*, *virus*), and those ending in an accented vowel followed by-s that require-es (*compás/compases*, *revés/reveses*, *país/aíses*, *obús/obuses*).

On the other hand, the verbs are classified into 91 categories based on the permissible inflectional forms. These categories are obtained by merging and, in some cases, splitting the categories generally found in the dictionaries or in the grammar literature. Traditionally, *dormir* and *morir* are placed in the same class, yet in the NooJ module they are kept separately since they have different past participle (*dormido/muerto)*. On the other hand, *huir* and *argüir* are placed in the same category because with respect to NooJ they have the same properties, i.e.-i changes to-y before a vowel and-u loses the diaeresis.

Morphological Grammar

In this section, first we present a simple NooJ grammar which recognises Spanish diminutives ending in-ito. In this grammar (Fig. 1) 9 cases are covered: the nouns and adjectives ending in-a,-e,-go,-co,-eo,-n,-l,-o (except for-eo,-go and-co), and-z. The respective derivatives (singular masculine) end in-ito,-ecito,-guito,-quito,-eíto,-ncito,-lito,-ito and-cecito.

However, the nominal lexemes incompatible with the diminutive as elaborated by Lázaro Mora (1999) are not rejected:

- The words ending in-ao (*cacao*, *nao*, *sarao*, *vaho*) with exception to *bacaladito*.
- The names of the days of the week except *sábado* and *domingo* reject the suffix.
- Territories or institutions in which an authority exercises the command: *decanato*, *priorato*, *maestrazgo*, etc.
- Professions or activities with the suffix-ista: *periodista*, *accionista*, *legalista*, etc.
- 'Abstract' nouns and nouns of 'action', especially those formed with specific suffixes denoting their type (*agudeza*, *alevosía*, *arrianismo*, *abundancia*, *competencia*, *venganza*, *torcimiento*, *abordaje*).

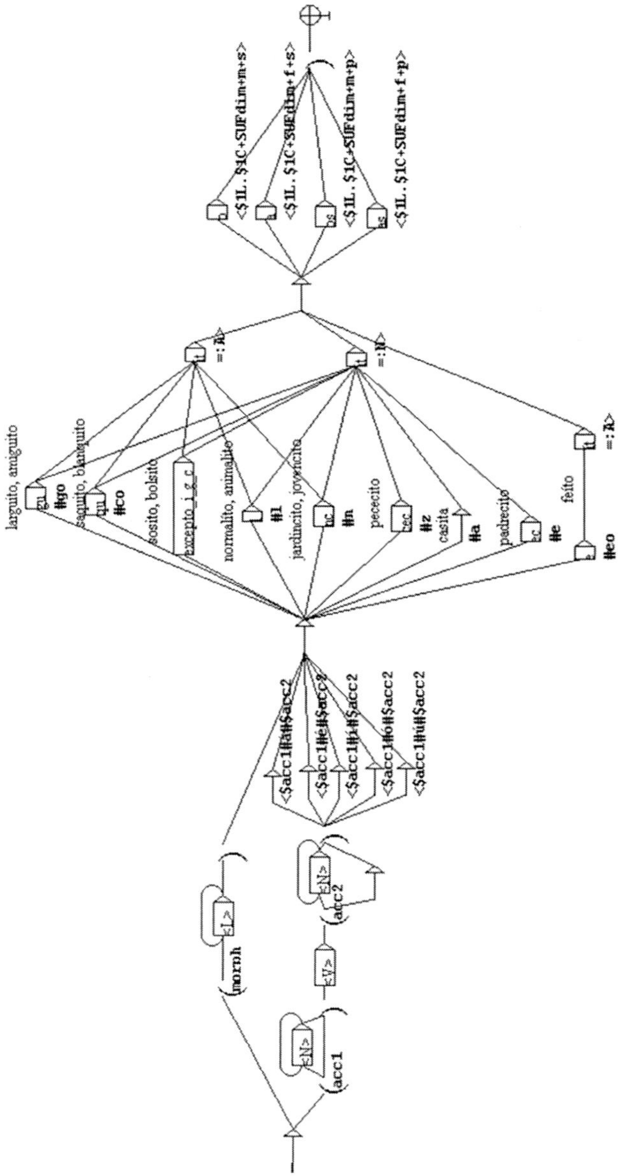
larguito, amiguito
#go
saquito, blanquito
#co
sosito, bolsito
excepto_i_g_c
normalito, animalito
#l
jardincito, jovencito
#n
pececito
#z
casita
#a
padrecito
#e
feito
#eo
morph
acc1
acc2

Fig. 1

The second grammar (Fig. 2) deals with superlatives ending in-ísimo. Again, 9 scenarios are outlined, which apply onlyto adjectives. The derivations are-e to -ísimo, -co to -quísimo ,-io to-ísimo,-go to-guísimo,-guo to -quísimo, -l to -lísimo, -n to -ncísimo,-o (but not in -co, -io, -go, -guo) to -ísimo, and -r to -rísimo. The grammar is rather simple and does not touch upon the exceptions discussed by Bosque (1999):

- When the relational adjectives behave as qualificative, they allow syntactic gradation but not lexical (*muy musical/??musicalísimo*; *bastante político/??politiquísimo*).
- The situational adjectives tend to reject-ísimo, but allow quantifiers: *muy próximo/ ??proximísimo*; *muy cercano/ ??cercanísimo*; *muy anterior/ ??anteriorísimo*. The most frequent adjectival suffixes in the formation of adjectives of relation (-ivo,-ero,-ista,-ario) are compatible with syntactic quantifiers; but most of them reject-ísimo).

  High-register adjectives [cultos] reject -ísimo, but allow syntactic gradation: *muy sagaz*, *bastante veraz*, *absolutamente ducho*, *algo bisoño*, *bastante cauto*, but not *??sagacísimo*, *??veracísimo*, *duchísimo*, *bisoñísimo* etc. Many compound adjectives of Greek origin also reject the relative suffix: *demagogo*, *ególatra*, *carnívoro,* which are mostly stressed on the antepenultimate syllable [esdrújulos].

- The adjectival nouns allow syntactic gradations, but tend to reject-ísimo: *muy rosa*, *bastante violeta*, *muy niño*, *algo cabezota*, as opposed to *??rosísima*, *??violetísima*, *??fierísima*, *??cabezotísima*.
- The adjectives ending in-ío (*sombrío*) also reject-*ísimo* with the exception of pío (*piísimo*), similarly for their feminine. The same applies for the endings in-io (*lapio*, *propio*) and their feminine. The exceptions are l*impio*, *amplio* and *sucio.* Neither the adjectives ending in-eo (*aéreo*),-uo (*vacuo*, *inicuo*), nor their feminine have the derivatives; *antigua* is an exception. In the same way, the adjectives stressed on the antepenultimate syllable [esdrújulos] in-ico (*lúdico*, *rústico* etc.) reject the derivation except *simpático* and *práctico*. The same applies for adjectives ending in-ante, such as *insinuante*, *boyante*, *frustante*, as well as those ending in-(i)ente, like *impaciente*, *insolente*, *pudiente*, with the exception of *frecuente*, *valiente*, *caliente*.
- The majority of the adjectives with a negative prefix do not allow derivation: *incierto*, *inusitado*, *inseguro*, *insólito*, *amorfo*.

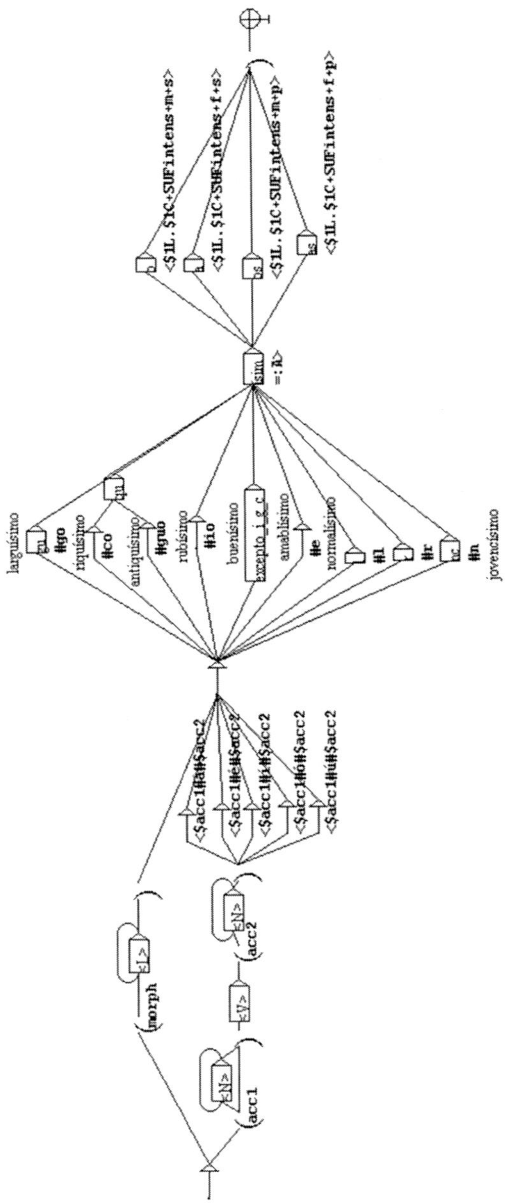
acc1
<N>
<V>
acc2
<N>
morph
<L>
<$acc1#a#$acc2
<$acc1#e#$acc2
<$acc1#i#$acc2
<$acc1#o#$acc2
<$acc1#u#$acc2
laguísimo
#go
riquísimo
#co
antiquísimo
#guo
rubísimo
#io
buenísimo
excepto_i_g_c
amabilísimo
#e
normalísimo
#l
#r
#n
jovencísimo
sim
<$1L.$1C+SUFintens+m+s>
<$1L.$1C+SUFintens+f+s>
<$1L.$1C+SUFintens+m+p>
<$1L.$1C+SUFintens+f+p>

Fig. 2

Clitics

In Spanish, with respect to the conjugated verbs, the pronoun appears in pre-verbal position (proclisis), while with the infinitives, gerunds and affirmative imperatives it assumes a post-verbal position (enclisis) (Soriano, 1999). The syntactic grammar (Fig. 3) written for this module recognises all possible combination of proclitics even the incorrect ones; such as the cases when two verbs are present or when an accusative pronoun is followed by a dative (Soriano, 1999):

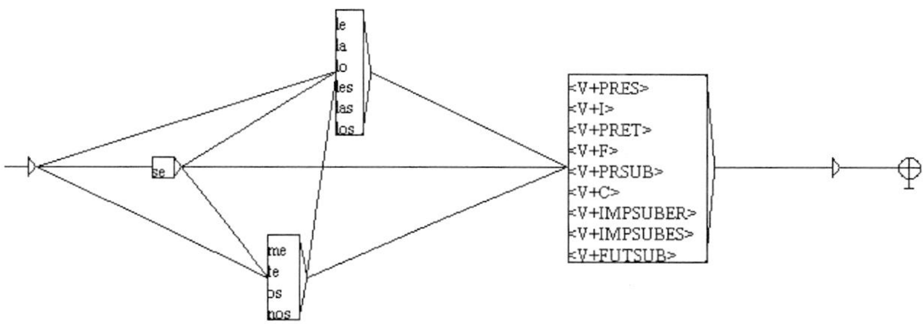

Fig. 3

- *Lo quiero que compres
- *Me le acerqué

Similarly, the grammar which recognises enclitics for gerunds (Fig. 4) and infinitives (Fig. 5) accepts all possible combinations of pronouns as demonstrated by Subirats-Rüggeberg (1989) using the verb *regalar*. However, the grammar does not reject the erroneous cases involving the pronoun *se* and transitive verbs such as *desear*, *odiar*; the ditransitive verbs such as *impedir*, *prohibir*; the verbs of perception; the causative verbs, and other verbs as detailed by Mendikoetxea (1999):

- *La gente desea [trabajarse menos].
- *La policía prohibió [entrarse al juzgado].
- *Vimos [aclamarse a los vencedores].
- *El gobierno hizo [construirse embalses].
- *{Debe/Puede/Suele/Quiere} *trabajarse* mucho aquí.

Nonetheless, the grammars are capable of identifying the lexical stress on the appropriate syllable. Generally, the infinitives and gerunds do not have the accent sign (except verbs with hiatus e.g. *reír*, *oír*):

- Juan quiso enseñar [el libro] [a María].
- Juan estuvo enseñando [el libro] [a María].

The presence of enclitics mandates a graphic stress on the third last syllable:

- Juan quiso enseñarlo a María.
- Juan quiso enseñarle el libro.
- Juan quiso **enseñárselo**.
- Juan estuvo **enseñándolo** a María.
- Juan estuvo **enseñándole** el libro.
- Juan estuvo **enseñándoselo**.

In case of enclitics for affirmative imperatives (Fig. 6) the position of the lexical stress is not fixed. If a word with the last syllable stressed [aguda] (including monosyllabic words) combines with two enclitics, the stressed vowel of the supporting verb will always have the tilde:

- Oír, reír = oírselo, reírse
- Da, di = dáselo, dímelo

When a word with the last syllable stressed [aguda] (including monosyllabic words) combines with only one enclitic, the verb keeps its original accent:

- da, oír = dale, oírlo

The plural imperative of the reflexive verbs has to be used without tilde, despite the fact that the form is stressed on the last syllable [aguda] and it has one enclitic:

- Marchaos, deteneos

However, second person plural affirmative imperative of-ir verbs have tilde because of the hiatus (except for the verb IR-idos)

- partíos, uníos, veníos

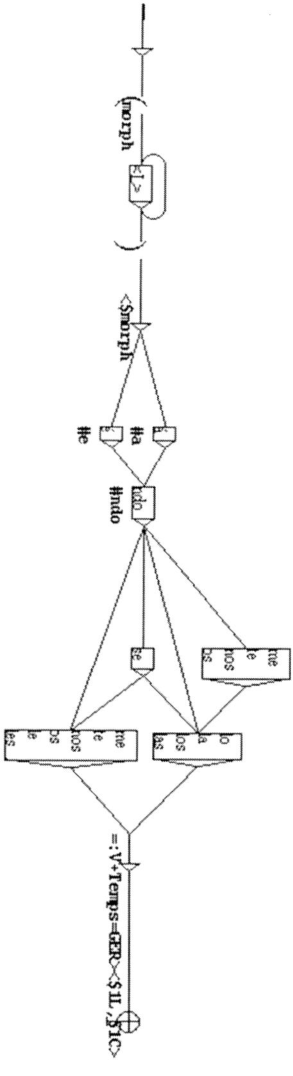
(morph
<$morph
#e
#a
#ndo
=:V+Temps=GER<$1L,$1C>

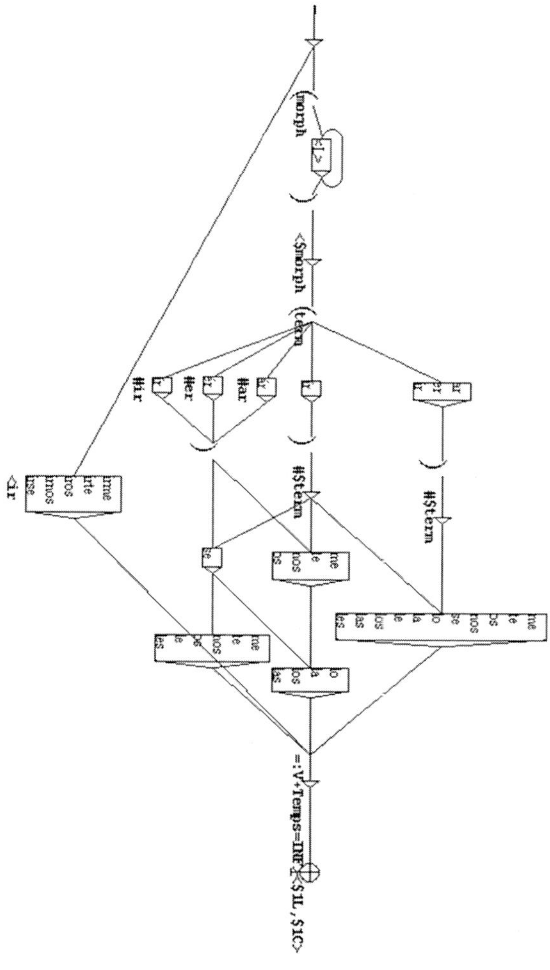
(morph
<$morph
(term
#ir
#er
#ar
#$term
#$term
=:V+Temps=INF<$1L,$1C>

g. 4

Fig. 5

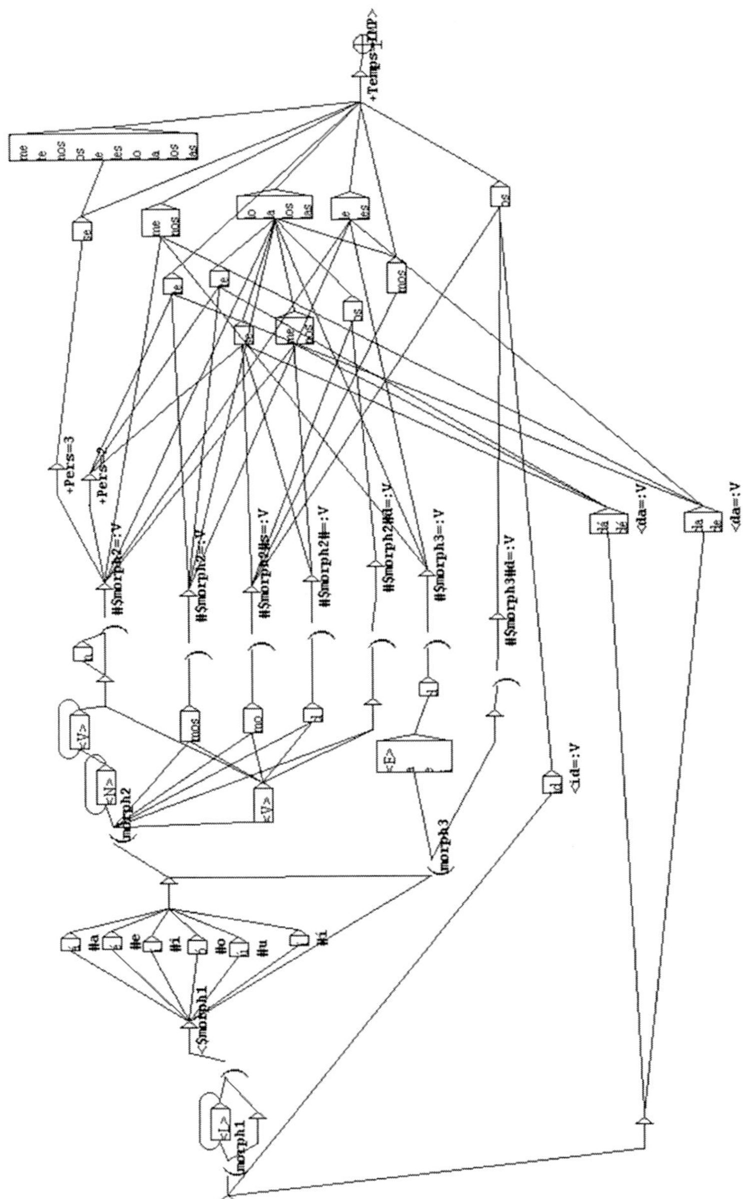

Fig. 6

Lastly, the imperatives also undergo orthographic changes. In front of the clitic *nos* the *s* disappears from the first person plural of the imperative:

- Regalemo**s** + nos = regal**émonos**
- Comamo**s** + nos = com**ámonos**

Similarly, the reflexive form of the second person plural of the imperative loses *d*:

- regala**d** + os + lo = regal**áoslo**
- espabila**d** + os = espabil**aos**
- come**d** + os = com**eos**

Conclusion

The present module contains the basic components of the Spanish dictionary and grammars to enable the recognition of diminutives, superlatives and clitics. The module functions well with both the .NET and the Java versions of NooJ. By regularly updating the resources, it is expected that they could eventually provide a stronger basis for future research, enhancing and refining the linguistic description and formalisation of Spanish.

References

Ambadiang, T. 1999. "La flexión nominal. Género y número." In Gramática descriptiva de la lengua española, ed. Ignacio Bosque and Violeta Demonte. Nebrija y Bello. Volume 3 : 4843-4913. Madrid: Espasa.

Blanco, X. 2000. "Les Dictionnaires électroniques de l'espagnol (DELASs et DELACs)." Lingvisticae Investigationes 23-2: 201-218.

Bosque, I. 1999. "El sintagma adjetival: Modificadores y complementos del adjetivo. Adjetivo y participio." In Gramática descriptiva de la lengua española, ed. Ignacio Bosque and Violeta Demonte. Nebrija y Bello. Madrid: Espasa.

Lázaro M. F. 1999. "La derivación apreciativa." In Gramática descriptiva de la lengua española, ed. Ignacio Bosque and Violeta Demonte. Nebrija y Bello. Madrid: Espasa.

Mendikoetxea, A. 1999. "Construcciones con se: Medias, pasivas e impersonales." In Gramática descriptiva de la lengua española, ed.

Ignacio Bosque and Violeta Demonte. Nebrija y Bello. Madrid: Espasa.

Piera, C. and Soledad V. 1999. “Relaciones entre morfología y sintaxis.” In Gramática descriptiva de la lengua española, ed. Ignacio Bosque and Violeta Demonte. Nebrija y Bello. Madrid: Espasa.

Soriano, O. F. 1999. “El pronombre personal: Formas y distribuciones.” In Gramática descriptiva de la lengua española, ed. Ignacio Bosque et Violeta Demonte. Nebrija Y Bello. Madrid: Espasa.

Subirats-Rüggeberg, C. 1989. “Verbal morphology in the electronic dictionary of Spanish.” Lingvisticae Investigationes XIII (1): 179–201.

DERIVATION OF MULTIPLY COMPLEX NEGATIVE ADJECTIVES FROM VERBAL STEMS IN GREEK

ZOE GAVRIILIDOU AND LENA PAPADOPOULOU

Abstract

This work focuses on Greek multiply complex negative adjectives from verbal stems. On the one hand, the derivation in one step from the verbal root using NooJ morphological grammars is presented. On the other hand, the idiosyncratic meanings of the deverbal adjectives in our Greek NooJ dictionaries of complex forms are listed.

Introduction

Greek deverbal adjectives of the type a[negative prefix]-metri[present perfect passive participle form of the verb metro 'count']-tos[suffix for the creation of deverbal adjectives] 'uncountable' (Anastasiadis 1994, Ralli 2005) form a productive derivational category, where the negative prefix a-'un' attaches productively to a deverbal adjective in-tós 'able' to form adjectives that express a negative property. In many cases, the intermediate adjective in-tós is only a possible word, which is not listed in the lexicon as in: aperiγraptos 'indescribable' (*periγraptós '*describable'), avástaxtos 'unbearable' (*vastaxtós '*bearable'), and in others it has acquired an idiosyncratic meaning (metró 'count'>metritós 'cash' vs. metrisimos 'countable'). Following Booj (2010), we derive multiply complex adjectives of this type in one step from the verbal root using NooJ morphological grammars. On the other hand we list the idiosyncratic meanings of the deverbal adjectives in –tós in our Greek NooJ dictionaries of complex forms.

Theoretical issues

The morphological analysis of Greek deverbal adjectives of the type a[negative prefix]-metri[present perfect past participle form of the verb metro 'count']-tos[suffix for the creation of deverbal adjectives] 'uncountable' is a puzzling phenomenon studied by a number of scholars in Greek (Anastasiadis 1994, Ralli 2005). The problems that follow from the morphological analysis of these constructions can be summarised as follows. First, in many cases there is a mismatch between the morphological structure of the word and its semantics causing a bracketing paradox. In other words, these constructions seem to require one constituent analysis at the morphological level:

(1) [a-[VERB-t(os)]]

and a different analysis at the semantic level:

(2) *[[a-VERB]-t(os)]

What these representations mean is that morphologically the above mentioned examples are structured by the attachment of the negative prefix a-'un/in' to a deverbal adjective in t(os) (see ex. 1), while semantically we see that aperiγraptos 'indescribable', for instance, means 'who can't be described', where there is a verbal base (see ex. 2). However, in Greek, the prefix a-'un/in' does not attach to verbal bases, only to adjectival and nominal bases. More over what is peculiar in these constructions is the fact that in many cases the adjective in t(os) is only a possible word which is not listed in the lexicon or, in other words, it has an idiosyncratic meaning (e.g. metri[present perfect passive participle form of the verb metro 'count']-tós[suffix for the creation of deverbal adjectives] 'cash money' and not 'who can be counted', xtipi[present perfect passive participle form of the verb xtipo 'knock']-tós 'vivid' (in expressions like xtipito kitrino 'vivid yellow') and not 'knocking'.

In order to account for these irregularities in the studied examples, we adopt the notion of embedded schemata (Booij 2010: 41) within the frame of construction morphology. According to the author (Booij 2010: 42), "possible complex words may form intermediate steps in coining new words". The proposed analysis of our data is thus as follows:

(3) [a-A]A+[VERB-(tos)]A=[a[VERB-t(os)]A]A
[un-A]A+[VERB-able)A=[un[VERB-able]A]A

where two schemas of Greek derivational morphology are unified in a more complex schema. On the basis of this complex schema we may derive multiply complex adjectives of this type in one step from a verbal base as, for instance, the adjective aperiγraptos 'indescribable' without an intermediate adjective *periγraptós 'describable' that is possible but not existing in Greek.

Three are the advantages of this analysis. First, it allows at the morphological level the co-occurrence and simultaneous application of two word formation processes, one that derives negative adjectives and one that derives deverbal adjectives, thus accounts adequately for the morphological analysis of the word. Second, at the semantic level it mirrors the language user's ability to establish a direct relation between the verbal base of these examples and the complex word "that is two or more derivational steps away from that base word" (Booij 2010: 43). Third, it implies that we are not forced to assume discontinuous affixes a-tos 'un-able' for the derivation of these Greek adjectives as Anastasiadis (1994) had assumed.

This theoretical analysis can find an application in natural language processing with NooJ as it will be described below.

Negative deverbal adjectives in NooJ

The processing of negative deverbal adjectives was carried out within the NooJ derivational grammar´s tool.

Before proceeeding with the elaboration of the derivational grammar, it is worthwhile to recall the morphological analysis of negative deverbal adjectives, which is threefold.

(4) negative prefix+present perfect participle form+tos

The first part is the negative prefix *a* (5), or its allomorph *an* (6), when the root strarts with a vowel:

(5) a-fore-tos 'unworn'
(6) an-amfisviti-tos 'unquestionable'

The second part concerns the present perfect passive participle form, which corresponds to the perfective verb stem. The perfective verb stem is normally sigmatic and it is made up regularly of the imperfective verb stem and a segmentable affix (-s-) with phonological stem changes. The perfective stem is used in order to construct the perfect tenses; simple past, simple future, present perfect, past perfect and future perfect. Finally, the third part is the suffix *–tos*, which is inflected in all cases – nominative, genitive, accusative and vocative, numbers – singular and plural, and genders – masculine, femenine and neutral.

As far as the grammar construction is concerned, the imperative form of the second person singular of simple past (IPT+s+2) had been set as the basis for the stem definition. IPT+s+2 form has been chosen for three reasons; first, it refers to a monolectical verb form, e.g. *kalese* 'invite', *milise* 'speak', second, it does not contain the stressed syllabic augment *e-*, which is used when the verb stem is monosyllabic and starts with a consonant, e.g. *apespases* 'you extracted', *epekses* 'you played' (second person of the indicative of simple past) and *apospase* 'extract', *pekse* 'play' (IPT+s+2), and, third, it follows the antepenultimate stress rule, according to which the past tense form has to be stressed in the antepenultimate syllable, e.g. ***γé**lase* (IPT+s+2) *γe**lá**sete* (IPT+s+2). Thus, the construction of negative deverbal adjectives is defined within NooJ grammar as the combination of the negative prefix *a(n),* the form of IPT+s+2, without the sigmatic form and the inflectional morpheme, and the suffix *–tos* (see Image 1), which is totally inflected in a subgraph of the same grammar (see Image 2):

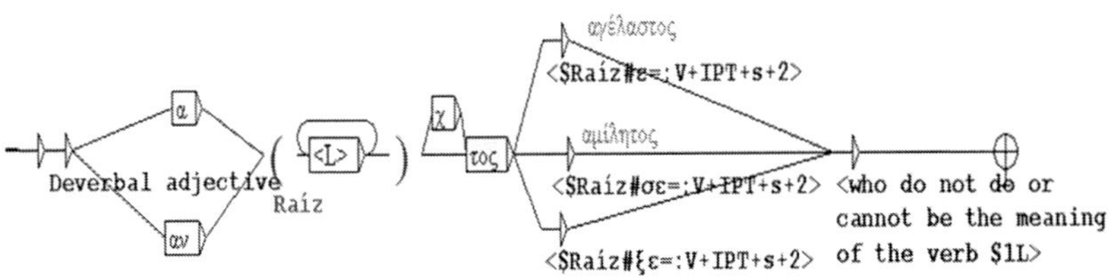

Fig.1: Graph for negative adjectives derived from verbs in active voice

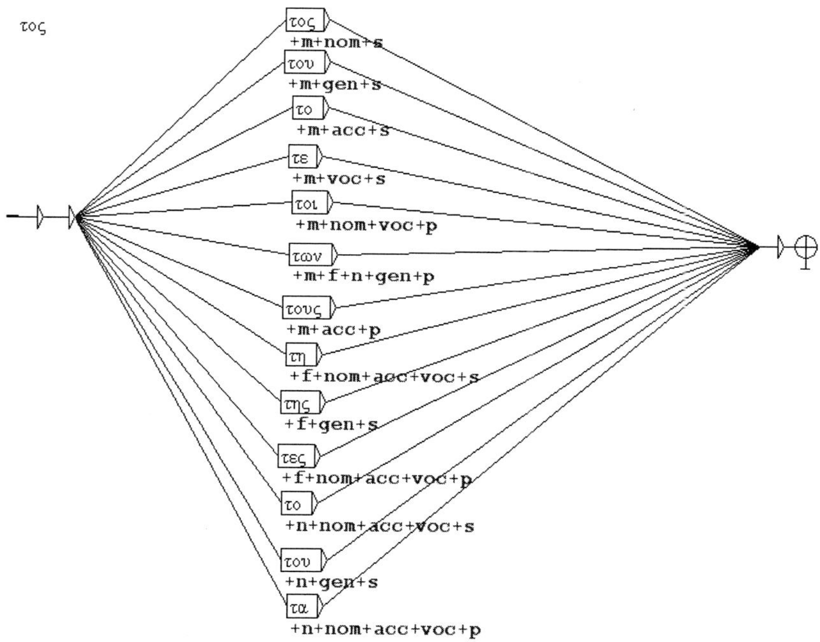

Fig.2: Subgraph for the inflection of the suffix-*tos*

Limitations – Conclusions

Our work has been subject to two main constraints. First, the derivational grammar is limited to the verbs of the second conjugation class. This limitation has been imposed because of the regular formation that the second conjugation class presents, especially considering the stress, as the verbs of this class are stressed on the inflectional suffix of the present tense (Clairis & Babiniotis 2005: 512), i.e. *γeláo* 'to laugh', *oδiγó* 'to drive'. Second, our derivational grammar is limited to recognise negative adjectives derived from verbs that are already inflectionally processed in NooJ (among others Gavriilidou, Z., Chatzipapa, E., Papadopoulou, E., 2007; Papadopoulou, E. 2010; Gavriilidou, Z., Papadopoulou, E. & Chatzipapa E. 2011) considering the reuse of certain perfective verb forms.

Although the initial scope of the work focuses on the second conjugation verb class, our grammar can also recognise negative adjectives derived from verbs of the first conjugation as well, such as verbs ending in *–óno aplírotos* (*<pliróno*) 'unpaid', in *–ázo aplisíastos* (*<plisiázo*) 'unapproachable',*-évo apísteftos* (*<pistévo*) 'unbelievable', in *–ízo* a*kaθóristos* (*<kaθorízo*) 'undefined', etc.

Finally, further work has to be done in order to incorporate in the derivational grammar verbs of the first conjugation class.

References

Anastasiadis, A. 1994. «Το τεμάχιο *–τος* στα ρηματικά επίθετα της Νεοελληνικής». *Studies in Greek Linguistics* 15: 473-484.

Booij, G. 2010. *Construction Morphology*. Oxford: Oxford University Press.

Clairis, C. and Babiniotis G. 2005. *Modern Greek Grammar [In Greek]*. Athens: Elinika Gramata.

Gavriilidou, Z. Chatzipapa E. Papadopoulou E. 2008. «The New Greek NooJ Module: morphosemantic issues», in Blanco, X.; Silberztein, M. (eds): *Proceedings of the 2007 NooJ International Conference*, Cambridge: Cambridge Scholars Publishing, pp. 96-103.

Gavriilidou, Z. Papadopoulou E. and Chatzipapa E. "Processing Greek frozen expressions with NooJ", in Vučković, K. Bekavac, B. and Silberztein, M. 2011: *Automatic Processing of Various Levels of Linguistic Phenomena: Selected Papers from the NooJ 2011 International Conference (Dubrovnik)*, Cambridge Scholars Publishing, pp. 63-74.

Papadopoulou, E. 2010. *Diccionario monolingüe coordinado para enseñanza/aprendizaje del griego moderno por parte de hispanohablantes y para traducción automática griego-español*, Tesis Doctoral, Bellaterra: Universitat Autònoma de Barcelona.

Ralli, A. 2005. *Morphology [In Greek]*. Αθήνα: Πατάκης.

Silberztein, M. 2003. *NooJ manual*. Available at http://www.nooj4nlp.net

THE NOOJ ENGLISH DICTIONARY

SIMONETTA VIETRI[1] AND MARIO MONTELEONE

Abstract

This paper describes the construction and revision phases of the NooJ English Simple Words Electronic Dictionary (NESWED). As a NLP software environment, greatly appreciated worldwide, today NooJ is used by a large international community of researchers to process several languages and to analyse texts dealing with multiple and diverse fields of knowledge. The most basic part of NooJ lingware consists of monolingual electronic dictionaries that need to be continually tested and updated. However, before we started this project, an efficient and reliable NESWED had not yet been built, even if the need of such a dictionary has always been strongly felt by the community who gathers around NooJ.

Foreword

This paper describes the construction and revision phases of the NooJ English Simple Words Electronic Dictionary (NESWED). As a NLP software environment, greatly appreciated worldwide, today NooJ is used by a large international community of researchers to process several languages and to analyse texts dealing with multiple and diverse fields of knowledge. The most basic part of NooJ lingware consists of monolingual electronic dictionaries that need to be continually tested and updated. However, before we started this project, an efficient and reliable NESWED had not yet been built, even if the need of such a dictionary has always been strongly felt by the community who gathers around NooJ. Therefore, in this paper we give a step-by-step description of the NEWSWED creation, complying with the definition of the word list (Section 1); the identification and assigning of inflection codes to entries (Section 2); and

---

[1] Simonetta Vietri is author of the Foreword, Sections 1, and 2 (including subsections). Mario Monteleone is author of Sections 3, 4 and 5, and of the Appendix. The authors would like to thank Max Silberztein for his crucial and constant support during all the construction phases of the dictionary.

the application of the NEWSWED within NooJ automatic textual analysis (Section 3), in terms both of procedures and result evaluation. The conclusive part of this paper (Section 4) discusses some possible implementation procedures, more specifically the semantic tagging of names. For several reasons related to the (rather long but necessary) creation and revision phases, the dictionary we present here is still a beta version, but we rely upon the support of the NooJ Community for error detection and suggestions on how to improve it.

The Dictionary

The starting point of NESWED construction was the list of lemmas extracted from the Wiki English Dictionary (WED)[2]; it counts about 287,000 entries, including both simple and compound atomic linguistic units (ALUs)[3]. The subsequent step was to isolate simple ALUs and separate them from compound ones. As for Parts of Speech (POS) classification, compound ALUs are subject to the same descriptive modalities and categorial tag set used for simple words, while they have specific formal and inflection characteristics, which makes it necessary to categorise them with ad hoc criteria. For example, compound ALUs also include verb idiomatic complex lexemes like *to take one's heels*, or phrasal verbs like *to slow down* and *to give up*, which have to be considered as V+Adverb constructions. In the same way, they include compound nouns like *apple pie* but also sequences like *a lot of*, which must instead be classified as a pre-determiner/pre-quantifier. A further step was to tag NESWED entries with proper POS labelson the basis of their concrete linguistic uses, essentially bearing in mind that apart from

---

[2] See http://en.wiktionary.org/wiki/Wiktionary:Main_Page.

[3] As for compound words, today the terms "collocations", "multi-words", "multiword expressions" and "multiword units" are often used in literature to indicate "strings of words having a unique overall meaning". These terms seem rather ambiguous and less effective than "compound ALUs" to distinguish between free word groups (i.e. compositional non-terminological free word formations) and all other kind of word formations (going from compound terminological words to proverbs). Besides, according to Maurice Gross' Lexicon-Grammar, which is our NLP theoretical and practical framework, only the items of the second group are to be lemmatized in electronic dictionaries. Therefore in this paper we will adopt the expressions "compound ALUs" to refer to any kind of lemmatisable "strings of words having a unique overall meaning", including terminological compound words, which even being very often semantically compositional, can be lemmatised due to their particular non-ambiguous information content.

average polysemy, in English simple words have a high categorial ambiguity level, and that often the same word may be used as a noun, an adjective, and also a verb. This happens for instance with words such as *level* and *yellow* (noun, verb, and adjective), or *clue* (noun and adjective). Subsequently, the word list so obtained was converted into the NooJ dictionary format and started to be examined in order to validate POS tagging and create inflection paradigms.

Detecting and Assigning Inflection Codes

The most important steps of this phase were the detection and assignment of appropriate inflection paradigms to each NESWED verb and noun; the revision and updating of the already existing inflection codes; and the creation and integration of new inflection paradigms.

English inflection morphology is less complex than those of Roman languages, and also than those of Slavic languages such as Czech[4]. For instance, Roman Languages may inflect even prepositions, as we can see in the following sentences:

(French) *Max a écrit (**au** dirécteur + **aux** dirécteurs)*
(Italian) *Max ha scritto (**al** direttore + **ai** direttori)*
(English) *Max wrote **to the** (director + directors)*

All this has made code detection and assignment reasonably complex. English paradigms are not numerous, rather regular and predictable, therefore easily formalisable. Noun paradigms present an almost constant number of inflected forms averagely going from 1 to 4, while verb paradigms have from 3 to 5 forms.[5] Subsequently, already existing inflection codes were revised, updated, and integrated into new ones.[6] The codes created anew were for example those of human nouns like

[4] Czech or Bohemian language presents a quite complex noun inflection, very similar to the one of Latin declensions. In fact, it has seven nominal cases, namely: nominative, genitive, dative, accusative, vocative, locative and instrumental. This complexity is due to the fact that Czech literary language was formed and consolidated during rather ancient historical periods, prior to other European languages.

[5] On the contrary, some Italian verbs like fare (to do, to make) exceeds the number of 70 inflected forms, not considering compound verb uses such as the past conditional avrei fatto (I shoud have done) or the past conjunctive avessi fatto (I had done).

[6] In the Appendix, we will present sample lists of English inflection paradigms.

administrator, inheritor, interlocutor, persecutor, tutor that inflect their feminine forms in *administratrix*, *administratrices, administratrixes* (but also *administratress*, *administratresses*); *inheritrix, inheritrices, inheritrixes* (but also *inheritress, inheritresses*); *interlocutrix, interlocutrices, interlocutrixes* (but also *interlocutress, interlocutresses*); *persecutrix, persecutrices*, *persecutrixes* (but also *persecutress, persecutresses*); *tutrix, tutrices, tutrixes* (but also *tutoress, tutoresses*). Usually, these word forms are considered rare, however, for a word like *administratrix* a Web search produced 820,000 results. The last step of this phase was the automatic assignment of the +FLX property to each entry. Even if the WED describes nouns and verbs morphology/inflection, the output had to be carefully checked (and still needs to), mainly because in some cases the inflection information given by the WED is imprecise; and also because even if extremely accurate, the automatic assignment of the +FLX property to each entry could not always account for particular meanings/ uses of some words, especially countable/uncountable nouns.

Using WED Inflection Information

A concrete example of WED lacking/incomplete inflection information is the class of Mineral nouns, which very often are given unreliable descriptions. For instance, the morphology of the word ***balangeroite* is described as follows:**

balangeroite
1. (mineralogy) A monoclinic-prismatic mineral containing hydrogen, iron, magnesium, manganese, oxygen, and silicon.

A similar description is given for *calciborite*:

calciborite
1. (mineralogy) An orthorhombic-dipyramidal white mineral containing boron, calcium, and oxygen.

On the contrary, ***uranite* is described as both countable and uncountable:**

uranite (countable and uncountable, plural uranites)
1. A dark, lustrous, heavy mineral, a source of uranium and radium.

Due to these inconsistent descriptions, countable inflection codes were assigned to all mineral names. However, a more careful analysis would lead to different choices on the basis of meanings, linguistic uses and descriptive taxonomy of minerals. In this sense, a great help comes from the Oxford Advanced Learner's Dictionary (OALD) and from its definition[7] of the term "mineral":

> Mineral
> noun
> [**countable, uncountable**] a substance that is naturally present in the earth and is not formed from animal or vegetable matter, for example gold and salt. Some minerals are also present in food and drink and in the human body and are essential for good health.

This description mentions two widely used mineral names, i.e. "gold" and "salt". Intuitively, they seem uncountable, i.e. mass-nouns, but they have attested plural forms: "golds" is used to indicate both coins made of gold, and the nuances of a bright yellow color, resembling the metal gold; "salts" is used to indicate the entire class of "compounds formed from the reaction of an acid with a base, where a positive ion replaces a hydrogen of the acid."[8] Therefore, it would seem reasonable to think that mineral nouns are uncountable only when referring specifically to substances naturally present in the earth, while their plural forms may be used in different ways. Consequently, in the NESWED mineral names have been (and will be) tagged as only singular by means of the specific code MAXIMAX:

```
balangeroite,N+FLX=MAXIMAX
calciborite N+FLX=MAXIMAX
gold N+FLX=MAXIMAX
salt N+FLX=MAXIMAX
uranite N+FLX=MAXIMAX
```

In addition, where necessary, they will also have a countable inflection:

```
gold,N+FLX=APPLE
salt,N+FLX=APPLE
```

with the code APPLE:

---

[7] See http://oald8.oxfordlearnersdictionaries.com/dictionary/mineral.

[8] See http://en.wiktionary.org/wiki/salt#English. As for Minerals, differences in meanings also occur in Italian. The name ori (golds) means "golden objects, jewels", while sali (salts) means "compound based on ammonium salts, added with flavoring essences and used for reanimation in case of fainting".

APPLE = <E>/s | s/p ;

accounting also for the plural forms "golds" and "salts". At any rate, additional linguistic analysis will be required to identify the correct inflection codes for all mineral nouns, the number of which in English exceeds 5000 units.

Problems of the +FLX Automatic Assignment

Among others, a specific problem coming from the +FLX automatic assignment concerns the nouns of nationalities and national languages. In the NEWSWED, entries such as *Czech*, *Italian*, and *Zulu* have been labelled with the code "YOKE", which is structured as follows:

YOKE = <E>/s | <E>/p | s/p ;

Besides, for *Italian*, the indication given by the WED is:

Noun
Italian (plural Italians)
1. An inhabitant of Italy, or a person of Italian descent.
Proper noun
Italian
2. The official language of Italy, also spoken in San Marino, the Vatican, and parts of Switzerland.

For *Czech* it is:

Noun
Czech (plural Czechs)
1. A person from the Czech Republic (Czechia) or of Czech descent.
Proper noun
Czech
2. A Slavic language primarily spoken in the Czech Republic.

The indication given for *Zulu* is slightly different:

Zulu
1. An African ethnic group living mainly in the KwaZulu-Natal Province in Eastern South Africa.
2. The language of these people, a Bantu language; isiZulu.

Due to specific linguistic use constraints, all the entries which merge names of nationalities with names of languages have been doubled. Actually, names of languages are always only singular, as in:

In Italian we say "bottega"; *In Italians we say "bottega"
In Czech we say "obchod"; *In Czechs we say "obchod"

From a sociolinguistic point of view, this constraint is not neutralised by the possible presence of language variants, i.e.: there is only an Italian language, despite the fact that in different regions of Italy different forms of Italian may exist. In addition, nationality names refer to humans and are consequently always countable, as in:

Italians say "bottega"; An Italian says "bottega"
Czechs say "obchod"; A Czech says"obchod"

The +FLX automatic assignment could not account for or formalise such differences directly pertaining to encyclopedia. Besides, we note that doubling is necessary also as far as semantic tagging is concerned. In fact, names of nationalities may be additionally labelled with the tag "Hum", while this would be incorrect for names of languages. Therefore, in the NEWSWED we will have doubled entries as:

Czech,N+FLX=APPLE+Hum
Czech,N+FLX=MAXIMAX
Italian,N+FLX=APPLE+Hum
Italian,N+FLX=MAXIMAX
Zulu,N+FLX=APPLE+Hum
Zulu,N+FLX=MAXIMAX[9]

[9] As for NooJ automatic textual analysis and parsing, we note that the correct distinction between these different inflection behaviours may help in the construction of more coherent FSA/FSTs, in the sense that with NooJ grammars it will be possible to rapidly process communication predicates such as "to communicate", "to write", "to say", "to speak" or "to talk" when they co-occur with names of languages, mainly if such names will be labelled with an *ad hoc* tag. For this reason in the following pages we will propose a set of semantic tags for nouns which the group of linguists at the "Maurice Gross" Computational Linguistics Laboratory are at present developing and applying to Italian electronic dictionaries. As we will see, such tags are based on universal and standard logic criteria, and may be used also for the NESWED.

Another specific problem coming from the +FLX automatic assignment concerns all abstract entries ending in "-ness", as *absentmindedness, abstruseness, bareness, bitterness*, which are almost always uncountable, a part from some few cases. For instance, the definition given by the WED for *absentmindedness* is:

Noun
absentmindedness (uncountable)
Alternative form of absent-mindedness.

The +FLX automatic assignment has labeled all these entries with the code "APPLE". A revision of these entries is still ongoing. Considering that their number exceeds 7000 units, we preferred to automatically substitute the code "APPLE" with "MAXIMAX", and to check these entries one by one, changing the code where necessary.

NESWED and WED Verb Syntactic Properties

An additional critical point for the NESWED was the fact that the information given by the WED on verb syntactic properties (i.e. transitivity/intransitivity) are inconsistent and difficult to reuse/formalise. For instance, there are several verbs for which no indication is given. This is the case of *to adlect*:

adlect (third person singular simple present adlects, present participle adlecting, simple past and past participle adlected)

1. To choose or elect, especially to promote someone to higher office before he has served in a lower capacity

Besides, an entry like *to read* is defined as follows:

1. read,V+DEF="To consist of certain text"
2. read,V+Intransitive+DEF="Of text, etc., to be interpreted or read in a particular way"
3. read,V+Transitive+DEF="To interpret or infer a meaning, significance, etc."
4. read,V+Transitive+DEF="To look at and interpret letters or other information that is written"
read,V+Intransitive+DEF="To look at and interpret letters or other information that is written"
5. read,V+Transitive+DEF="To speak aloud words or other information that is written. Often construed with a 'to' phrase or an indirect object."

read,V+Intransitive+DEF="To speak aloud words or other information that is written. Often construed with a 'to' phrase or an indirect object."
6. read,V+Transitive+DEF="To substitute (a corrected piece of text in place of an erroneous one); used to introduce an emendation of a text"
7. read,V+Transitive+DEF="To make a special study of, as by perusing textbooks" +DOM="British"
8. read,V+Transitive+DEF="To be able to hear what another person is saying over a radio connection"+DOM="telecommunications"
9. read,V+Transitive+DEF="to recognise (someone) as being transgender" +DOM="transgenderism"

For example, in (5) the verb *to read* is considered transitive since it enters a sentence construction like *He **read** us a passage from his new book*. On the other hand, it is considered intransitive because of a sentence structure like *All right, class, who wants to **read** next?* A correct syntactic analysis would assign to *to read* only the property +Transitive, since the supposed intransitive construction is due to the object deletion, i.e. in Lexicon-Grammar terms it is a substructure of a transitive use. However, even being fuzzy and imprecise, WED syntactic information have been imported in NESWED along with verb definitions, but they are not yet available because they need further revisions and validations.[10]

NESWED Inflecting and Testing

The first NESWED inflected version includes 281,317 entries, of which 76,629 are verb forms and 131,970 are noun forms. Also, it includes 59,413 adjectives and 11,031 adverbs, besides minor categories like prepositions, determiners, conjunctions, and pronouns. The total number of inflection paradigms is 150 for nouns and 122 for verbs. Some sample NESWED noun and verb inflection codes are presented in the Appendix. As for nouns, they were subdivided into the following morphological and formal groups, i.e.: apostrophe; -y ending; singular only; plural only; mass and no-mass; regular; internal inflection; irregular; others; derivations. At the same time, verb codes were subdivided into: regular verbs; verbs with regular and irregular forms; auxiliaries and modals; irregular verbs.

---

[10] To achieve this task, other on-line dictionaries will be consulted, such as the Merriam-Webster (http://www.merriam-webster.com/), and the Oxford On-line Dictionary (http://www.oxforddictionaries.com/). In order to specify transitivity/intransitivity, this last one regularly makes use of the indication "with object/no object". However, it is worth noting that also these two dictionaries do not clearly account for eventual direct object deletions.

A first testing of the NEWSWED has been carried out on the text file reut2-000.txt (1.217 KB, 317 pages, 167.741tokens), extracted from the Reuter Corpus «**Reuters-21578**», freely downloadable at http://www.dav iddlewis.com/resources/testcollections/reuters21578/. After the processing, NooJ highlighted 927 texts units, 167,741tokens, 122,316 word forms, 23,789 digits, 21,366 delimiters, 998,591 annotations (98,381 different), 531 unknown words. These last ones are mostly proper nouns, acronyms, neologisms, place names and typos, as it is evidenced by the following examples:

ABSB,UNKNOWN
absorbant,UNKNOWN
adition,UNKNOWN
adverserial,UNKNOWN
alows,UNKNOWN
ananta,UNKNOWN
ARGENTINA,UNKNOWN
AUSTRALIA,UNKNOWN
authorizerd,UNKNOWN
autoparts,UNKNOWN
avearge,UNKNOWN
avg,UNKNOWN
aymah,UNKNOWN
azpurua,UNKNOWN
balace,UNKNOWN
BALO,UNKNOWN
BankAmerica,UNKNOWN
BankEast,UNKNOWN
bankrupcty,UNKNOWN
bankrupcy,UNKNOWN
BanPonce,UNKNOWN
BC,UNKNOWN
BCF,UNKNOWN
BCOM,UNKNOWN
benficiaries,UNKNOWN
bilion,UNKNOWN
BOLIVIA,UNKNOWN
bourse,UNKNOWN
BPCL,UNKNOWN
bpd,UNKNOWN
CAC,UNKNOWN
CAECL,UNKNOWN
cale,UNKNOWN
CANADA,UNKNOWN

This is a fairly satisfactory result as it provides reassuring indications on the current coverage of the NESWED. However, a testing on the entire Reuters corpus is already in progress, and its results will be very useful to provide additional entries with which to update the NEWSWED.

Conclusions: Further Steps to Take

As we have seen, the actual NESWED still needs revision, validation and updating, not only in order to produce a reliable beta version, but mainly to become a more consistent, flexible and versatile tool for NooJ NLP operations. Schematically, to this end the steps to achieve are: the revision of verbs transitivity/intransitivity; the study of verb syntactic behaviours/profiles (more specifically the individuation of all those transitive verbs which produce substructures and are hence erroneously defined as intransitive by the WED or by any other English on-line/paper dictionary); the consequent labelling of verbs with the appropriate transitive/intransitive tags; also, the consequent deletion of all incorrect intransitive tags; the syntactic tagging of verbs (using already existing LG classes or where necessary, completing English Lexicon-Grammar description); the creation of a typology for English semantic predicates; the building of any other necessary/lacking NooJ English dictionaries (acronyms, proper nouns, place names, etc.); the revision and eventually updating/upgrading of noun inflection codes; the syntactic tagging of English nouns, adjectives and of any POS likely to play the role of a predicate inside simple sentences; the semantic tagging of English nouns, i.e. the creation of a set of semantic tags likely to formally resume LG rules of co-occurrence and selection restriction; the creation of a more vast English corpus on which to test the NESWED; the analysis of the testing results to achieve further updating/upgrading.

Noun semantic tagging

The utility of assigning semantic labels to names is strictly linked both to the definition of (sets of) English semantic predicates, and to the creation of NooJ FSA/FSTs for coherent English text processing. The definition of semantic predicates was originally introduced by Gross (1981); subsequently, by means of NooJ, it was concretely formalised and applied to Italian by Elia et alii (2010). Gross' definition is based on the fact that for each given language analysed, Lexicon-Grammar can establish sets of lexical-syntactic structures on the basis of the semantic features of each verb. These features are made explicit directly by the application of the rules of co-occurrence and selection restriction, through which verbs select semantically their arguments to construct acceptable simple sentences. Also, the arguments selected by each verb are given the value of attants (subjects included). Therefore, we may have semantic predicates expressing the intuitive notion of "exchange" (i.e. "Transfer Predicates" as "to give" or "to receive"), "motion" ("Movement Predicates" as "to go" or "to move") or "production" ("Creation Predicates" as "to build", "to assemble"). Each set of semantic predicates will select only and exclusively those arguments with which they have compatible semantic roles. For instance, "Transfer Predicates" will select a "giver", an "object to transfer" and a "receiver", as in:

Max (giver) gives a present (object to transfer) to John (receiver)
John (receiver) receives a present (object to transfer) from Max (giver)

"Movement Predicates" will select an "agent of motion", eventually an "object to move", and a "locative name", as in:

Max (agent of motion) goes to Rome (locative name)
Max (agent of motion) moves the table (object to move) from the living room to the kitchen (locative names)

"Creation Predicates" will select a "creator" and a "creation", as in:

Max (creator) assembles the train (creation)
Max (creator) paints a picture (creation)

On such basis, electronic dictionary nouns may also be labeled predicting their likelihood of becoming arguments of (a specific set of) semantic predicates. However, the list of semantic tags likely to be used is not easily identifiable, due to the polysemy of simple nouns. In fact, from the above examples, it can be seen that "agent of motion" and "creator" are sub-classes of the class "Hum", and that "object to move", and "creation" are sub-classes of the class "Conc" (concrete objects). Moreover, the words *abbey* and *train* can be selected by both "Motion" and "Creation":

Max (entered + built) the (abbey + train)

and also occur as human nouns:

The (abbey + train) laughed at Max's joke

On this basis, in the NESWED *abbey* and *train* could be labelled as follows:

abbey,N+FLX=APPLE+Conc
abbey,N+FLX=APPLE+Hum
abbey,N+FLX=APPLE+Loc[11]
train,N+FLX=APPLE+Conc
train,N+FLX=APPLE+Hum
train,N+FLX=APPLE+Loc

Despite all possible and evident difficulties, an attempt to define a comprehensive set of semantic tags is currently in progress for the Italian DELAS-DELAF. The first results of this research have produced the following list of semantic categories and labels:

NAbb: clothing article
NAlimE: edible substance
NAlimP: potable substance
NAnim: animal/animate
NArr: (piece of) furniture
NAst: abstract
NAtmo: weather event
NBot: botanical
NChim: chemical
NColl: collective human
NConc: concrete
NCosm: cosmetic
NCreat: creation

In terms of sets, the semantic features specified in this list overlap to a variable extent, especially with regard to all the possible subclasses of concrete nouns. For this reason, during the labeling of nouns, it will be possible to assign more than one tag. As previously declared, this system of semantic classification is still in an embryonic state. However, it is already possible to say that it could simplify and improve the efficiecy of building NooJ FSA/FST grammars, allowing for verbs and nouns the insertion into nodes of one or more tags which could be used to identify classes of words instead of single words. In this sense, it could be also possible to build large-coverage grammars for single sets of semantic

[11] We note that a double tagging "Conc_Loc" would be inaccurate, as while accounting simultaneously for movement and creation, it would make it impossible to distinguish between the argument selections of the two semantic predicates.

predicates, as the one in Figure 1, which accounts for 105 simple sentences of the following kind:

(He + Max) (draws + is drawing) (a picture + pictures)
(We + Paul and John) (outline + are outlining) (a drawing + drawings)

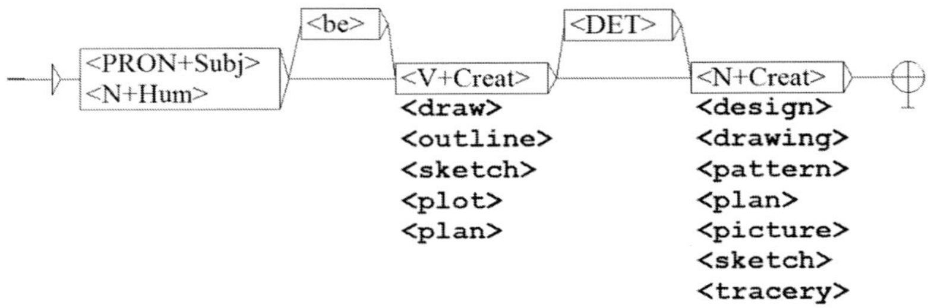

Fig.1: Sample Local Grammar for Creation Semantic Predicates

References

De Bueris, G., Elia, A. (eds.), 2008: *Lessici elettronici e descrizioni lessicali, sintattiche, morfologiche ed ortografiche*, Plectica, Salerno.

Elia, A., Vietri, S., Postiglione, A., Monteleone, M., Marano, F., 2010: "Data Mining Modular Software System", in ARABNIA H.R., MARSH A., SOLO A.M.G (eds.), *Proceedings of The 2010 International Conference on Semantic Web & Web Services*, CSREA Press, Las Vegas Nevada USA.

Gross, M., 1981: "Les bases empiriques de la notion de prédicat sémantique", in Guillet, A., Leclère. C. (eds.), *Formes syntaxiques et prédicats sémantiques*, Langages No. 63, Larousse, Paris.

—. 1989: "La construction de dictionnaires électroniques", in *Annales des Télécommunications*, vol. 44, No. 1-2: 4-19, CENT, Issy-les-Moulineaux/Lannion.

Harris, Z. S., 1970: *Papers in Structural and Transformational Linguistics*. Reidel, Dordrecht.

Monteleone, M., 2004: *Lessicografia e dizionari elettronici. Dagli usi linguistici alle basi di dati lessicali*, Fiorentino & New Technology, Napoli.

Silberztein, M., 1993: *Dictionnaires électroniques et analyse automatique de textes*, Masson, Paris.

—. 2003: *NooJ Manual* available at www.nooj4nlp.net

Vietri S., Elia A., D'Agostino E., 2004: "Lexicon-grammar, Electronic Dictionaries and Local Grammars in Italian", in Laporte, E., Leclère, C., Piot, M., Silberztein M. (eds.), *Syntaxe, Lexique et Lexique-Grammaire. Volume dédié à Maurice Gross*, Lingvisticae Investigationes Supplementa 24, John Benjamins, Amsterdam/Philadelphia.

Vietri, S., 2004: *Lessico-grammatica dell'italiano. Metodi, descrizioni e applicazioni*, UTET, Torino.

—. 2008: *Dizionari elettronici e grammatiche a stati finiti. Metodi di analisi formale della lingua italiana*, Plectica, Salerno.

Appendix

Samples of Noun Inflection Codes:

Apostrophe
A = <E>/s | 's/p;
KO = <E>/s | 's/p | s/p ;
-y ending
ABILITY = <E>/s | <B>ies/p | s/p ;
ACTIVITY = <E>/s | <B>ies/p ;
MONEY = <E>/s | <E>/p | <B2>ies/p | s/p ;
PENNY = <E>/s | <B>ies/p | <B2>ce/p ;
TONY = <E>/s | <B>ey/p ;
Singular only
MAXIMAX = <E>/s;
Plural only
SERIES = <E>/p ;
CLOTHES = <E>/p | es/p ;

Samples of Verb Inflection Codes:

ABOLISH=<E>/INF | <E>/PR+1+2+s | <E>/PR+1+2+3+p | es/PR+3+s | ed/PT+1+2+3+s+p | ed/PP | ing/G;
abolishES,abolishED,abolishING
ADMIT=<E>/INF | <E>/PR+1+2+s | <E>/PR+1+2+3+p | s/PR+3+s | <D>ed/PT+1+2+3+s+p | <D>ed/PP | <D>ing/G;
admitS, admiTTED, admiTTING
LIVE=<E>/INF | <E>/PR+1+2+s |<E>/PR+1+2+3+p | s/PR+3+s| d/PT+1+2+3+s+p | d/PP | <B>ing/G;
liveS, livED, living

PART II:

SYNTACTIC AND SEMANTIC GRAMMARS

SEMANTIC RELATIONS AND LOCAL GRAMMARS FOR THE ENVIRONMENT[1]

PILAR LEÓN-ARAÚZ

Abstract

Terminologists often tend to rely on manual work to extract all the information they need for the description of specialized domains, but this can be very tedious and time-consuming. Nevertheless, knowledge representation would be more efficient and objective if knowledge extraction techniques were more systematic and semi-automatized. In this paper we show how some of the manual processes that we have developed in the extraction and representation of environmental semantic relations and can be partially automatized with the help of NLP applications such as NooJ. We have developed an English environmental NooJ dictionary and a series of local grammars based on the lexico-syntactic patterns that convey semantic relations in real texts. Grammars are designed to identify, so far, hyponymic and meronymic relations among the terms previously defined in the dictionary.

Introduction

Terminologists often tend to rely on manual work to extract all the information they need for the description of a particular specialised domain, but it can be very tedious and time-consuming. This has been the case of EcoLexicon[2], an environmental terminological knowledge base (TKB), developed at the University of Granada. Up to the present, all conceptual propositions (concept-relation-concept) in EcoLexicon (more than 6,000) have been manually extracted from our environmental corpus and represented in semantic networks. However, knowledge representation

[1] This research has been carried out within the framework of the project RECORD: Representación del Conocimiento en Redes Dinámicas [Knowledge Representation in Dynamic Networks, FFI2011-22397], funded by the Spanish Ministry of Science and Innovation

[2] ecolexicon.ugr.es

would be more efficient if knowledge extraction techniques were more systematic and, at least, semi-automatised. Yet, this requires a well-defined set of selection criteria based on previous manual identification of which types of information are useful, why they are useful and how they can be structured.

In this chapter we show how some of the manual processes that we have developed in the extraction and representation of semantic relations can be partially automatised with the help of NLP applications such as NooJ (Silberztein, 2003). We have developed an English environmental NooJ dictionary and a series of local grammars based on the knowledge patterns (KPs) that convey semantic relations in real texts. Grammars are designed to identify, so far, hyponymic and meronymic relations between terms already defined in the dictionary.

EcoLexicon: an environmental TKB

EcoLexicon is a multilingual TKB that represents environmental terms, concepts and their relations in different formats, i.e. semantic networks, controlled-language definitions, graphical resources and linguistic contexts, such as knowledge-rich contexts and concordances (Figure 1). Currently, it has 3,343 concepts and 17,413 terms in English, Spanish, German, French, Modern Greek, Russian and Dutch.

Semantic networks are one of the main forms of knowledge representation in EcoLexicon, where concepts appear related to others by means of a closed inventory of semantic relations. This inventory has been especially conceived for the environmental domain and includes both hierarchical and non-hierarchical relations. According to our corpus data, semantic relations depend on concept types and their relational power. For instance, the relation *has_function* can be activated by both entities and processes, but the relation *made_of* only occurs between two entities.

This is what we have called relational natural constraints, since the potential activation of certain semantic relations is determined by the nature of the concept. However, the relational behaviour of concepts can also be affected by context (León-Araúz and Faber 2010). In EcoLexicon we represent contextual variation by showing how concepts and propositions are not equally prototypical across all environmental subdomains, such as Atmospheric sciences, Coastal Engineering, or Geology (León-Araúz et al. 2013). In this sense, the following figures show how the concept SAND is recontextualised according to the domains of Coastal Engineering (Figure 2) and Wastewater Treatment and Supply (Figure 3).

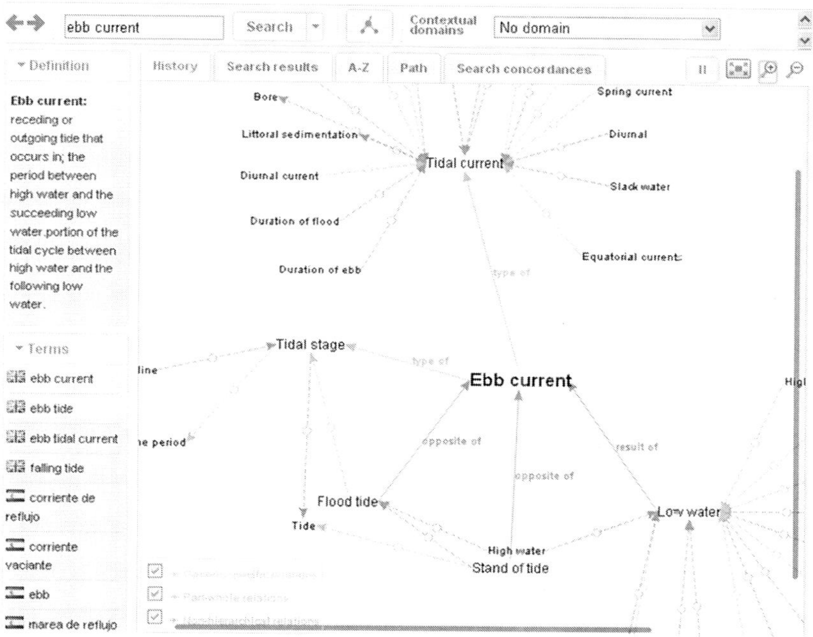

Fig.1: EcoLexicon's user interface

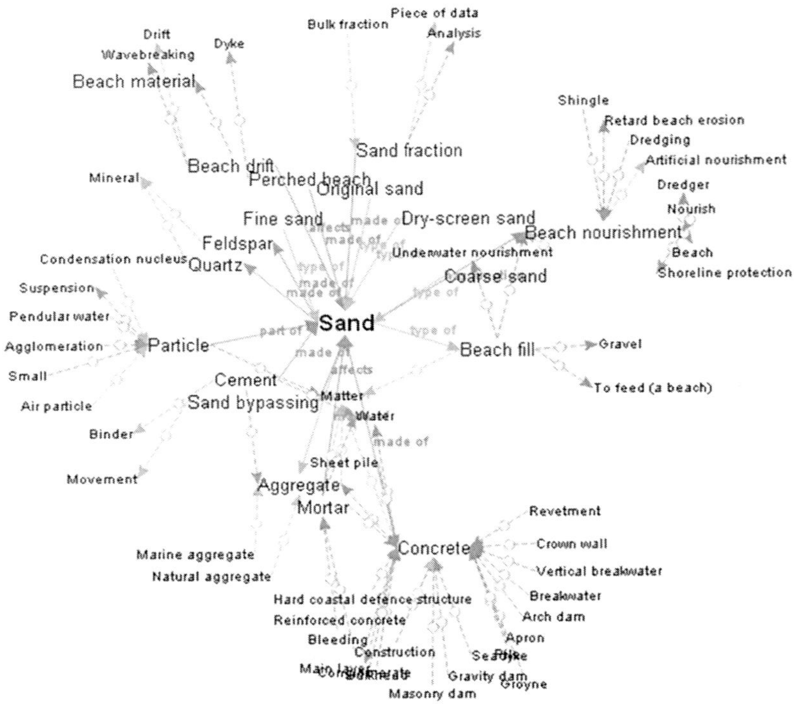

Fig.2: SAND in the Coastal Éngineering domain

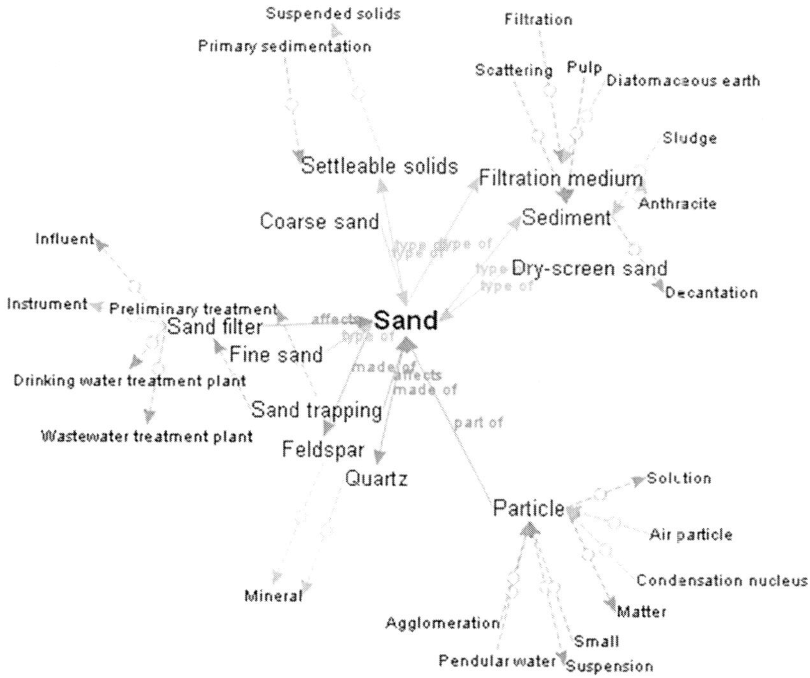

Fig.3: SAND in the Wastewater treatment and supply domain

Recontextualisation involves highlighting or supressing conceptual propositions regarding their prototypicity within a list of environmental domains in which our corpus has also been divided. This has also been a powerful and cognitively-sound way of reducing information overload (Faber et al. 2014, León-Araúz and Magaña 2010), which was mainly caused by the great deal of multidimensionality shown in the environmental domain. Multidimensionality (Kageura 1997) occurs when concepts can be classified according to different points of view or conceptual facets. For instance, as can be found in the corpus, SAND may be categorised as a subtype of very different – and sometimes incompatible – hypernyms: SEDIMENT, BEACH FILL, AGGREGATE, SUSPENDED SOLID, or PROPPANT. This vast array of possible hypernyms highlights the relevance of dynamic conceptualisations as opposed to traditional static representations.

Manual extraction of semantic relations: collecting KPs

KPs are the lexico-syntactic patterns that occur between – or near – two specialised terms making semantic relations explicit. According to many research studies, KPs have long been considered one of the most reliable methods for the extraction of semantic relations (Condamines, 2002; Marshman et al., 2002; Barrière, 2004; Cimiano and Staab, 2006). Since Hearst (1992) much has been written about them. Nevertheless, despite their popularity, KPs have never been fully studied and exploited, especially in specialised domains. Furthermore, as stated by Bowker (2004), there are still major problems with regards to noise and silence, pattern variation, anaphora, domain and language dependency, etc. Moreover, not all relations have been analysed in the same depth.

In EcoLexicon we firstly studied the combinatorial potential of specialised terms in the corpus by manually looking for this type of meaningful patterns based on keyword searches. For instance, in Figure 4 we find several lexicalisations of causality associated with the seed term *erosion*.

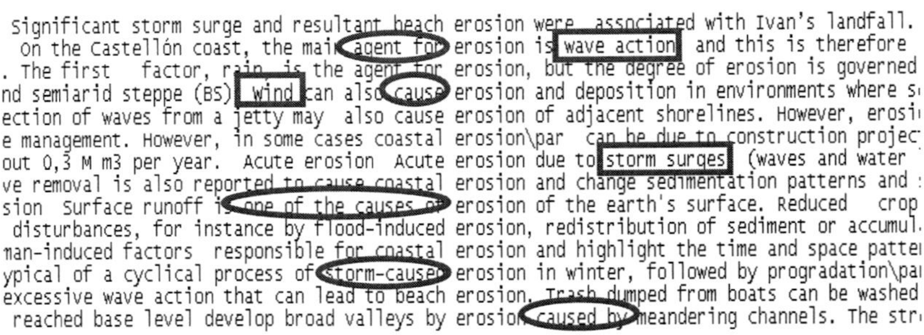
Significant storm surge and resultant beach erosion were associated with Ivan's landfall.
On the Castellón coast, the main agent for erosion is wave action and this is therefore
. The first factor, rain, is the agent for erosion, but the degree of erosion is governed
nd semiarid steppe (BS) Wind can also cause erosion and deposition in environments where s
ection of waves from a jetty may also cause erosion of adjacent shorelines. However, erosi
e management. However, in some cases coastal erosion\par can be due to construction projec
out 0,3 M m3 per year. Acute erosion Acute erosion due to storm surges (waves and water
ve removal is also reported to cause coastal erosion and change sedimentation patterns and
sion Surface runoff is one of the causes of erosion of the earth's surface. Reduced crop
disturbances, for instance by flood-induced erosion, redistribution of sediment or accumul
man-induced factors responsible for coastal erosion and highlight the time and space patte
ypical of a cyclical process of storm-caused erosion in winter, followed by progradation\pa
excessive wave action that can lead to beach erosion. Trash dumped from boats can be washed
reached base level develop broad valleys by erosion caused by meandering channels. The str

Fig.4: Concordances for *erosion* showing causal KPs

*Agent for * is*, *cause*, *may also cause*, *due to*, *one of the causes of*, **-caused*, **-induced*, etc. are all different structures expressing the causal relation between EROSION and other specialised concepts such as STORM SURGE, WAVE ACTION, JETTY or LANDFALL. After collecting all useful KPs activated by the seed terms, a pattern-based search was also conducted in order to find new relations among other concepts. In a cyclic way, once we extracted new term pairs, we applied them as seeds in order to find new meaningful patterns. This time-consuming process has been extremely worthwhile in that it has provided us with the knowledge needed to formalise the structure of KPs for automatic corpus searches and to determine the prototypicality of conceptual propositions.

Automatic extraction of semantic relations: formalising KPs

Now that we have a thorough knowledge of the domain, we have converted the English part of our TKB into an environmental NooJ dictionary and we have developed a series of local grammars based on all of the collected KPs. So far our grammars aim at identifying hyponymic and meronymic relations among the terms previously included in the dictionary.

The dictionary comprises 5,054 entries, which are used in the grammars to identify specialised propositions (e.g. <N+Term> is a noun previously annotated as a Term using the dictionary). This means that we leave out anaphora cases and relations where non-environmental concepts occur. Furthermore, dictionary entries add different types of information based on the features that may influence KPs' interpretation, since the correct identification of meaningful concordances depends on the semantic and syntactic structure of the text that precedes or follows any KP (León-Araúz and Faber 2012). For instance, noise or polysemy may be avoided thanks to the addition of semantic features such as +Landform, +Structure, +Water_body, etc., or morpho-syntactic features such as uncountable or countable. In this way, grammars are constrained according to different parameters and are not only based on purely structural patterns.

Local grammars for hyponymy

Figure 5 shows a local grammar specifically designed for hyponymy extraction.

It is composed of five subgraphs (type_of_1 to type_of_5), each of which in turn contains two other subgraphs (hypernym and hyponym). The five subgraphs lexicalise five different forms of the hyponymic or IS_A semantic relation, which can be found in Figure 6. They are the formalised expression of common KPs such as *x is the most common example of y* or *x such as y*.

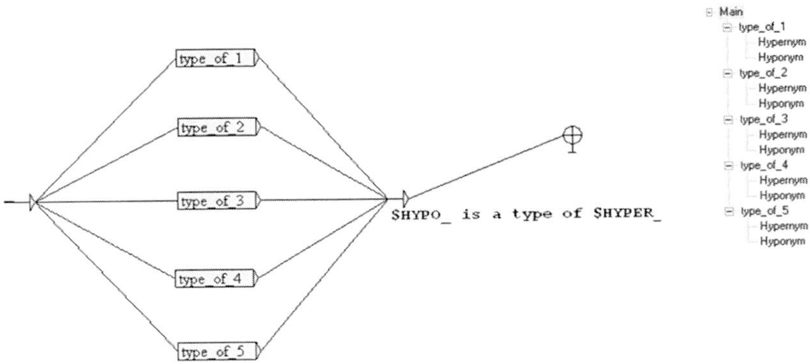

Fig.5: Hyponymic local grammar

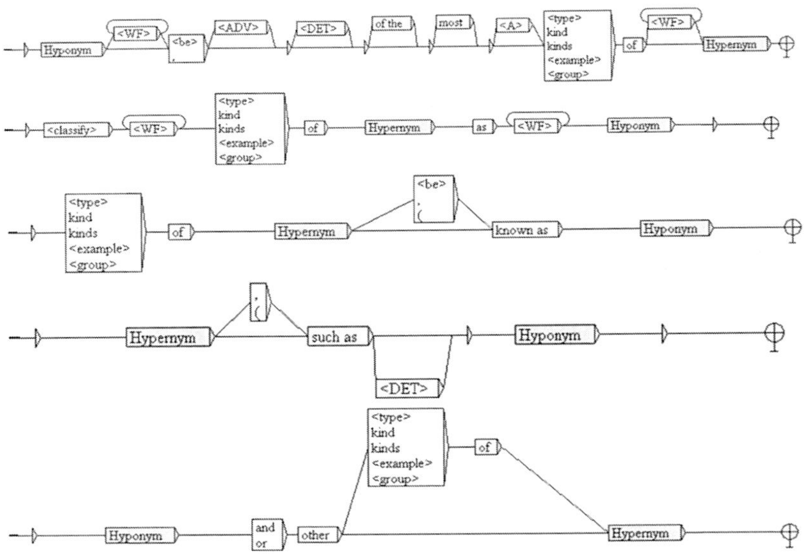

Fig.6: Different lexicalisations of the hyponymic relation

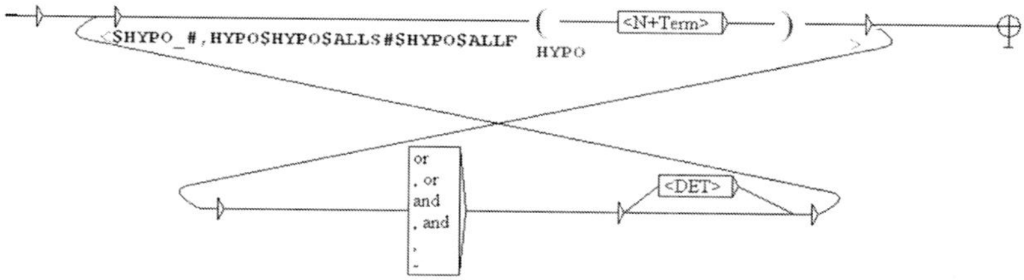

Fig.7: Recursive grammar for multiple hyponyms extraction

As it can be observed, hyponyms and hypernyms do not always appear in the same order. For this reason they are stored in variables (e.g. $(HYPO) in Figure 7), so that the main grammar (Figure 5) can produce the right output: *x is a type of y*, where *x* is always the hyponym and *y* the hypernym. Once we filter out incorrect matches, we export every term pair and apply new searches in order to enrich the grammars with new KPs.

Moreover, both hyponym and hypernym subgraphs are recursive grammars that let us extract multiple conceptual relations from a single sentence by applying the *All matches* feature. This can be seen in Figure 8. For instance, from the sentence *Coastal structures such as jetties, groins, seawalls, bulkheads, and revetments*, five different outputs are produced, as the recursive grammar collects all possible cases of hyponym enumerations. Figure 8 also shows different KPs lexicalisations producing the same output (*such as*, *and other*, *be * examples of*, *known as*, *be * type of*, etc.).

Finally, the hyponymic grammar (Figure 7) also produces a dictionary annotation every time the term is found in the text within a hyponymic structure ($HYPO_#,$HYPO$HYPO$ALLS#$HYPO$ALLF). This helps us constrain our searches in order to observe different phenomena in a more straight-forward way. For instance, Figure 9 shows part of the result of the following simple query: <HYPO+Structure>, which lets us analyse multidimensionality based on category membership and dynamic conceptualisations. In this case, we can easily observe that structures are generally classified according to the following facets: *place* (coastal, marine); *position* (shore-perpendicular); *attribute* (hard); *material* (rubble); *function* (protective, load-bearing) and *origin* (man-made). Not surprisingly, these are the dimensions that are usually activated in the definition of each of the structures' subtypes.

Seq.
bedrock, such as sandstone, conglomerate, limestone/limestone is a type of bedrock
bedrock, such as sandstone, conglomerate/conglomerate is a type of bedrock
bedrock, such as sandstone/sandstone is a type of bedrock
clay and other substances/clay is a type of substance
CO2 and other greenhouse gases, such as methane/methane is a type of greenhouse gas
CO2 and other greenhouse gases/carbon dioxide is a type of greenhouse gas
Coastal structures such as jetties, groins, seawalls, bulkheads, and revetments/revetment is a type of coastal structure
Coastal structures such as jetties, groins, seawalls, bulkheads/bulkhead is a type of coastal structure
Coastal structures such as jetties, groins, seawalls/seawall is a type of coastal structure
Coastal structures such as jetties, groins/groyne is a type of coastal structure
Coastal structures such as jetties/jetty is a type of coastal structure
estuaries and other wetlands/estuary is a type of wetland
Fjords are particularly good examples of highly stratified estuaries/fiord is a type of stratified estuary
infrastructure (such as a port/port is a type of infrastructure
kinds of cyclones, known as extratropical cyclones and subtropical cyclones/subtropical cyclone is a type of cyclone
kinds of cyclones, known as extratropical cyclones/extratropical cyclone is a type of cyclone
material such as rock/rock is a type of material
material, such as a steel/steel is a type of material
metals such as steel/steel is a type of metal
metals, such as carbon/carbon is a type of metal
reefs are a specific type of hard bottom habitat/reef is a type of habitat
Roll clouds and shelf clouds both are types of arcus clouds/roll cloud is a type of arcus cloud
Roll clouds and shelf clouds both are types of arcus clouds/shelf cloud is a type of arcus cloud
Roll clouds, shelf clouds, and wall clouds are examples of accessory clouds/eyewall is a type of cloud
Tropical Storm Franklin, an example of a strongly sheared tropical cyclone/tropical storm is a type of tropical cyclone
wall clouds are examples of accessory clouds/eyewall is a type of cloud

Fig.8: Concordances resulting from the hyponymic grammar application

Coastal structures such as jetties,	groins
some other structures such as	groins
using hard structures, such as	groins
shore-perpendicular structures, such as	groins
rubble structures such as seawalls,	groins
load-bearing structures such as	groins
marine structures such as jetties,	seawalls
or protective structures such as	seawalls
Man-made structures, such as	seawalls

Fig.9: Concordances resulting from the query <HYPO+Structure>

As previously stated, an important feature in EcoLexicon is the representation of how conceptual propositions are more or less prototypical across different contextual domains. We understand prototypicity in the same sense as the standard score provided in the statistical module of NooJ. Now, the salience of conceptual propositions can be automatically cross-checked by making queries such as the following:

(<gravel,HYPO><WF>*<sediment,HYPER>)|(<sediment,HYPER><WF>*<gravel,HYPO>)
(<gravel,HYPO><WF>*<detritus,HYPER>)|(<detritus,HYPER><WF>*<gravel,HYPO>)

As found in the corpus, GRAVEL is usually categorised as a kind of SEDIMENT or as a kind of DETRITUS. When we apply the hyponymic grammar and those queries to a context-based classified corpus, we can easily infer that the proposition GRAVEL *is_a_type_of* SEDIMENT is activated in the Soil Sciences domain, whereas GRAVEL *is_a_type_of* DETRITUS belongs to the Coastal Engineering domain (Figure 10).

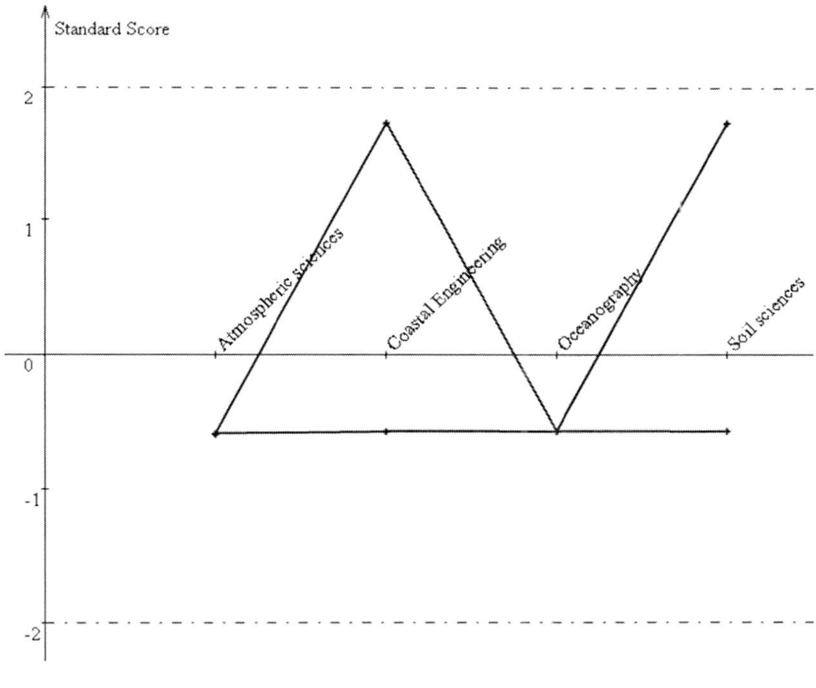

Fig. 10: Dynamic categorisation of GRAVEL across different domains

Local grammars for meronymy

Figure 11 shows a local grammar designed to identify meronymy, which contains two subgraphs in order to store both Parts and Wholes. These subgraphs are also recursive grammars, since parts, materials and the like usually occur in the form of enumerations too. KPs in this grammar are based on general constitutive predicates such as *compose*, *form*, *consist*, *contain*, etc., but there are also certain predicates that are domain-specific, such as *build* or *reinforce*. Prepositions also play an important role in each of the different paths conveying meronymy. When applying this grammar, meaningful meronymic occurrences can be retrieved, such as *ocean beaches consist of sand*, *seawalls are made of concrete*, *a typical revetment consists of broken rock*, or *the gorge is the deepest part of an inlet*.

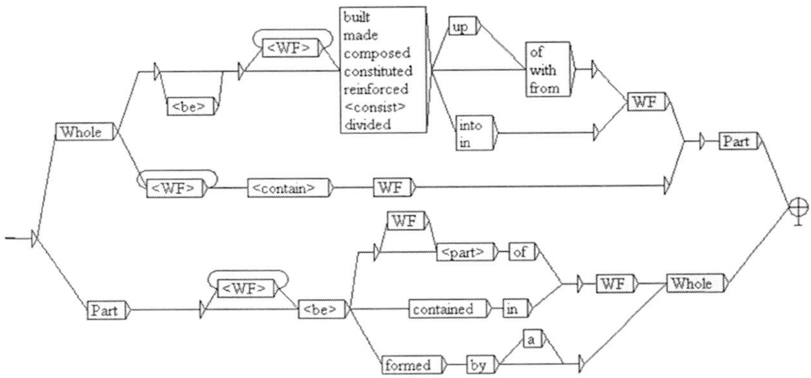

Fig. 11:. Meronymic local grammar

However, meronymy poses two additional challenges. First of all, there are different types of meronymy, since not all parts are linked to their wholes in the same way. In EcoLexicon this semantic relation has been divided into six different types for reasoning purposes. Depending on their natural type, concepts are related through meronymy according to these relations: *part_of, made_of, located_at, takes_place_in, delimited_by and phase_of*. Secondly, one of the problems stemming from the use of KPs is that they may be polysemic structures. For instance, it is evident that *form*, which is usually involved in meronymy, does not have the same meaning in the following sentences: *clouds* are *formed of water* and *clouds are formed by condensation*. In this case prepositions play an important role, but also do argument fillers. The second arguments of each sentence (*water* and *condensation*) have a different conceptual nature (entity and process) and imply different relations (*made_of* and *caused_by*). However, even if we include the preposition *by* within the pattern, we still find that *formed by* may convey three relations, as depicted in Figure 12:

```
RESULT

force of a seiche. Seiche is a wave formed by the rocking of water in an
From Space   Delta coasts are those formed by the deposition of sediment
p gorge in rock avalanche   debris, formed by headward erosion of seepage
edge outcrops. Boulder beaches were formed by glacial scouring  and depos
 The higher berm, or storm berm, is formed by wave action during storm c
. Consequently,   coastal sediments formed by evaporation of seawater ar
ns (Fig. 1). The alluvial fans were formed by the deposition of vast quan
 , and secondary coasts, which were formed by marine action. Primary coas

PART

 Barents Sea bottom water (BSBW) is formed by cold, hyper-saline cascades,
ngs. Some of the laminae are solely formed by alveolar septal structures.

MATERIAL

h units correspond to alluvial fans formed by breccia and conglomerates, wh
ity.     The  cuspated  delta  was  formed by  alluvial  sediments  carried
and regular with different laminae, formed by dark micrite with few detrita
```

Fig.12: *formed by*: a polysemic KP

Therefore, we need to disambiguate not only the polysemic patterns but also the different dimensions of the meronymic relation. Figure 13 shows how these two problems are approached.

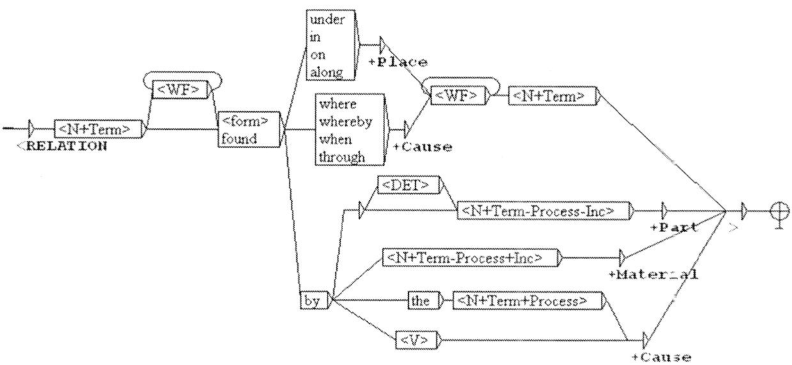

Fig.13: KP disambiguation: syntactic annotation for different dimensions

In this grammar we use different semantic and morphosyntactic features in order to disambiguate the polysemic KP *formed by* and the different dimensions it may convey. Since we have this kind of information in our dictionary, constraints on *formed by* are based on the concept type [process (+Process) or entity (-Process)], whether the terms are countable or not and whether they are nouns or verbs.

If the KP is followed by a verb, it is definitely related to the *cause* dimension. On the contrary, if the KP is followed by a noun, it can be linked to any of the three dimensions. Then the difference lies in two factors: if the noun is a process concept type, the concept still falls into the *cause* dimension; if the noun is an object concept type, the dimension can be either *part* or *material*, but if the noun is uncountable, it will always refer to the *material* dimension, whereas countable nouns will always link wholes with *parts*.

Thus, in this case, we use syntactic annotations in order to classify meronymic types and then we proceed in the same way as with the hyponymic grammar.

Conclusions and future research

Local grammars are a powerful way of automatising semantic relation extraction. In this chapter we have shown an approach for the formalisation of hyponymic and meronymic patterns. Our grammars have been proven effective at: (1) extracting useful concordances for our users, where environmental concepts appear meaningfully related to others; (2) accessing multidimensionality in a more straightforward way; (3) comparing the salience of conceptual propositions across different contexts in a more reliable way; (4) disambiguating polysemic KPs. In the near future we plan to improve these grammars with new possible lexicalisations of both hyponymy and meronymy, but we will especially focus on developing new grammars for other non-hierarchical relations, with the final aim of building automatic definitions.

References

Barrière, C. 2004. Building a concept hierarchy from corpus analysis. *Terminology* 10: 2, 241-263.

Bowker, L. 2004. Lexical knowledge Patterns, Semantic Relations, and Language Varieties: Exploring the Possibilities for Refining Information Retrieval in an International Context. *Cataloging and Classification Quarterly*, 37(1): 153 - 171

Cimiano, P., Staab, S. 2005 Learning Concept Hierarchies from Text with a Guided Agglomerative Clustering Algorithm, *Workshop on Learning and Extending Lexical Ontologies with Machine Learning Methods*, Bonn.

Condamines, A. 2002. Corpus analysis and conceptual relation patterns. *Terminology* 8:1, 141-162.

Faber, P., León-Araúz, P., Reimerink, A. 2014. Representing Environmental Knowledge in EcoLexicon. *Languages for Specific Purposes in the Digital Era*. Springer. 19: 267-301.

Hearst, M. 1992 Automatic Acquisition of Hyponyms from Large Text Corpora. *Proc. of the Fourteenth International Conference on Computational Linguistics*, Nantes, France.

León-Araúz, P., Reimerink, A., Aragón, A.G. 2013. Dynamism and Context in Specialized Knowledge. *Terminology* 19 (1): 31–61.

León-Araúz, P., Faber, P. 2012. Causality in the specialized domain of the environment. In Proceedings of the *Workshop "Semantic Relations-II. Enhancing Resources and Applications" (LREC'12)*, edited by Verginica Barbu Mititelu, Octavian Popescu, and Viktor Pekar, 10-17. Istanbul: ELRA.

León-Araúz, P., Magaña, P.J. 2010. EcoLexicon: contextualizing an environmental ontology. In *Proceedings of the Terminology and Knowledge Engineering (TKE) Conference 2010*. Dublin: Dublin City University.

León-Araúz, P., Faber, P. 2010. Natural and contextual constraints for domain-specific relations. *Proceedings of the Workshop Semantic Relations. Theory and Applications*, ed. Verginica Barbu Mititelu, Viktor Pekar, and Eduard Barbu, 12-17. Valletta

Marshman, E.; Morgan, T.; Meyer I. 2002. French patterns for expressing concept relations. *Terminology* 8:1, 1-29.

Meyer, I. 2001. Extracting knowledge-rich contexts for terminography: A conceptual and methodological framework. In Bourigault, D., Jacquemin, C. and L'Homme, M.C (eds.), *Recent Advances in Computational Terminology*. Amsterdam: John Benjamins. 279-302.

Silberztein, M. 2003. *NooJ Manual*. Available at: http://www.nooj4nlp.net

DESCRIBING SET AND FREE WORD COMBINATIONS IN BELARUSIAN AND RUSSIAN WITH NOOJ

YURY HETSEVICH, SVIATLANA HETSEVICH, ALENA SKOPINAVA, BORIS LOBANOV, YAUHENIYA YAKUBOVICH AND YURY KIM

Abstract

This paper focuses on developing NooJ grammars and linguistic resources in order to identify and classify set word combinations (phrasemes) and syntax-free word combinations (including quantitative expressions with measurement units) in Belarusian and Russian texts.

Introduction

The goal of this research is to further improve the Belarusian and Russian dictionaries presented previously at the International NooJ Conferences (Hetsevich et al. 2013). A complete set of resources for a given language requires dictionaries and grammars that describe not only words but also word combinations. Hence, it is planned to develop NooJ grammars and linguistic resources in order to identify and classify set word combinations (phrasemes) and syntax-free word combinations (including quantitative expressions with measurement units) in Belarusian and Russian texts.

Set word combinations can also be defined as *phrasemes* in the sense of the Meaning-Text Theory (Mel'čuk 2013), i.e. bound multiword phrases consisting of at least two lexemes, e.g.: *пойдзем сваёй дарогай* 'let's go our own way', *перайсці ўброд* 'to ford', *зоологический сад* 'zoological garden', *медовый месяц* 'honeymoon' etc. Phrasemes are indivisible multiword units and thus need to be processed as a whole by NooJ. To achieve this, we will describe them primarily in dictionaries and, if necessary, will develop linked grammars.

Free word combinations are viewed as sequences of words bound together by means of standard language rules, e.g.: *новая кватэра* 'a new flat', *посматривал на часы* 'looked at the watch from time to time'. Words in free combinations can be easily replaced, e.g.: *новая (камфартабельная, сучасная...) кватэра* 'a new (comfortable, modern…) flat', *посматривал на часы (картину, девушку...)* 'looked at the watch (painting, lady…) from time to time' etc. As these sequences are constructed ad hoc, they will be described primarily by means of syntactic grammars.

Special attention is given to processing **quantitative expressions with measurement units (QEMUs)**, which are a specific subclass of free word combinations. For example, *Цягнік рухаўся з хуткасцю 200 км/г у Саарбрукен* 'The train was moving at a speed of 200 km/h to Saarbrücken'. The aim is to identify *200 км/г* '200 km/h', classify it as an expression with a SI-derived unit of speed, and turn it into orthographical words *дзвесце кіламетраў у гадзіну* 'two hundred kilometers per hour'. The problem of their processing is important due to the ubiquity of QEMUs, and at the same time it is not easy to solve because of their language-dependent character and the variety of ways in which QEMUs are expressed in writing. Texts containing QEMUs require resources for identification and processing in the following areas:

— Corpora and database management systems, libraries, information retrieval systems: to formulate extended search queries, locate specific expressions on the Internet, support automatic text annotation and summarisation;
— Text-to-speech synthesis systems: to generate orthographically correct texts, their tonal and prosodic peculiarities;
— Publishing institutions: to automatically locate specified lists of expressions with measurement units and check quickly if the extended names of units are used correctly.

Building NooJ dictionaries and grammars for the above-mentioned problems will enable automatic recognition and annotation of these expressions in Belarusian and Russian texts. For instance, search engines should suggest the most common word combinations, and if they don't have sufficient statistical data, their suggestions can be based on resources describing structural types of word combinations. Such resources could be of great importance for text-to-speech synthesis. Speech synthesisers need to make pauses between free word combinations and set word combinations (as single units), but not inside them (not between their components), which is impossible to accomplish if only basic dictionaries of single tokens are applied. Such resources can be built in Belarusian and Russian NLP applications for many areas, e.g. syntactic parsing, prosody prediction, text-to-speech synthesis etc., and also as a didactic material for academic courses on computational linguistics and phraseology.

Identification of Set Word Combinations

Native speakers and those who seek to master a language often use phrasemes – bound multiword combinations. Therefore, a complete electronic dictionary should contain not only unigrams with necessary grammatical information but also syntactically and semantically composed multiword units. In the NooJ terminology we find two terms which are close to the specific term phraseme, namely frozen expressions and multiword units. The typology of phrasemes includes the classes of collocations, idioms, clichés and pragmatemes. These classes differ from each other mainly by the level and type of semantic fusion. However, phrasemes of all classes have been collected into dictionaries regardless the degree of fusion.

Pragmatemes constitute a specific class of phrasemes and denote expressions which are formed according to the grammar rules of a given language but with certain limitations. In a strictly defined situation, they convey a certain meaning, and only one of various grammatically and semantically possible expressions is used. For example, while riding a Belarusian or Russian bus (train, etc.), one might hear *Асцярожна, дзверы зачыняюцца! Осторожно, двери закрываются!* ('Attention, the doors are closing!'), but not *Увага, зараз я зачыняю дзверы! Внимание, закрываются двери!* ('Attention, right now I'm closing the doors!'). Pragmatemes can be conveniently collected in a database and managed by means of MS Access. The pragmatemes databases are further converted into dictionaries in the NooJ format (Figure 1).

Currently the dictionaries include over 300 Belarusian and over 170 Russian pragmatemes, subdivided into several categories according to the form of use (written or spoken); function (similar to the speech acts types: commands, prohibitions, advice, warnings, wishes, etc.); situation (regarding temporal and spatial circumstances). For instance, the pragmateme *Асцярожна, злы сабака* 'Beware of the dog' is usually expressed in the written form, implies a warning, and is used to protect property. The pragmateme *Приятного аппетита!* 'Bon appétit!' is used as an oral expression to wish someone enjoyment at the table during a meal. In order to detect phrasemes in Belarusian and Russian NooJ texts, the first step was to collect them manually from the corpora. According to the syntactic functions which can be fulfilled by the phrasemes, we have subdivided them into nominal, verbal, adjectival, adverbial and phrasal (Table 1).

Pragmateme	Form	Act	Situatio
Не паліць	written	prohibit	sign
Да пабачэння	oral	valediction	parting
Дзяжурныя на лінію!	oral	order	military
На плячо!	oral	order	military
За ваша здароўе!	oral	wish	drinking
Калі ласка!	oral	request	politeness
Спадары прысяжныя!	oral	greeting	court

```
# Input Language is: be
Не паліць,PRAGMATEME+Form=written+Act=prohibit+Situation=sign
Да пабачэння,PRAGMATEME+Form=oral+Act=valediction+Situation=parting
Дзяжурныя на лінію! ,PRAGMATEME+Form=oral+Act=order+Situation=military
На плячо! ,PRAGMATEME+Form=oral+Act=order+Situation=military
За ваша здароўе!,PRAGMATEME+Form=oral+Act=wish+Situation=drinking
Калі ласка!,PRAGMATEME+Form=oral+Act=request+Situation=politeness
Спадары прысяжныя!,PRAGMATEME+Form=oral+Act=greeting+Situation=court
```

Fig.1: An excerpt of the Belarusian pragmatemes database, converted into a NooJ dictionary

Type and function	Model	Example
Nominal (subject or object)	[Adjective + Noun]	*вадзяная курачка* 'a water hen'
	[Noun + Noun]	*зямлі маці* 'Mother Earth'
	[Noun + Preposition + Noun]	*кража со взломом* 'a break-in'
Verbal (predicate)	[Verb + Noun]	*выскаляў зубы* 'bare one's teeth'
	[Verb/Imperative + Noun]	*пабойцеся Бога* 'have a heart'
Adjectival (attribute)	[Preposition + Noun]	*з капрызамі* 'with whims'
	[Adjective + Conjunction + Noun]	*белыя як снег* 'white as snow'
Adverbial (adverbial modifier)	[Preposition + Noun]	*по обыкновению* 'as usual'
	[Preposition + Noun + Preposition + Noun]	*ад краю да краю* 'from edge to edge'
Phrasal units (sentences themselves)	Common models can hardly be stated. They are unique. Most often, such phrasemes turn out to be proverbs and pragmatemes.	*Лепей недаесці, як ястраб, чым пераесці, як свіння.* 'It is better to eat like a bird than to overeat like a pig.'

Table 1: Types of phrasemes according to the syntactic functions they perform

The analysis of Belarusian and Russian phrasemes has led to conclusions about some common features between these two languages. The word order is not always strict: *обратил внимание* = *внимание обратил* 'drew attention'. Some phrasemes admit lexical insertions: *с благоговением* 'with reverence', *с тем же благоговением* 'with the same reverence'. Often elements of set word combinations can appear in various morphological forms: *судебный следователь* 'an investigator', *судебного следователя* 'investigator's', *судебные следователи* 'investigators', etc. Almost every syntactic type of phraseme needs a local grammar. For example, nominal phrasemes of the type [ADJECTIVE+NOUN] can be found by means of the following simple graph (Figure 2):

Fig.2: A graph for nominal phrasemes of the type [ADJECTIVE+NOUN]

Phrasemes which have a similar structure (e.g. *ад краю да краю* 'from edge to edge', *ад цямна да цямна* 'from dawn to dusk') are organised into groups, each of which requires a separate local grammar (Figure 3):

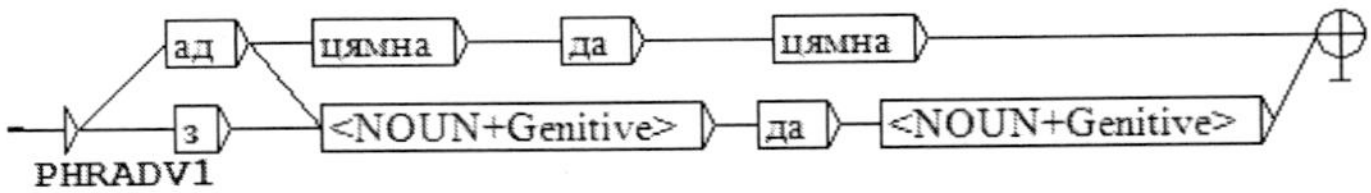

Fig.3: A graph for nominal phrasemes with similar structures

Those phrasemes which do not vary grammatically and do not admit any insertions must be included in NooJ dictionaries (Figure 4).

На назе бот рыпіць, а ў гаршку трасца кіпіць,
PHRASEME+PHRType=PHRASE+PHRSource=Kalasy04not

Fig. 4: An excerpt of the Belarusian phrasemes dictionary in NooJ format

In order to locate phrasemes in Belarusian or Russian texts, firstly, the dictionaries are applied, and secondly, the query PHRASEME (enclosed in angle brackets) is made through the "locate pattern" option (Figure 5).

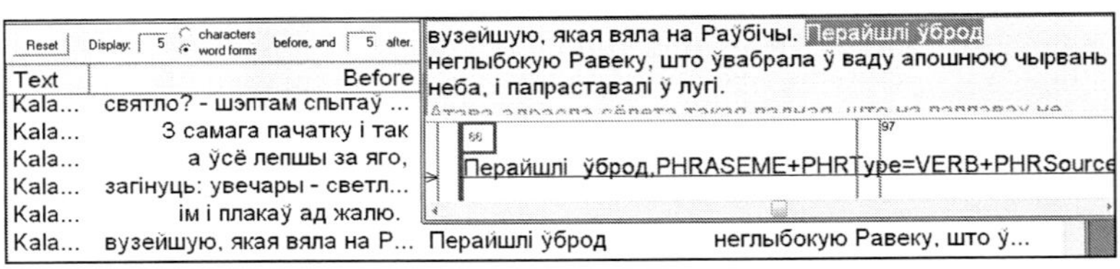

Fig.5: Locating phrasemes in Belarusian texts

To sum up, the practical results of the first part of the research include a dictionary of over 300 Belarusian and 174 Russian pragmatemes; a dictionary of over 420 Belarusian and 131 Russian phrasemes; graphs for 6 main types of free word combinations.

Describing Free Word Combinations

Usually, sentences contain at least one free word combination. For instance, in the sentence *Разам з лазняй сплыла чорная гісторыя* 'The dark story together with the bathhouse disappeared' two free word combinations can be identified: *разам з лазняй* 'together with the bathhouse' [Adverb + Preposition + Noun], *чорная гісторыя* 'the dark story' [Adjective + Noun]. Free word combinations are easier to be described with graphs or regular expressions. Depending on the part of speech of the first word, free word combinations are subdivided into several groups (Figure 6).

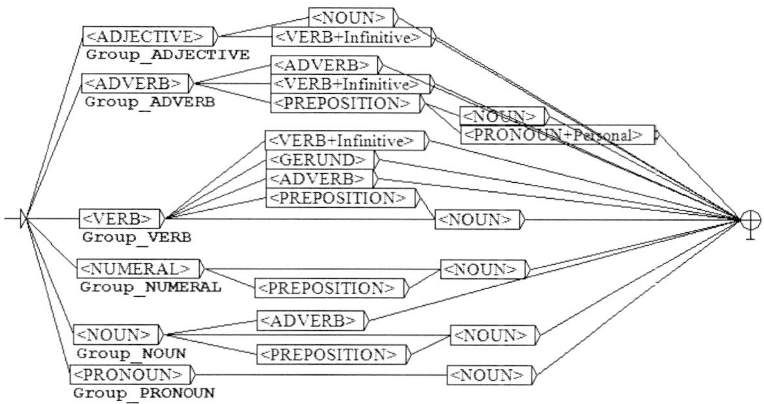

Fig.6: A graph for identifying Belarusian or Russian free word combinations

Table 2 gives examples of Belarusian and Russian free word combinations found by the constructed grammar.

	Free word combinations	Types	Sources
Bel.	*абыякавыя галасы* 'indifferent voices'	Group_ADJECTIVE	Kalasy_12.not
	адразу зразумець 'at once to understand'	Group_ADVERB	Kalasy_03.not
Rus.	*потом подобрать* 'to pick up later'	Group_ADVERB	Dom s mezoninom.not
	горе с счастьем 'grief with happiness'	Group_NOUN	Drama na ohote.not

Table 2: Some results from the identification of Belarusian (Bel.) and Russian (Rus.) free word combinations

Processing of Quantitative Expressions with Measurement Units

To start with, under the term "a quantitative expression with a measurement unit QEMU", we mean a character-literal expression, combining two elements: a numeral quantifier (a number or a numeral) and a symbol or a word denoting a metrological unit, e.g. *123 мА* '123 mA', *пяць кілаграмаў* 'five kilograms', *200 кДж* '200kJ', *36°C* '36°C', etc. When dealing with units of measurement, many difficulties arise. Numeral quantifiers and names of units exhibit a great variety, both in writing and formation (Skopinava et al. 2013). Another difficulty lies in the different types of agreement of a unit with different numbers/numerals (e.g. *25 метраў* '25 meters', *21 метр_*'21 meter_', *23 метры* '23 meters'), synonymous written forms (e.g. *2000 метраў* '2000 meters' = *2000 м* '2000 m' = *2×10³ м* '2×10³ m' = *2 кіламетры* '2 kilometers' = *2 км* '2 km' = *два км* 'two km', …). Therefore, creating localisation rules for all cases is practically impossible, and it is extremely important to use tools that allow users to easily modify previously developed rules and add new ones. QEMUs are language-dependent: *гадзíна* (Belarusian) = *час* (Russian) = *hour* (English) = *Stunde* (German), etc. Thus, it is essential to make accurate provisions for each language.

Significant results have already been achieved by European researchers and developers of the Quantalyze semantic annotation and search service[1], and Numeric Property Searching service in Derwent World Patents Index on STN[2] (Hetsevich et al. 2013). However, language specificity and limited thematic coverage are the reasons why these theoretical or practical results cannot be readily applied for Belarusian or Russian.

Our first goal was to create **resources for identification and classification of QEMUs for Belarusian and Russian in accordance with the International Bureau of Weights and Measures**[3] (Figure 7).

The main graph (Figure 7a) includes four subgraphs. Any text fragment is initially parsed using the first subgraph (Figure 7b) if it has a numeral descriptor. Very often it is recorded not only with integer, decimal and fractional numbers, but also as compound expressions with exponential parts, periods, etc. This subgraph is language-independent. If the graph detects a numeral quantifier, it keeps moving along one of the tree branches in accordance with the SI-classification: SI-basic (Figure

---

1 http://www.stn-international.com/numeric_property_searching.html
2 https://www.quantalyze.com/en/
3 http://www.bipm.org/en/si/si_brochure/general.html

7c), SI-derived and extra-systemic units. In each subgraph, units are differentiated, e.g.: *секунда* ‘a second’ is a unit of time. After applying the graph to the text, different search requests are possible via “Locate Pattern” (Figure 8).

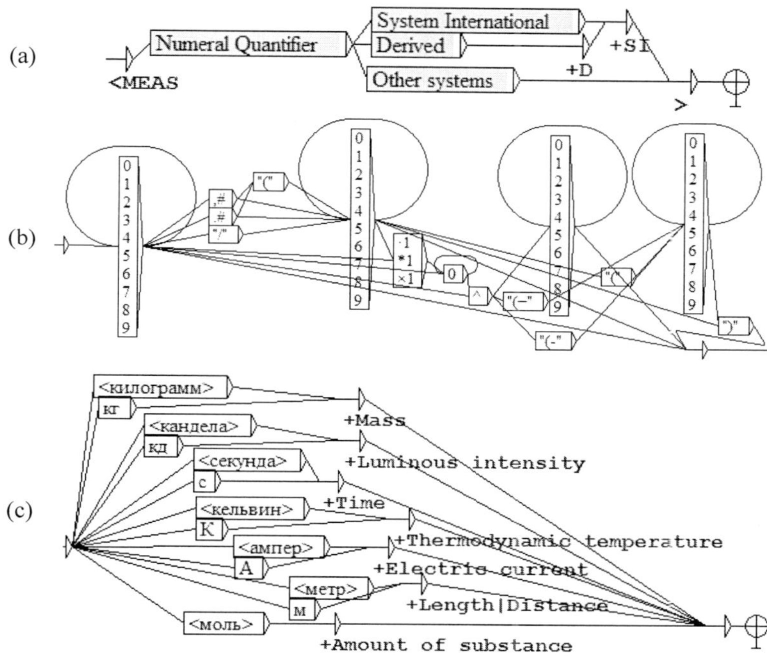

Fig.7: Graphs for identifying and classifying QEMUs according to the SI

Before	Seq.	After	
з разрашэннем да 1–	5 м	. З улікам камерцыйных	5 m
інфармацыі на ўзроўні 1–	10 м	. Такая дэталёвасць неабход	10 m
стартавая маса перавышае	3600 кг	. Разліковы тэрмін актыўнага	3600 kg
масай меней за	10 кг	, а праз 10–20 гадоў	10 kg
гадоў – масай парадку	1 кг	, якія змогуць устанаўліваць	1 kg
этым складала парадку 150–	500 метраў	. У 70–80-х гг	500 metres

Fig.8: Search results for the request <MEAS+SI-D> (quantitative expressions with SI-basic MUs) for Belarusian (English translations provided)

According to the values of precision, recall and their average harmonic mean, the graphs achieve 72% accuracy.

Our next goal was to develop **resources for identifying and classifying QEMUs according to word formation peculiarities**. The solution is based on successive application of three blocks (Figure 9). The first block includes resources with basic stems, metrological prefixes and prefix symbols. At this stage, morphemic and lexical analysis is performed. Metrological word stems and prefixes are identified. Stems can be either full (*Ампер* 'ampere') or shortened (*А* 'amp'), while prefixes or prefix symbols can be either multiple (*кілаампер* 'kiloampere') or submultiple (*мА* 'mA'). Measurement units with several sequences of prefixes (e.g. *мікрамегафарад* 'micromegafarad') are uncommon and need to be extracted separately. All these variants are considered by the second block, which consists of four morphological, language-independent grammars. The next stage of morphological analysis is performed, where words denoting units of measurement are identified. They also receive certain markers: *Mump* (with multiple prefixes), *Musp* (with submultiple prefixes), *Muhp* (with several prefixes), *Mub* (basic units without prefixes). Identified measurement units with prefixes inherit all grammatical and inflectional characteristics from the initial words. For example, *дэкалітрамі* 'deciliters (in the Instrumental case)' correlates with the dictionary word *літр* 'liter'. The graph lets *дэкалітрамі* remain the noun with all its inflectional endings and grammatical features, though it is not included in the resource dictionary. The third block is represented by two syntactic grammars which accumulate morphological data and, finally, identify QEMUs and give them the marker <MUEXPR> (Figure 10).

Finally, we proceed to the third complex of resources, which is aimed **at generating QEMUs or turning them into orthographical word sequences**. Tokens such as *7000 м* '7000 m' are supposed to turn into *сем тысяч метраў* 'seven thousand meters'. The graph (Figure 11) contains subgraphs of two types: for generating numeral quantifiers (numbers from 0 to 999999999999) and for generating words denoting units of measurement. QEMUs pass from input to output by means of one of seven ramifications, depending on the inflection of Belarusian/Russian nouns following numbers. The graph which processes numbers resembles Russian dolls: the subgraph for numbers of one triad (0-999) includes the subgraph *ThMlnMlr* for numbers of two triads (1000-999999) with the in-built subgraphs *MlnMlr* (three triads) and *Mlr* (four triads). After generating numbers the graph proceeds to processing nouns which denote MUs. At present, the graph can generate basic SI units and some frequently used ones. Thanks to finite-state automata, the graph can be easily and rapidly improved by adding more MUs. Figure 12 demonstrates some results using the graph.

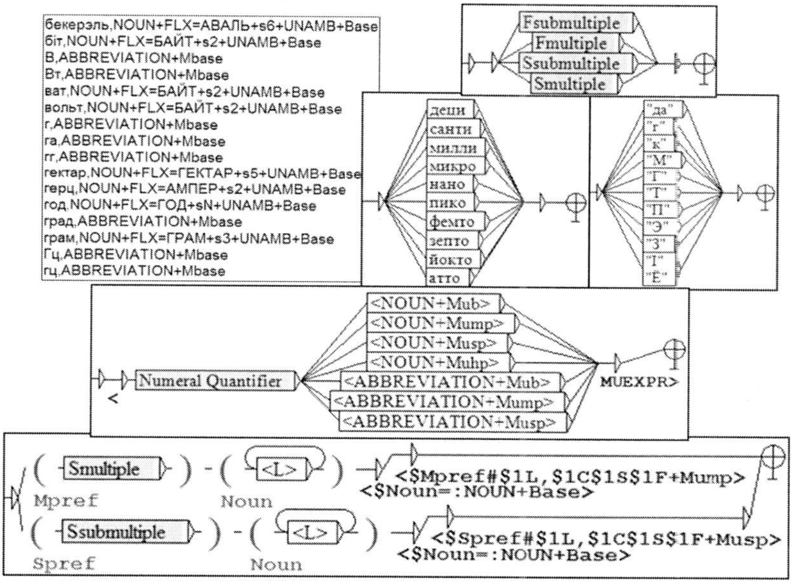

Fig.9: Resources for identifying and classifying QEMUs according to word formation peculiarities

Before	Seq.	After	
ок не превышал	1 мА	. На человека токи ст	1mA
сказать «файл в	100 килобайт	»). При обозначении	100 kilobytes
личиной от 1 до	100 МОм	, чтобы протекающий	100 Mohm
д пикотеравольт	13 йоттайоктограммов	Каждая строка соде	13 yottayoktograms
до 64 Мбит/с) и	137,4 МГц	(метровый диапазон	137,4 MHz
зумруд» массой	1383,95 каратов	. Изумруды выращи	1383,95 carats
мюонов - около	2.2 мкс	- осложняет задачу	2.2 µs
казалась равной	22 фемтограммам	(1 фг = 1•10^(-15) г).	22 femtograms
ались равными:	8.1·10^21 Дж	(уменьшение массы	8.1·10^21 J
км - наклонение	98,00 град	. Срок активного сущ	98,00 deg

Fig.10: Search results for the request <MUEXPR> for Russian (English translations provided)

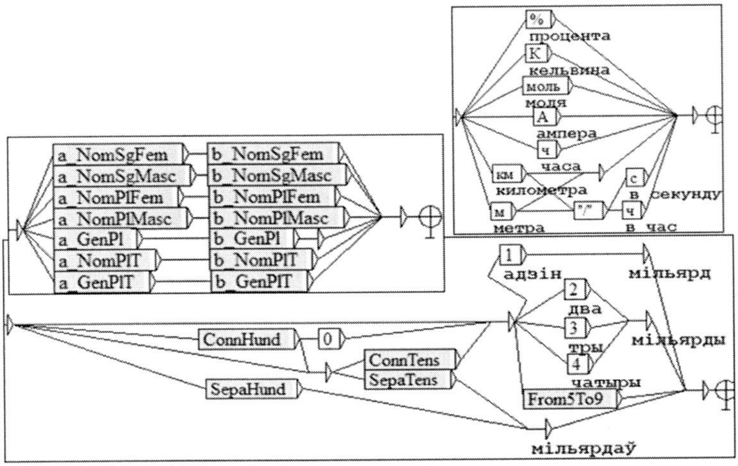

Fig.11: Resources for expanding QEMUs into orthographical form

Seq.
15 т/пятнаццаць тонаў
123 кг/сто дваццаць тры кілаграмы
5678904 К/пяць мільёнаў шэсцьсот семдзесят восем тысяч дзевяцьсот чатыры кельвіны
123 А/сто дваццаць тры амперы
6785672 м/шэсць мільёнаў семсот восемдзесят пяць тысяч шэсцьсот семдзесят два метры
787879 сут/семсот восемдзесят сем тысяч восемсот семдзесят дзевяць сутак
6761 сут/шэсць тысяч семсот шэсцьдзесят адны суткі

Fig.12: After applying the resources for expanding QEMUs into orthographical form to the Belarusian text corpus

Conclusion

It can be concluded that the goal of developing resources which find set and free word combinations in Belarusian and Russian text corpora has been achieved. Particular attention is paid to analysing quantitative expressions with measurement units as a specific subclass of free word combinations. Three complexes of NooJ visual morphological and syntactic grammars have been developed. They identify, classify (with two approaches) and expand QEMUs into orthographical word sequences. In the future it is planned to build local grammars for phrasemes, expand the resources for describing wider groups of free word combinations, and disambiguate cases when the graphs "confuse" some units (e.g. the same initial letter г for год 'year', грам 'gram', гадзíна 'hour').

Acknowledgements

We would like to thank the linguist Adam Morrison for his help in revising the language of this paper.

References

Hetsevich, Y., Sviatlana H., Boris L., Alena S. and Yauheniya Y. 2013. "Accentual expansion of the Belarusian and Russian NooJ dictionaries". In: *Formalising Natural Languages with NooJ: Selected Papers from the NooJ 2012 International Conference*, edited by Anaïd Donabédian, Victoria Khurshudian and Max Silberztein, 24–36. Newcastle: Cambridge Scholars Publishing.

Mel'čuk, I. 2013. "Tout ce que nous voulions savoir sur les phrasèmes, mais". In: *Cahiers de lexicologie. Revue internationale de lexicologie et de lexicographie*, 129-149.

Skopinava, A., Yuras H. and Boris L. 2013. "Processing of quantitative expressions with units of measurement in scientific texts as applied to Belarusian and Russian text-to-speech synthesis". In: *Компьютерная лингвистика и интеллектуальные технологии: По материалам Международной конференции «Диалог»*, 634–651 Moscow: Russian State University for the Humanities Publishing.

Silberztein, M. 2003. *NooJ Manual*. Available at: http://www.nooj4nlp.net

POLITICAL MONITORING AND OPINION MINING FOR STANDARD ARABIC TEXTS

DHEKRA NAJAR AND SLIM MESFAR

Abstract

Since the continuous advent of the journalistic content online and the changing political landscape in many Arabic countries, we started our research for the implementation of a media monitoring system for opinion mining in the political field. This system allows political actors, despite of the large volume of online data, to be constantly informed about opinions expressed on the web in order to properly monitor their actual standing, orient their communication strategy and prepare election campaigns. For this purpose, the developed system is based on a linguistic approach using NooJ's linguistic engine to formalise the automatic recognition rules and apply them to a dynamic corpus composed of journalistic articles. The first implemented rules allow identifying and annotating the different political entities (political actors and organisations). These annotations are used in our system for media monitoring in order to identify the opinions associated with the extracted named entities. The system is mainly based on a set of local grammars developed for the identification of different structures of political opinion phrases. These grammars are using the entries of the opinion lexicon that contain the different opinion words (verbs, adjectives, nouns) where each entry is associated with the corresponding semantic marker (polarity and intensity). Our developed system is able to identify and annotate the opinion holder, the opinion target and the polarity (positive or negative) of the phraseological expression (nominal or verbal) expressing the opinion.

Introduction

Since the democratic transitional phase that the Arab spring's countries are passing through, Arabic citizens are becoming more actively engaged in political issues and more and more relying on online newspapers (than the traditional media) to get informed of the latest news and events. It's a normal change that is due to the high rapidity and ease of use of the Internet. So, online media publish constantly a wide variety of political information and opinions. As a result, it began to have the power to influence people's political decisions (elections, voting, etc.) in a much stronger manner. That's why political actors see that they must have knowledge about their actual standing on the web media (online newspapers, etc.). In this paper we describe an opinion mining system capable of measuring sentiments vis-à-vis political actors in the content of web media using NooJ's linguistic engine. The paper is divided into four parts. The first part deals with previous studies in the domain of opinion mining. The second part of this paper begins by laying out the theoretical dimensions of the research in order to specify the adopted approach. The third part presents a description of the approach we have adopted using the platform NooJ. The fourth part describes the evaluation and synthesis of our opinion mining system and some of the challenges faced. Finally, we discuss the results and perspectives of our research.

Opinion mining

Definition

Opinion mining is a new area in NLP that is born from the advent of the Internet and online media. It's the process that allows a user to analyse a huge amount of unstructured text data transmitted over the web in order to extract information related to the opinions and evaluations of the author as they are expressed vis-à-vis objects (a product, organization, etc.) or a concept (a service, an individual, a decision).

While a variety of definitions of the opinion have been suggested, this paper will use the definition formulated by Bing Liu who saw it as:

> *«a quintuple (oj, fjk, ooijkl, hi, tl), where oj is an object, fjk is a feature of the object oj, ooijkl is the orientation or polarity of the opinion on feature fjk of object oj, hi is the opinion holder and tl is the time when the opinion is expressed by hi. The opinion orientation ooijkl can be positive, negative or neutral. For feature fjk that opinion holder hi comments on, he/she chooses a word or phrase from the corresponding synonym set Wjk, or a word or phrase from the corresponding feature indicator set Ijk to describe the feature, and then expresses a positive, negative or neutral opinion on the feature.» (Bing, 2010)*

In the following section we discuss some related work in the field of opinion mining and particularly in the Arabic language.

Related work

There is a large volume of published studies describing various methods of opinion mining, especially in Latin languages.

Several studies have led to the creation of lexical resources, in particular for English, such as the dictionary WordNet-Affect (Strapparava & Valitutti, 2004), which contains 1903 concepts related to mental or emotional condition, and SentiWordNet (Esuli & Sebastiani, 2006). For the French language there is the lexicon of feelings developed by (Y.Yannick, 2005) which has a thousand simple words expressing feelings, emotions and psychological states. It is an ontology containing words which are divided into 38 different classes. Previous studies have based their methods on using large-coverage linguistic resources.

In contrast, several studies have been introduced in the literature based only on machine learning techniques. Pang and Lee (Pang, Lee, & Vaithyanathan, 2002) tested different learning techniques (Naive Bayes , Maximum Entropy and SVM) in the field of ' movie reviews ' in order to classify comments and advices into two classes (positive, negative). They showed that the use of Maximum Entropy classifier gave a higher value of F-measure. As for Wiebe and his co -authors (Wiebe, Bruce, & O'hara, 1999), they used a naive Bayes classifier to determine whether a sentence is objective or negative. This system has obtained an F-measure equal to 81.5%.

Thus, we mention the study of (Farra, Challita, Assi, & Hajj, 2010) that used a SVM classifier to automatically classify sentiments in the political field. The classification is performed at two levels: document level or sentence level. This system has achieved 89.3% F-measure for classification at the sentence level and 87% for the document level. Generally, manually developed dictionaries and resources (SentiWordNet, WordNet-Affect) are often combined with automatic techniques (SVM) in order to take advantage of machine learning approaches. In this context, the work of (Vernier & Monceaux, 2009) attempts to construct automatically a lexicon of subjective terms from 5,000 blog posts and comments. This method relies on the indexation of the language constituents (adjectives, adverbs, nominal and verbal expressions) by using a web search engine and a large number of queries.

On the other hand, in Arab world not much literature has been published on opinion mining and sentiment analysis. Most of the studies are mainly based on machine learning techniques. In a study of (Abdul-Mageed & Diab, 2012), which is an extension of their work (Abdul-Mageed, Diab, & Korayem, 2011), the authors present the system AWATIF, which is an Arabic multi-genre annotated corpus for sentiment and subjectivity analysis. The corpus is tagged using two methods of sourcing[1] (regular sourcing and crowd sourcing). It can be used to assist in the construction of subjectivity and sentiment analysis systems, such as the attempt of (Abdul-Mageed & Diab, 2012). We note that this corpus is not available to the public. In another major recent study, (Abdul-Mageed, Diab, & Kübler, 2013) have developed the system SAMAR, which is a supervised machine learning system for subjectivity analysis in Arabic. The advantage of this study is that the authors have created a multi-genre corpus (from 4 types of social media) of texts written in Standard Arabic (MSA) and Dialectal Arabic (DA).

In fact, this is the first research that addresses the dialectal Arabic language (Egyptian dialect). The authors have created manually a lexicon of 3982 adjectives. Each of the adjectives is marked as positive, negative or neutral adjective. For classification, they have adopted a two-phased approach: (objective/subjective classification and positive/negative classification).

Indeed, most of the proposed automatic approaches in Arabic are based on the semantic similarities between words in order to classify the words with unknown polarity. For example, (Amira F, Torky I, Maha A, & Mohamed M, 2013) propose an automatic approach for emotion detection in Arabic texts.

This approach relies on the construction of a moderate size lexicon that contains emotions and feelings terms to annotate stories for children. The SVM model aims to classify these stories into six basic emotions (joy, fear, sadness, anger, disgust, and surprise) by calculating the degree of similarity between words and already annotated emotions. This approach has achieved 64.5% F-measure for the six emotions.

According to the recent study of (Alaa El-Dine & Fatma El-zahraa, 2013), the authors have developed an annotated corpus in Arabic for sentiment analysis. This corpus is used to classify new comments. Then, they used various learning algorithms (decision tree, SVM, etc.) to implement the sentiment analyser. The best result was obtained by the SVM classifier with an F-measure reached 73.4 %.

We also include the study of (Abdul-Mageed & Korayem, 2010), who annotated a corpus of 200 documents from the Penn Treebank Arabic (Maamouri, Bies, Buckwalter, & Mekki, 2004), composed of subjective journalistic texts. They applied three different learning algorithms on the

---

[1] Le sourcing est le terme par lequel on désigne l'ensemble des opérations, préalables à la collecte de données, qui visent à identifier des sources (sites web, blogs, forums, etc.) susceptibles de contenir de l'information.

corpus to automatically classify sentences. This approach has achieved a very high F-measure equal to 99.48% with the SVM classifier.

Adopted approach

The approach we follow for developing our Arabic opinion mining system is mainly based on a linguistic approach, but makes use of some machine learning techniques.

Named Entities recognition is a potentially important pretreatment for the opinion mining field. However, this task presents a serious challenge, given the specificities of the Arabic language.

For this purpose, we have adapted a rules-based approach to recognise Arabic named entities and political organisations, using different grammars and gazetteer. We also use the Al-DicAr dictionary *(Mesfar, 2008)* as the basis for our sentiment analysis system.

Implementation

We use the linguistic engine NooJ to deal with all morpho-syntactic searches such as lemmatisation, annotation, submission of various linguistic queries so that we provide access to advanced features (syntactic and morphological queries) without being expert in the field. NooJ is a linguistic engine based on large-coverage dictionaries and grammars. It parses text corpora made up of hundreds of text files in real time.

Resources

We use the Al-DicAr dictionary (Mesfar, 2008), which stands for "Electronic Dictionary for Arabic", as the basis for our sentiment analysis system. In addition, we build a new lexicon representing the different opinion and political vocabularies (verbs expressing opinions, adjectives, nouns). Each opinion word is integrated in the dictionary associated with a set of linguistic and semantic information: grammatical category, gender and number, syntactic information. We have extracted 933 subjective terms from our training corpus, which are commonly used in the journalistic media.

Category	Number of entries	Polarity		
		Positive	Negative	Total
Verbs	127	46	71	117
Nouns	480	225	335	560
Adjectives	256	132	124	256
Total		403	530	933

Table 1. Number of the opinion dictionary entries

Since we have limited our research in one field (politics), we consider these rates high. We note that the nouns represent more than half of all entries in the opinion lexicon (60%), followed by adjectives (27.5%), verbs (12.5%). All the recognised subjective words in our dictionary are associated with the corresponding semantic markup:

- *+Polarite= pos; for positive terms;*
- *+Polarite= neg; for negative terms.*

Grammars

The political opinion mining application first requires the corpus to be annotated with political and party entities. For this we have also developed a series of grammars in order to annotate, in a first stage, the political organisations and actors.

The approach we take for Named Entity recognition is a rule based one which is quite similar to that used by *(Mesfar, 2008)*. The Named Entity recognition module is able to find mentions of Persons, Locations and Organisations, as potential opinion targets. For this purpose, the NER system is based on the use of lists containing gazetteers and lexical markers that are known beforehand and have been classified into named entity types. We also use lists of trigger words which indicate that the surrounding tokens are probably named entity constituents and may reliably permit the type of the political named entity to be determined (minister, president, etc.). Lists of triggers are produced manually from the training corpus.

The key words are tagged as result of the morphological analysis, and are used in named entity grammar rules. A syntactic grammar represents word sequences described by manually created rules, and then produces some kind of linguistic information such as function of the recognised political actor.

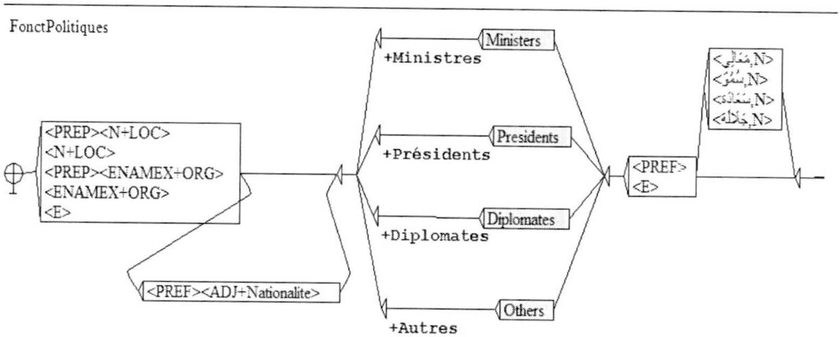

Fig. 1: ENAMEX NooJ syntactic grammar

Beyond the recognition of the political actors names and their functions, NooJ also allows saving a recognised sequence in a variable to be used later. We employ this functionality to store the name of the named entity in the variable "NOM" and its function in the variable "FONCTION". We use these variables later in our opinion mining system in order to identify different variables of an extracted opinion.

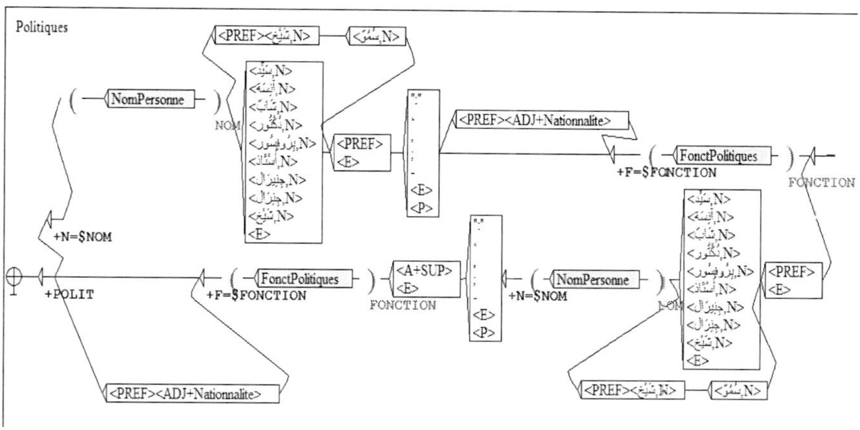

Fig. 2. ENAMEX NooJ syntactic grammar

The NER grammar "ENAMEX PERS" is launched in the linguistic analysis of the corpus in order to enhance it by associating annotations to its various textual segments: named entities, political organisations. The generated annotations are used in the description of syntactic rules for the identification of opinions in the journalistic texts.

The approach we take for sentiment analysis is a rule based one based on the entries of our opinion lexicon. Initially, we try to collect the maximum of information for contextual recognised forms. Then, this information is used within syntactic grammars to locate relevant opinion sequences. The main body of the opinion mining application involves a set of NooJ grammars which create annotations on segments of text. The grammar rules use information from gazetteers combined with semantic regular expression (+Polarite=neg etc.) and contextual information to build up a set of annotations.

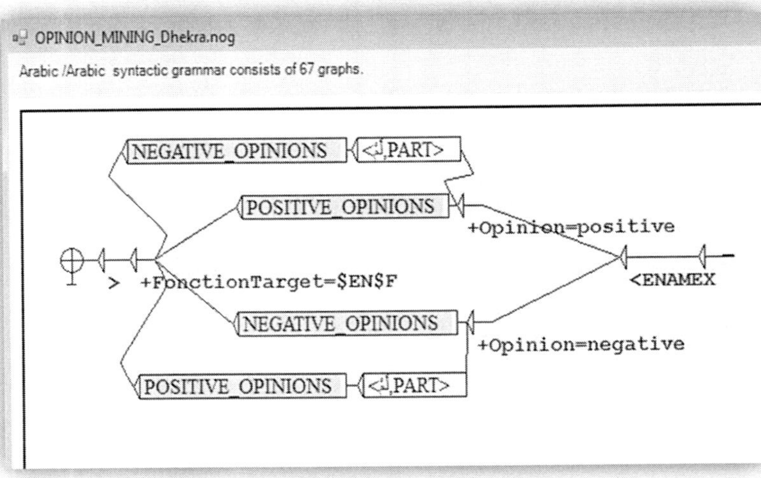

Fig. 3: Opinion mining syntactic grammar

To classify opinions in journalistic texts, we create annotations (Opinion=positive or Opinion=negative) on the subjective segments in the corpus, as shown in Fig. 3.

A grammar rule is generally made of a trigger word and tagged words from the opinion lexicon. NooJ syntactic grammars employ some heuristics when applying rules. They locate the longest match for one grammar and all matches for the whole set of grammars.

Evaluation

Data were collected *using* a program for extracting regular journalistic texts online. Then the corpus is analysed using the NooJ linguistic engine. All downloaded items are filtered by automatically removing HTML tags, advertisements, images and other added elements to extract plain text. These texts are then analysed using the linguistic NooJ engine. In addition to using our linguistic resources such as electronic dictionaries, with large coverage and local grammars, we use some other filtering dictionaries to resolve the most frequent ambiguous cases. The studied corpus is composed of a set of journalistic articles published during the period between 05/12/2013 and 12/08/2013: at this time we loaded 100 articles from different web media.

Traditionally, the scoring report compares the answer file with a carefully annotated file. The system was evaluated in terms of the complementary precision (P) and recall (R) metrics. Briefly, precision evaluates the noise of a system while recall evaluates its coverage. These metrics are often combined using a weighted harmonic called the F-measure (F).

Evaluation of the dictionary

To test the lexical coverage of our dictionary, we launch the linguistic analysis of our corpus. The linguistic analysis shows that the corpus contains about 19,319 different forms, of which we have recognized 18991 forms (328 unknown forms). In other words, the result of lexical analysis shows that the vocabulary of the corpus is recognised to 98.3% by our lexical and morphological resources. In fact, the non-recognition is due to two main reasons: the absence of certain words in our dictionaries or the frequent mistakes in journalistic texts. For example:

- False voyellation of words such as (أيضا, too);
- Common typographical errors such as confusion between Alif and Hamza or the substitution of (ه ,ة) and (ي ,ى) at the end of the word;
- The false writing of Hamza (جاءوا ,جاؤوا, they arrived);
- The addition or omission of a character in a word;
- The lack of whitespace between two terms as (وهذا, andthis);
- The transcription of foreign names (ديفيد David);
- Neologisms such as (ديبلوم, Diploma) (twitter, تويتر) .

Discussion: The recognition rate in the corpus is high. This shows that the developed resources in the thesis of (Mesfar, 2008), as well as our specialised political lexicons, are rich and wide. They can probably cover the journalistic discourse used in articles. This will ensure a maximum of lexical recognition for our opinion mining system.

Evaluation of the NER grammar

To evaluate our NER local grammars, we analyse our corpus to extract manually all named entities. Then, we compare the results of our system with those obtained by manual extraction. The application of our local grammar gives the following result:

Precision	Recall	F-Measure
0.86	0.77	0.81

Table 2. ENAMEX grammar experiments on our corpus

The table above presents the recall, precision and F-measure obtained by the application of the NER grammar on our corpus. It is clear that we have reached a reasonable result of recognition with F-measure of 0.81. This result is encouraging given the rate achieved by the systems participating in MUC. In fact, in our system, we consider only the completely extracted information (named entities and their functions).

In the figure below there are several sources of error. The main error consists in bad formalisation of the recognition rules. Concerning the silence of our NER module, it is often due to the absence of some recognition rules; naive indices (upper case) and triggers. This explains why the rate of recall is low (0.77) Among the other reasons, we can mention the obstacle of the transcription into Arabic (different variants of a single word). The application of the NER grammar gives the results below.

```
الرئيس الإسلامي محمد مرسي/<ENAMEX+PERS+Présidents+F=الرئيس الإسلامي+N=محمد مرسي+POLIT>
وزير الخارجية المصري نبيل فهمي/<ENAMEX+PERS+Ministres+F=وزير الخارجية المصري+N=نبيل فهمي+POLIT>
الرئيس الحالي عدلي منصور/<ENAMEX+PERS+Présidents+F=الرئيس الحالي+N=عدلي منصور+POLIT>
وحيد عبد المجيد، مدير مركز/<ENAMEX+PERS+N=وحيد عبد المجيد+Autres+F=مدير مركز+POLIT>
الوزير محمد إبراهيم/<ENAMEX+PERS+Ministres+F=الوزير+N=محمد إبراهيم+POLIT>
زعيم المعارضة سوثيب ثاوجسوبان/<ENAMEX+PERS+Présidents+F=زعيم المعارضة+N=سوثيب ثاوجسوبان+POLIT>
رئيس الحكومة علي زيدان/<ENAMEX+PERS+Présidents+F=رئيس الحكومة+N=علي زيدان+POLIT>
الملك محمد السادس/<ENAMEX+PERS+Présidents+F=الملك+N=محمد السادس+POLIT>
رئيس الحكومة عبد الإله بن كيران/<ENAMEX+PERS+Présidents+F=رئيس الحكومة+N=عبد الإله بن كيران+POLIT>
والرئيس فرنسوا هولاند/<ENAMEX+PERS+Présidents+F=والرئيس+N=فرنسوا هولاند+POLIT>
أحمد فؤاد نجم شاعر الغلابة/<ENAMEX+PERS>
الرئيس الراحل أنور السادات/<ENAMEX+PERS+Présidents+F=الرئيس الراحل+N=أنور السادات+POLIT>
مؤسسة الأمير كلاوس الهولندية/<ENAMEX+PERS+Autres+F=مؤسسة الأمير+N=كلاوس الهولندية+POLIT>
الرئيس السوداني عمر البشير ان/<ENAMEX+PERS+Présidents+F=الرئيس السوداني+N=عمر البشير ان+POLIT>
الرئيس السوداني عمر البشير الى/<ENAMEX+PERS+Présidents+F=الرئيس السوداني+N=عمر البشير الى+POLIT>
حكم الرئيس السوداني عمر البشير/<ENAMEX+PERS+Présidents+F=الرئيس السوداني+N=حكم عمر البشير+POLIT>
وزير الخارجية اليمني أبوبكر القربي/<ENAMEX+PERS+Ministres+F=وزير الخارجية اليمني+N=أبوبكر القربي+POLIT>
صائب عريقات وزير الخارجية الأميركي/<ENAMEX+PERS+N=صائب عريقات+Ministres+F=وزير الخارجية الأميركي+POLIT>
رئيس الوزراء الإسرائيلي بنيامين نتنياهو/<ENAMEX+PERS+Présidents+F=رئيس الوزراء الإسرائيلي+N=بنيامين نتنياهو+POLIT>
السيد صائب عريقات/<ENAMEX+PERS+N=صائب عريقات>
```

Fig. 4: Named entity recognition concordancer

Discussion: Despite the problems described above, the used techniques seem to be adequate and display very encouraging recognition rates. Indeed, a minority of the rules may be sufficient to cover a large part of the patterns and ensure coverage. However, many other rules must be added to improve the recall.

Evaluation of the Opinion mining grammar

To evaluate our opinion mining local grammars, we also analyse our corpus to extract manually the opinion sequences and expressions related to the political actors. Then, we compare the results of our system with those obtained by manual extraction. The application of our local grammar gives the following result:

Precision	Recall	F-Measure
0.92	0.77	0.83

Table 3. Opinion Mining grammar experiments on our corpus

According to these results, we have obtained an acceptable identification of political opinion sentences. Our evaluation shows F-measure of 0.83. We note that the rate of silence in the corpus is low, which is represented by the recall value 0.77. This is due to the fact that this assessment is mainly based on the results of the NER module. Therefore, we can say that some cases of silence in the corpus are due to silence at the named entity recognition module. It is very important to note that journalistic texts of our corpus are heterogeneous and extracted from different resources. For this reason, we find an infinite structure of sentences expressing opinions (each journalist or author expresses the information in their own way). Another major source of uncertainty is the absence of some recognition rules for a given structure. The application of the opinion mining local grammar produces the results below.

<ENAMEX+Opinion=negative+Structure=verbal+Target=بشار الأسد+FonctionTarget=الرئيس السوري>/استخدم الرئيس السوري بشار الأسد القوة ضد شعبه
<ENAMEX+Opinion=negative+Structure=nominal+Target=فارح شردون+FonctionTarget=رئيس الوزراء>/سحب الثقة من السيد فارح شردون رئيس الوزراء
<ENAMEX+Opinion=positive+Structure=verbal+Target=فارح شردون+FonctionTarget=رئيس الوزراء>/أبدى رئيس الوزراء فارح شردون ترحيبه

Fig. 5: Opinion mining concordancer

As shown in the correlation table, our system is able to extract and classify the expressions of opinion in journalistic texts and identify their different variables.

We are able to identify for each extracted opinion:

- *oj*: opinion target;
- *fjk*: features of the target;
- *soijkl*: the polarity of the opinion (positive, negative) ;
- *hi*: opinion holder (opinion holder) .*

In fact, the target of the opinion and polarity are two obligatory variables for the categorisation and classification of an opinion sentence. The other two variables are complementary and optional depending on the structure of the opinion sentence. We note that in our system it is useful to implement the task of identifying the source of the opinion (which can be a person or organisation).

By visualising the extracted terms in concordance tables after the application of our syntactic grammars, we see the emergence of some false sequences. This is due to:

- Problems related to the procedure for recognition of named entities;
- A word can be both a personal name and an entry in our lexicon of opinion. This can lead the system to extract noisy information (noise).

Discussion: Errors are often due to the complexity of opinion sentences or the absence of their structure in our system (and in the learning corpus). In fact, the Arabic sentences in news articles are usually very long, which sets up obstacles for opinion mining analysis. Despite the problems described above, the developed method seems to be adequate and shows very encouraging extraction rates. However, other rules must be added to improve the result.

Conclusion and perspectives

Using our opinion mining system, we analysed sentiment in newspapers in Arabic, and identify the different variables of an extracted opinion sentence. Our experiments show that our method for extracting political opinion is consistent.

More broadly, research is also needed to compress the long sentences in news articles, which can set up obstacles for further opinion mining steps. Sentence compression is the task of producing a brief summary at the sentence level.

References

Abdul-Mageed, M., and Mohammed K. «Automatic Identification of Subjectivity in Morphologically Rich Languages: The Case of Arabic.» 2010: 2-6.

Abdul-Mageed, M., and Mona D. «AWATIF: A Multi-Genre Corpus for Modern Standard Arabic Subjectivity and Sentiment Analysis.» 2012.

Abdul-Mageed, M., Mona D., and Mohammed K. «Subjectivity and sentiment analysis of modern standard Arabi.» 2 (juin 2011): 587-591.

Abdul-Mageed, M., Mona D., and Sandra K. «SAMAR: Subjectivity and sentiment analysis for Arabic social media.» *Computer Speech and Language (2013)*, mars 2013.

Abdul-Mageed, M., and Mouhammed D.. «Toward building a large-scale arabic sentiment lexicon.» 2012.

Alaa El-Dine, A., and El-taher F. E. «Sentiment Analyzer for Arabic Comments System.» *International Journal of Advanced Computer Science and Applications*, 2013.

Amira F, El Gohary, S. Torky I, Hana M. A, et El Dosoky M. «A Computational Approach for Analyzing and Detecting Emotions in Arabic Text.» *International Journal of Engineering Research and Applications (IJERA)* 3 (May-Juin 2013): 100-107.

Bing, L. «Sentiment analysis and subjectivity.» *Handbook of Natural Language Processing*, 2010: 627–666.

Esuli, A, and F Sebastiani. ««SentiWordNet : a Publicly Available Lexical Resource for Opinion Mining .» 2006.

Farra, N., Elie C., Rawad Abou Assi, and Hazem H. «Sentence-Level and Document-Level Sentiment Mining for Arabic Texts.» *IEEE International Conference*, December 2010: 1114-1119.

Maamouri, M., Ann B., Tim B., and Mekki.W. «The Penn Arabic Treebank: Building a Large-Scale Annotated Arabic Corpus.» Septembre 2004: 102-109.

Mesfar, S.. «analyse morpho-syntaxique et reconnaissance des entités nommées en arabe standard.» Thèse, Université de franche comté école doctorale «LANGAGES, ESPACES, TEMPS, SOCIETES», 2008.

Pang, B., Lillian L., and Shivakumar V. «Thumbs up? Sentiment Classification using Machine Learning techniques.» 2002: 79-86.

Vernier, M.,and Laura M. «Enrichissement d'un lexique de termes subjectifs à partir de tests sémantiques.» 03 2009.

Wiebe, J. M., Rebecca F. B., and Thomas P. O. «Development and use of a gold-standard data set for subjectivity classifications.» 1999: 246-253.

Yannick, M. «Annotation of Emotions and Feelings in Texts.» (Springer Berlin Heidelberg) 2005: 350-357.

CO-REFERENCE RESOLUTION USING NOOJ RECOGNITION PROCESS OF ARABIC NAMED ENTITIES

HELA FEHRI , KAIS HADDAR AND ABDELMAJID BEN HAMADOU

Abstract

In this paper, we are going to resolve the co-reference problem in the Arabic language. Co-reference in our context occurs when multiple expressions in a sentence or a document refer to the same named entity. To resolve the co-reference problem, we propose a method which is based on two phases: the recognition phase and the co-reference resolution. Each phase of our method is based on NooJ transducers.

Introduction

The present paper focuses on resolving the coreference problem in the Arabic language. This problem is prevalent and difficult. In computational linguistics, coreference resolution is a well-studied problem in discourse. In order to derive the correct interpretation of a text, or even to estimate the relative importance of various subjects mentioned, referring expressions need to be connected to the corresponding named entity. Coreference in our context occurs when multiple expressions in a sentence or a document refer to the same named entity (Crystal 1997, Radford 2004). For example, in the named entity "ملعب الطيب المهيري" "Stadium of Taieb el Mhiri", " هذا الملعب" "this stadium" and "الطيب المهيري" "Taeib El Mhiri" and "الملعب" "Stadium" are most likely referring to the same named entity.

The pattern in this example is typical: when first introducing a place name or another topic for discussion, the author or the speaker will use a relatively long and detailed description. However, later mentions are briefer. When dealing with pronouns, references are frequently ambiguous. When looking back to the previous context, coreference is called "anaphoric reference". When looking forward, it is named "cataphoric reference" (Jurafsky and H. Martin 2000). Let us note that the problem of referring expressions in relationship to acronyms does not exist because acronyms have never been adopted in writing Arabic proper names.

The problem becomes more complex especially when a part of a named entity that appears in the following sentence, does not refer to this named entity. For example, in a text we can find a sentence mentioning the named entity "ملعب الطيب المهيري" "Stadium of Taieb el Mhiri" and in the next sentence of the text, we can find "الطيب المهيري" "Taieb el Mhiri" which is a part of the named entity "Stadium of Taieb el Mhiri" but is not a referring expression. It is used to indicate that this stadium was named after Taieb el Mhiri, and is in this case a personal name.

To resolve the coreference problem, we propose a method which is based on two phases: recognition phase and coreference resolution. In the second phase we identify the referring expressions and their position, and match them to the named entity in question. Then, we browse the text and replace each referring expression with the named entity in question. Each phase of our method is based on NooJ transducers.

Our paper deals with, firstly, the resources being constructed and their implementation in the linguistic platform NooJ; secondly, with experimenting and evaluating the developed resources; and finally, concluding with some perspectives.

Proposed approach

The proposed approach requires two-phase process: recognition of Arabic NEs phase and coreference resolution. Each phase involves construction of the respective transducers.

Arabic NE recognition and the extraction of referring expressions are based on rules. These rules are manually built to express the structure of the information to recognise and take the form of transducers which to be directly implemented in the linguistic platform NooJ (Silbeztein 2004). These transducers use morphosyntactic information, as well as information contained in the resources (lexicons or dictionaries). In addition, they allow the description of possible sequences of Arabic NEs constituents belonging to the sports domain and particularly to the category of place names. It should be noted that the sport venues NEs recognition requires the identification of other types of NEs from the same domain (player names, team names, sports names, etc.) or another domain (personal names, city names, numeric entities, etc.).

The steps of the proposed approach are illustrated in Fig. 1.

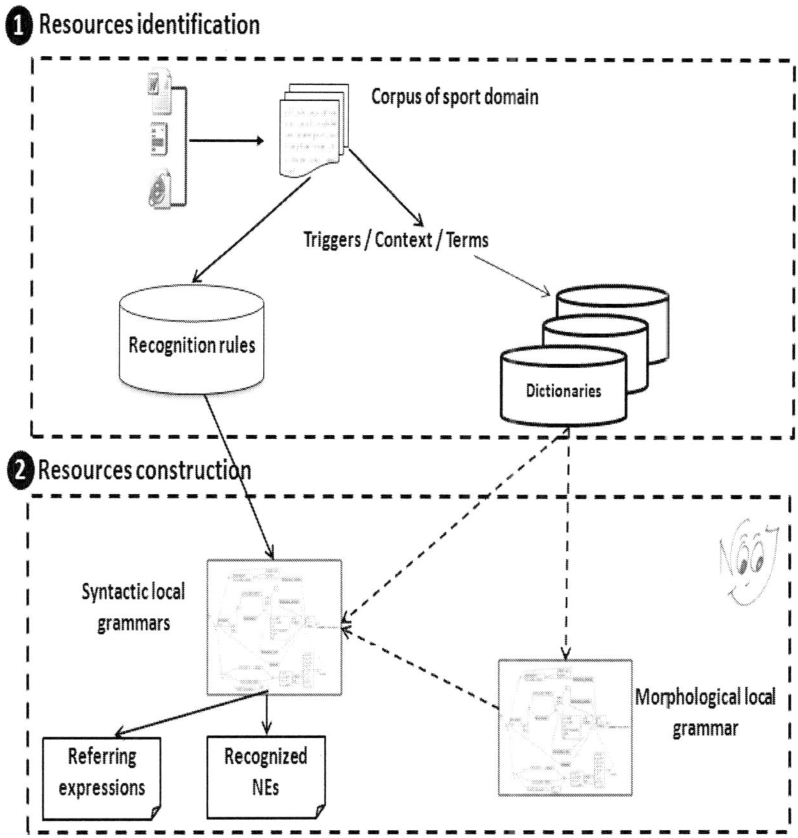

Fig. 1. Proposed approach

As shown in Fig. 1, the recognition process consists of identification of lexical entities using dictionaries and grammars (or syntactic patterns), and the transformation of grammars into transducers.

Identification of lexical entities

In the sport domain, object of our study, we apply the following dictionaries:

- A dictionary of simple names
- A dictionary of adjectives (e.g., أولمبي ' uwlamby , وطني Watany)
- A dictionary of team names (e.g., الملعب التونسي Almal ` ab eltuwnisy)

- A dictionary of player names
- A dictionary of sport names (e.g., كرة قدم Korat qadam)
- A dictionary of toponyms
- A dictionary of days and months
- A dictionary of first personal names
- A dictionary of names of individuals (e.g., خالد بن الوليد Khaalid bin alwalyd)
- A dictionary of domain trigger words (eg., ملعب mal` ab)
- A dictionary of functions (e.g., أمير ' amyR)

The entry structure of different dictionaries is not the same. It may vary from one dictionary to another but contains at least:

- the grammatical category of the entry (noun, adjective); and
- the semantic feature that defines the type of input (Function, First name, team, player name,)

In addition to this information, we can find, depending on the dictionary, additional information such as:

- Gender (masculine or feminine) and number (singular, dual and plural)
- Derivation Model to recognise the derived forms of the lemma contained in the input
- The inflectional model for recognising inflected forms of the lemma of in the entry.
- The feature "determination" of nouns to such as الرياض elriyaD. This is not the case with the name تونس tuwnis .

All this information is used by the transducers to guide the recognition process and resolve ambiguities.

Identification of syntactic patterns

To facilitate the work of transducers required for NE recognition, we identify syntactic patterns which give the arrangement of the various NE components and can be easily represented as graphs.

We distinguish between seven syntactic patterns that describe the Arabic NEs for sport venues. These patterns are generated by a common constituent from the identified NEs. In what follows, we detail some patterns.

Pattern2 describes the NEs where the personal name is an obligatory element. It represents NEs beginning with one or more trigger words followed by many adjectives followed by the name of a personality followed by a place name. It also describes the NEs beginning with one or more trigger words followed by a personal name, followed by adjectives or by one or more toponyms.

<Pattern2> := <Trigger word>+ ([<Adjective>]* <Pattern1> | <Pattern1> [<Adjective>]*) [<Toponym>]*

Pattern 1 describes different forms of a personal name.

Transformation of syntactic patterns into transducers

At this step we formalise the already built rules using the transducers. Fig. 2 shows the main transducer for the recognition of sport venues. In all, there are 5 graphs that represent the different types of sports venues (Stadium, Complex, swimming pool, and city).

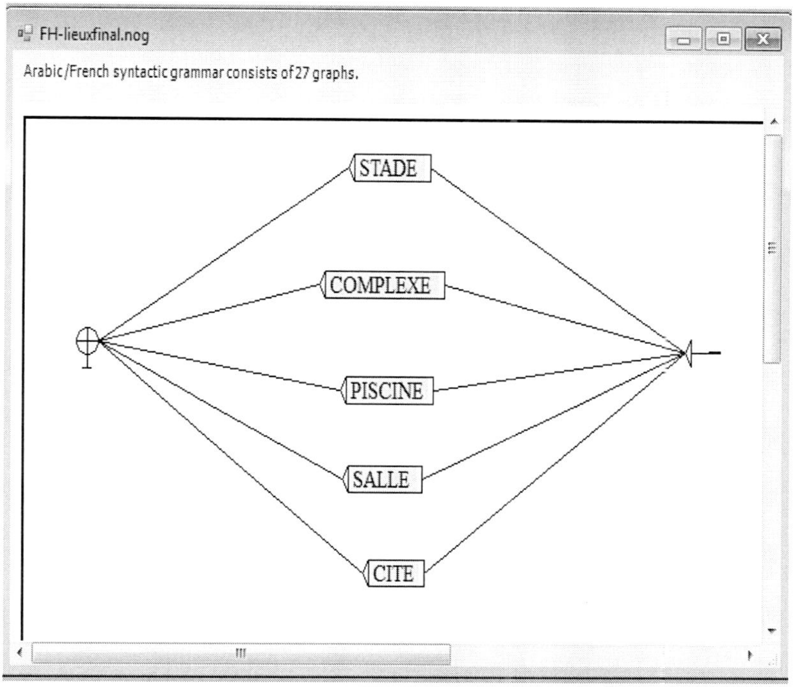

Fig. 2. Main transducer of NE' recognition

The transducer in Fig. 2 contains 27 subgraphs. These subgraphs represent the embedded NEs contained in the main NE. Each path of a subgraph describes a syntactic pattern.

To illustrate this transformation, below we give details about the subgraph "STADE".

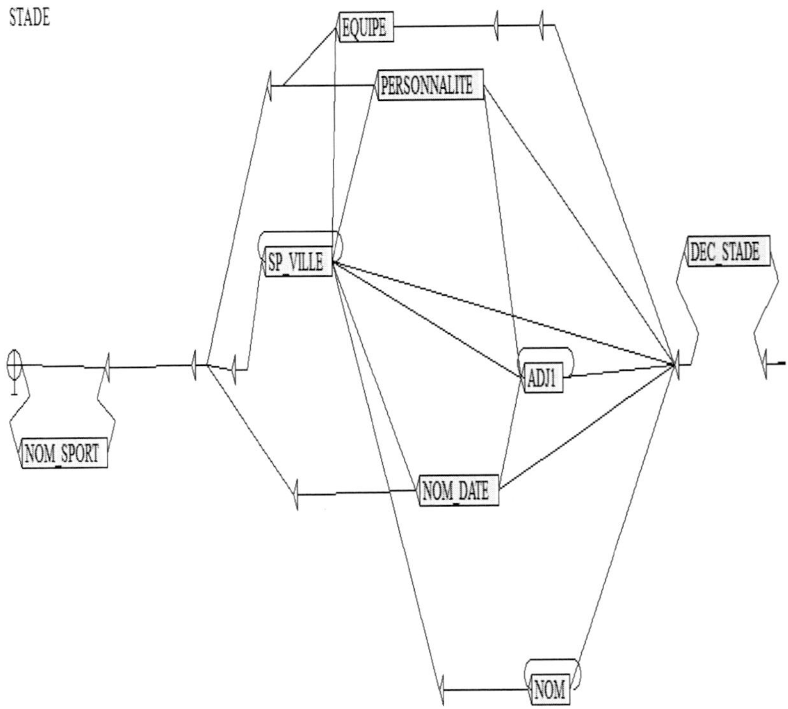

Fig. 3. The sub-graph "STADE"

The transducer in Fig. 3 shows that a stadium name may contain a personal name, a noun, an adjective, a city, a geographic category or a date. A personal name can be preceded by an adjective. After a personal name, the stadium name can be followed by a city name (presented by the subgraph "SP_VILLE"), a team name (represented by the subgraph "EQUIPE") or a sport name (represented by the subgraph "NOM_SPORT") or nothing (the "PERSONNALITE" node is linked directly to a final node). The combination of an output with an input identifies a rule. To recognise a place name, we have built other graphs for different types of NEs.

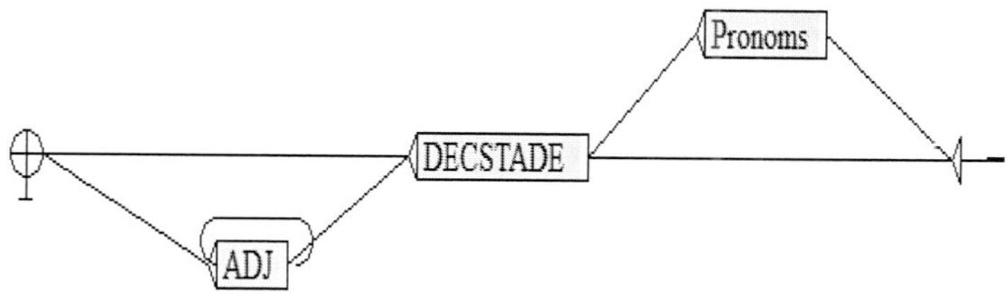

Fig. 4. Main transducer of coreference expressions

The subgraph in Fig 4 allows the recognition of the referring expressions like "هذا الملعب". The subgraph "Pronoms" describes pronouns that can appear at the beginning of the referring expression.

Below we describe the subgraph "DECSTADE".

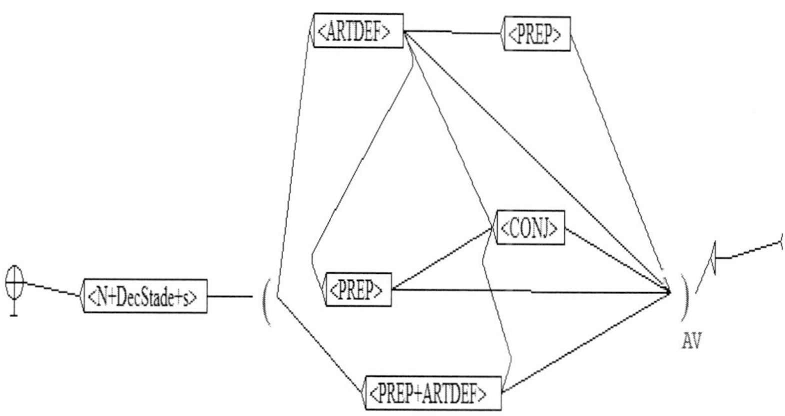

Fig. 5. The subgraph "DECSTADE"

The subgraph "DECSTADE" represents different forms that can be agglutinated to the words constructing a referring expression (Fehri, Haddar and Ben Hamadou 2011).

Experimentation and evaluation

To evaluate the recognition phase, we began by applying our resources to a corpus formed by 4000 texts from the sport domain, different from the study corpus. Fig. 6 shows a fragment of the obtained results.

0,27 , استاد الأمير عبدالله الفيصل
157,184 , استاد الأمير عبدالله الفيصل
725,747 , استاد الملك فهد الدولي
760,782 , استاد الملك فهد الدولي
4265,4287 , استاد الملك فهد الدولي
5344,5366 , استاد الملك فهد الدولي
6929,6944 , استاد الملك فهد
6955,6977 , استاد الملك فهد الدولي
7153,7175 , استاد الملك فهد الدولي
7308,7324 , أستاد بونغ كارنو
7402,7418 , أستاد جاكا بارنغ
7831,7853 , المدينة الرياضية بتونس
8503,8526 , الملعب الأولمبي بالمنزه
8585,8608 , للملعب الأولمبي بالمنزه
8825,8848 , الملعب الأولمبي بالمنزه
8884,8903 , ملعب 7 نوفمبر برادس
9118,9139 , الملعب الأولمبي بباجة
12187,12202 , ستاد الإسكندرية
12203,12218 , ستاد الإسكندرية
12743,12759 , ستاد الإسماعيلية
13000,13016 , ستاد الأمير محمد
13202,13222 , استاد البحرين الوطني
13684,13705 , لاستاد البحرين الوطني

Fig. 6. Extract of Arabic NE recognition result

Further, we have applied resources allowing the recognition of referring expression in the corpus. An extract of the obtained result is shown in Fig. 7.

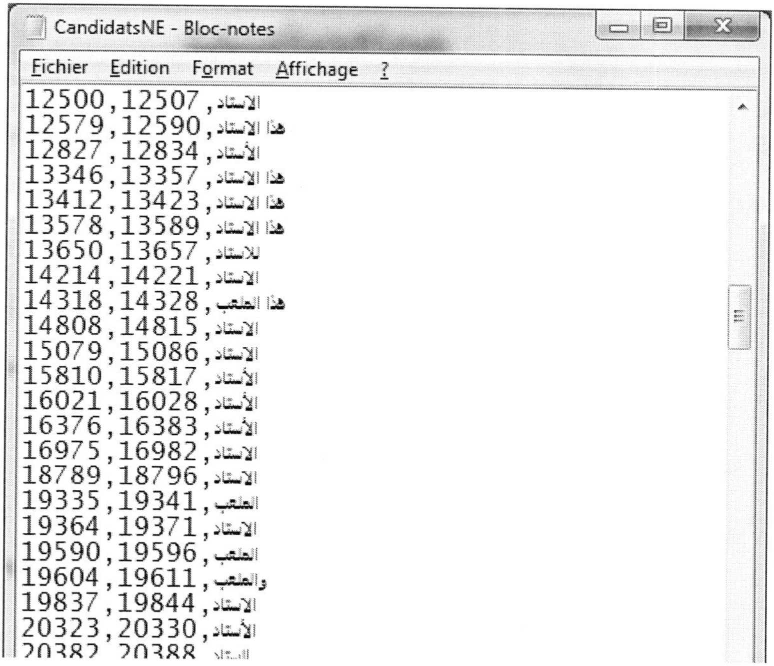
CandidatsNE - Bloc-notes

Fichier Edition Format Affichage ?

12500,12507,الاستاد
12579,12590,هذا الاستاد
12827,12834,الأستاد
13346,13357,هذا الاستاد
13412,13423,هذا الاستاد
13578,13589,هذا الاستاد
13650,13657,للاستاد
14214,14221,الاستاد
14318,14328,هذا الملعب
14808,14815,الاستاد
15079,15086,الاستاد
15810,15817,الأستاد
16021,16028,الأستاد
16376,16383,الأستاد
16975,16982,الاستاد
18789,18796,الاستاد
19335,19341,الملعب
19364,19371,الاستاد
19590,19596,الملعب
19604,19611,والملعب
19837,19844,الاستاد
20323,20330,الأستاد
20382,20388,

Fig. 7. Extract of the extracted referring expressions result

In Fig. 6 and Fig. 7, each referring expression or recognised NE, respectively, is extracted and labelled with its position in the text. So, we obtain the position of a referring expression and we can match it to the corresponding NE by verifying its location according to the pairs of successive NE positions. For example, we take the referring expression "الاستاد", which is indexed by "12500, 12507", we extract the position "12500" and browse the recognised NEs in Fig. 6. As a result, we find that this position is between the two successive positions 12203 and 12743, and we can conclude that the expression "الاستاد" refers to the NE "ستاد الاسكندرية", indexed by 12203.

Finally, we browse the text and replace each referring expression with its antecedent. After applying this process to our corpus, we obtain the text in the following form as illustrated in the figure below:

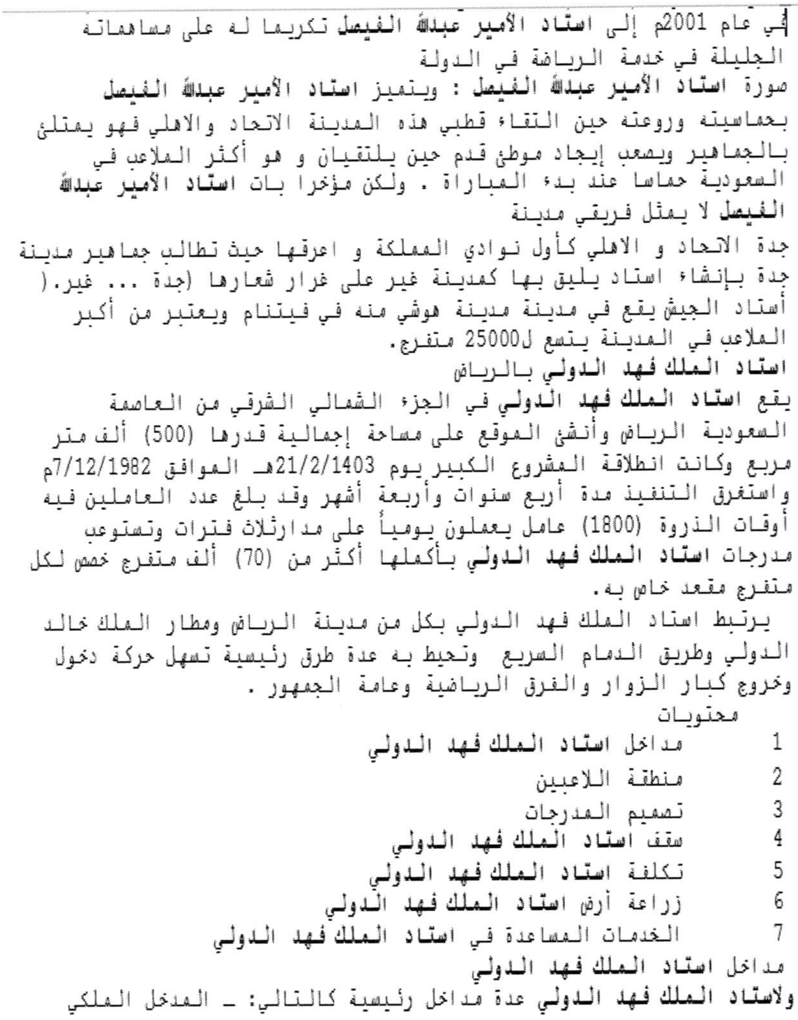
في عام 2001م إلى **استاد الأمير عبدالله الفيصل** تكريما له على مساهماته
الجليلة في خدمة الرياضة في الدولة
صورة **استاد الأمير عبدالله الفيصل** : ويتميز **استاد الأمير عبدالله الفيصل**
بحماسيته وروعته حين التقاء قطبي هذه المدينة الاتحاد والاهلي فهو يمتلئ
بالجماهير ويصعب إيجاد موطئ قدم حين يلتقيان و هو أكثر الملاعب في
السعودية حماسا عند بدء المباراة . ولكن مؤخرا بات **استاد الأمير عبدالله
الفيصل** لا يمثل فريقي مدينة
جدة الاتحاد و الاهلي كأول نوادي المملكة و اعرقها حيث تطالب جماهير مدينة
جدة بإنشاء استاد يليق بها كمدينة غير على غرار شعارها (جدة ... غير.(
أستاد الجيش يقع في مدينة مدينة هوشي منه في فيتنام ويعتبر من أكبر
الملاعب في المدينة يتسع ل25000 متفرج.
استاد الملك فهد الدولي بالرياض
يقع **استاد الملك فهد الدولي** في الجزء الشمالي الشرقي من العاصمة
السعودية الرياض وأنشئ الموقع على مساحة إجمالية قدرها (500) ألف متر
مربع وكانت انطلاقة المشروع الكبير يوم 21/2/1403هـ الموافق 7/12/1982م
واستغرق التنفيذ مدة أربع سنوات وأربعة أشهر وقد بلغ عدد العاملين فيه
أوقات الذروة (1800) عامل يعملون يومياً على مدارثلاث فترات وتستوعب
مدرجات **استاد الملك فهد الدولي** بأكملها أكثر من (70) ألف متفرج خصص لكل
متفرج مقعد خاص به.
يرتبط استاد الملك فهد الدولي بكل من مدينة الرياض ومطار الملك خالد
الدولي وطريق الدمام السريع وتحيط به عدة طرق رئيسية تسهل حركة دخول
وخروج كبار الزوار والفرق الرياضية وعامة الجمهور .
محتويات
1 مداخل **استاد الملك فهد الدولي**
2 منطقة اللاعبين
3 تصميم المدرجات
4 سقف **استاد الملك فهد الدولي**
5 تكلفة **استاد الملك فهد الدولي**
6 زراعة أرض **استاد الملك فهد الدولي**
7 الخدمات المساعدة في **استاد الملك فهد الدولي**
مداخل **استاد الملك فهد الدولي**
ولاستاد الملك فهد الدولي عدة مداخل رئيسية كالتالي: ـ المدخل الملكي

Fig. 8. Extract of the obtained text

The replaced referring expressions are written in bold.

Our method produces 70% well replaced referring expressions with the correct NE. The obtained result is promising and shows that there are some problems not yet resolved, which are related to the: clitic pronouns and empty pronouns (pro-drop projection phenomena).

Conclusion

Through this paper we have described our proposed method to resolve the problem of coreference related to NEs, especially sportive place names. We have also developed a system allowing the replacement of each referring expression with the corresponding NE at the syntactic level, discourse the linguistic (not the sentential linguistic) and anaphoric relation.

The developed system can be integrated into an automatic comprehension system and can be used for semantic improvement. Further, we intend to resolve the coreference problem at the cataphoric relation level and at the lexical level.

References

Crystal, D., 1997,. «A dictionary of linguistics and phonetics». 4th edition. Cambridge, MA: Blackwell Publishing. 1997.

Jurafsky, D. and H. Martin, J.., 2000, «Speech and language processing: An introduction to natural language processing, computational linguistics, and speech recognition». New Delhi, India: Pearson Education. 2000.

Radford, A... «English syntax: An introduction»., 2004, Cambridge, UK: Cambridge University Press. 2004.

Fehri, H., Haddar K.. and Ben Hamadou. A., 2011, «Recognition and Translation of Arabic Named Entities with NooJ Using a New Representation Model.» *FSMNLP 2011*. France, 2011.

Silbeztein, M., 2004, «NooJ : an Object-Oriented Approach». In Muller, C., Royauté, J. & Silberztein, M., eds. INTEX pour la Linguistique et le Traitement Automatique des Langues. Proceedings of the 4th and 5th INTEX workshop. Besançon. Presses Universitaires de Franche-Comté. 2004.

Adapting Existing Japanese Linguistic Resources to Build a NooJ Dictionary to Recognise Honorific Forms

Valerie Collec-Clerc

Abstract

We have been working on the generation of Japanese sentences in order to automatically produce exercises for intermediate learners. The first stage of our work consists in identifying valid sentences for exercises, which implies the study of corpora rich in syntactic structures using advanced analysers like NooJ. This work will enable us to rebuild sentences which comply with identified patterns. In this paper we describe our method for creating Japanese resources for NooJ from existing resources or from scratch.

***Keywords**: Japanese Honorifics, NLP, Lexical analysis, Segmentation*

Japanese writing system

The Japanese writing system uses three kinds of characters (kanji, hiragana and katakana). Sentence constructs are formed with inflectional forms of verbs, agglutination of suffixes and casual particles. Plain words are mainly composed of only about 2000 adapted Chinese characters (kanji). The Japanese language does not separate words and thus segmentation is a significant problem for NLP researchers. Classical longest match algorithms are not powerful enough for lexical disambiguation. Thus parsers based on statistical data about POS sequences, like ChaSen or MeCab, are generally introduced in the processing chain but carry errors and disregard possible alternatives. As a result, syntactic information must be introduced, for instance, with the help of NooJ graphs.

Dictionary

We wrote a PERL program which has enabled us to extract 15000 entries from one of the linguistic resources of Jim Breen's JDIC, a free multilingual dictionary (Japanese, English and German) with additional information and corrections: cf. JDIC Monash University's interface for EDICT Projects: From Kana, kanji, or Romanised Japanese to English and from English to Japanese, text or URL word dictionary files.

We chose to reject input lines that contain tags annotating archaisms or rarely used expressions.

The basic parts of speech (POS) are defined according to the data found in the input JDIC lexicon. Japanese grammars which are adapted for Western learners of Japanese commonly use grammatical categories that are partially equivalent to the Western grammatical system. Since no standard conventions seem to have been established for NooJ dictionaries, we define ours so that they comply with annotations used in other resources. We used syntactic information given by the input JDIC dictionary to extract the basic categories which are partially equivalent to Western parts of speech: A (adjective), N (noun),V (verb), AV (adverb), etc., and other categories specific to the Japanese language: CTR (counter), PART (particle), PREF (prefix), SUF (suffix). Sub-categories are introduced to describe specific Japanese POSsuch as i-adjectives (ADJI), no-adjectives (ADJNO), etc.

N	noun
ENAM	named entity
A	adjective
AV	adverb
V	verb
CONJ	conjunction
INTJ	interjection
NUM	numeral
CTR	counter
PART	Particle
PN	Pronoun
PREF	prefix**
SUFF	suffix**
EXP	complete expression

There are no ENAM in the basic dictionary, but we have kept this category to be able to adjust our dictionary to future requirements.

PART was added to the input dictionary and was distinguished from "suffix". We think that "prefix" and "suffix" categories are misleading forms for disambiguation. As a result, they are only used for the forms that do not belong to other categories. We preferred regarding combination of nouns as "compound noun" to a "noun + suffix" form.

EXP implies +UNAMB and means that we have to deal with multi-word units.

The 15000 entries of the dictionary as well the inflectional and derivational grammars enable NooJ to generate around 65000 Japanese lexical forms.

Inflections

Japanese inflections are mainly applicable to 15 types of verbs and i-adjectives. For instance, 浴びる,V+VT+FLX=TABERU means that the verb 浴びる ABIRU (to have a wash) is a transitive verb which belongs to the same category as the verb TABERU.

To link two adjectives, the Japanese language uses the て(TE) suspensive form. In the case of an i-adjective, its ending in I turns into KUTE. For instance, the adjective おいしい(OISHII: delicious) is turned into おいしくて.

おいしくて安い店 (OISHIKUTE YASUI MISE – a restaurant which is both delicious and cheap.) In our example, the くて(KUTE) inflection links OISHII (delicious) to YASUI (cheap).

Not only do inflections express verb tenses, mode, polarity (negative/affirmative), but they also convey the level of deference in register (formal/informal) and special constructions with different usages.

Adjectival verbs (i-adjectives)

The main inflections that are extracted for i-adjectives are

- Tense: p (past) np (non-past)
- Polarity: aff (affirmative, declarative) neg (negative)
- Suspensive: susp (to link an i-adjective to other adjectives)

We have created 5 different categories designated by a variable:

- TAKAI (高い): this category gathers i-adjectives whose inflectional behaviour is the same as the i-adjective takai (high, expensive).
- ABUNAI (危ない): this category comprises i-adjectives whose inflectional behaviour is the same as the i-adjective abunai (dangerous),

- MUZUKASHII (難しい): this category includes i-adjectives whose inflectional behaviour is the same as the i-adjective muzukashii (difficult),
- SHIROI (白い): this category gathers i-adjectives whose inflectional behaviour is the same as the i-adjective shiroi (white),
- SAMUI (寒い): this category gathers i-adjectives whose inflectional behaviour is the same as the i-adjective samui (cold),

All these categories enable the recognition of the adjectival verbs combined with the humble form of the copula desu (です) or dearu (である): gozaru, in hiraganaござる or its full kanji form 御座る.

Verbs

Verbal categories

Japanese verbs fall into three categories: ichidan, godan and irregular verbs. On the same principle, we have gathered verbs which correspond to the same conjugation models.

一段動詞chidan verbs:

We have chosen TABERU (食べる: eat) as a model to describe all the regular ichidan verbs.

五段動詞Godan verbs:

We have used the following verbs as conjugating patterns:

KAKU (書く: write) for the verbs ending in KU;

IKU (行く: go) even if this verb mainly complies with the KAKU model, it exhibits some irregular behaviours;

OYOGU (泳ぐ: swim) for the verbs ending in GU;

HANASU (話す: speak) for the verbs ending in SU;

MATSU (待つ: wait) for the verbs ending in TSU;

SHINU(死ぬ: die) for the verbs ending in NU;

AU (会う: meet) for the verbs ending in U;

TOU (問う: ask, inquire) even if this verb mainly complies with the AU model, it exhibits some irregular behaviours;

YOBU (呼ぶ: call) for the verbs ending in BU;

YOMU (読むb: read) for the verbs ending in MU;

NORU (乗る: get on/in, to board) for the verbs ending in RU;

NASARU (なさる), which is one of the irregular ARU-verbs whose masu-form is “aimasu” instead of “arimasu”. This verb is used to form either the honorific form of the verb “SURU” or the polite imperative.

Irregular verbs

サ変 (sahen) verbs – This category consists of verbs with a noun followed by the auxiliary するsuru (do).

We have used SURU as a variable for all the verbal inflections of the verb suru (する). As a result, it acts as conjugating model for all the suru-verbs

カ変 – 来る kuru (to come)

We have used HIRAKURU as a variable for the hiragana transcription of this verb. When this verb is written in kanji, it behaves like a regular ichidan verb.

感じるkanjiru (to feel, to experience)

It was necessary to create a variable KANJIRU to gather all the verbs ending in JIRU.

Copula だ DA is a variable which gathers all the forms the copula can take. The value だ (da) is the lemmatised form of this copula.

ある aru (to exist, to be, to have) The variable ARU refers to conjugated forms of this verb.

Tenses

The tenses p (past) and np (non-past) are described for all the polarities and registers that are mentioned below.

Polarities

The polarities include aff (affirmative, declarative) and neg (negative).

The term “affirmative and declarative” is used to clearly mark the difference with “affirmative and interrogative”.

Registers

The register f (formal 丁寧 (teinei)) corresponds to the masu-form. The form is used when the speaker does not recognise the listener as a member of his or her group.

The register if (informal or plain 普通 (futsuu)) corresponds to the lemmatised form of a verb or the different plain forms used for every tense. This form is either used in written language for newspaper or magazine articles or in oral language to show that the listener is part of the speaker's group.

Suspensive forms

Here suspensive forms will be here coded susp when they define the te-form. They are mainly used to link a verb to another element of the sentence and are commonly called renyou kei (連用形).

te-form informal: teform+if (ex 読む (yomu – read) ->読んで (yonde)),

te-form formal: teform+f (ex 読む (yomu – read) -> 読みまして (yomimashite))

Form: renyou - we have chosen to only keep the term "renyou" to describe the connective form used to build the masu-form .

Imperative

Rough imperative (kake: write) 書け and literary imperative (tabeyo: eat) 食べよ for ichidan verbs only.

Rough negative imperative (kakuna: don't write) 書くな and polite imperative (kakinasai: don't write please) 書きなさい.

Provisional

Since the provisional tense is also used as a conditional form, for our purposes we have chosen to call it conditional 1 (cond1). It consists of the affirmative non-past (kakeba: if /subject/write) 書けば and negative (kakanakereba: if/subject/not write) 書かなければ .

Potential

Informal

Affirmative – non-past (kakeru: can write) 書ける

Negative – non-past (kakenai: cannot write) 書けない

Negative – past (kakenakatta: could not write) 書けなかった

Formal

Affirmative – non-past – formal (kakemasu: can write) 書けます

Negative – non-past – formal (kakemasen: could not write) 書けません

Negative – past – formal (kakemasen deshita: could not write) 書けませんでした

Passive

Informal

Affirmative – non-past (kakareru: be/written) 書かれる

Negative – non-past (kakarenai: be/not/written) 書かれない

Negative – past (kakarenakatta: be (past)/not/written) 書かれなかった

Formal

Affirmative – non-past (kakaremasu: be/written) 書かれます

Negative – non-past (kakaremasen: be/not/written) 書かれません

Negative – past (karemasen deshita: be (past)/not/written) 書かれませんでした

Causative

Informal

Affirmative non-past書かせる (kakaseru: subject/let or make/ someone (object)/write)

Negative non-past 書かせない (kakasenai: subject/not/let or make/ someone (object)/write)

Negative past 書かせなかった (kakasenakatta: subject/not/let or make (past tense)/ someone (object)/write))

Formal

Affirmative non-past 書かせます (kakasemasu: subject/let or make/ someone (object)/write)

Negative non-past 書かせません (kakasemasen: subject/not/let or make/ someone (object)/write)

Negative past書かせませんでした (kakasemasen deshita: subject/not/let or make (past tense)/ someone (object)/write))

Standard endings of verbs

In this category we separate formal endings of verbs from those that are informal. We also take into account the lemmatised form of the verbs (JISHO_VERB)

(masu – non-past – affirmative formal) ます
(masen – non-past – negative formal)ません
(mashita – past – affirmative formal) ました|
(masen deshita – past – negative formal) ませんでした
Standard endings of verbs for non-past/past negative informal
(nai – non-past – informal negative ending) ない
(nakatta – past – informal negative ending) なかった
(nakareba – negative provisional) なかれば.

Derivation

The derivational process is mainly used for verbal nouns and nouns.

Verbal nouns

This process generates verbs ending in suru from verbal nouns (e.g.: 散歩sanpo (verbal noun)+するsuru: to go for a walk) and enables the extraction of all the inflectional forms that are associated.

Nouns

It turns nouns into adjectives by adding the particle の (no) (e.g. ドイツの自動車):

ドイツ (doitsu: noun - Germany)の自動車 (jidousha: noun - car) corresponds to German (adj) car (noun).

As a result, the initial pattern NOUN+particleNO+NOUN is turned into ADJ+NOUN. This class has been introduced to meet requirements for translation into a Western language and does not correspond to Japanese linguistics.

Some nouns (and adverbs) can be transformed into verbs using the verbal suffix する (SURU), or noun to no-adjective, and those derivations have to be defined.. For instance, 歩, N+VS+DRV=VSURU:SURU (SANPO(walk),N+VS (verb in suru)+DRV=VSURU:SURU).

Additional data

NooJ Tag	
+Onoma	Onomatopoeia
+Ateji	Ateji
+ Hira	used with kana form

Ateji refers to lemma in which the kanji are only used for its phonetic form and bear no connection with the word meaning.

+Hira The lemma is rarely used with its kanji form, thus the kana formbecomes the "superlemma" for NooJ and the kanji form a complementary lemma.

NooJ Tag	
+KANA=	kana form
+DE=	Simple translation in German
+EN=	Simple translation in English

"Translation" is only a suggested equivalence (especially when a lemma has more than, one signification)

NooJ Tag	Semantic Domain
+Anat	Anatomy
+Archi	Architecture
+Astron	Astronomy
+Bota	Botany
+Buddh	Buddhism
+Biol	Biology
+Business	Business
+Chemis	Chemistry
+Comp	computer science
+Econ	economy
+Engineer	engineering
+Energ	Energy
+Finance	Finance
+Food	food domain
+Geol	Geology
+Ling	linguistics
+Law	law domain
+Math	mathematics
+Med	medicine

+Mil	Military
+Music	Music
+Phys	Physics
+Shinto	Shinto
+ Sport	Sports
+Zool	Zoology

Honorific system

We have applied these resources to study the honorific system used in standard Japanese. The honorific system mainly describes two situations of communication:

- Act of speech that is oriented to the partner of the conversation;

- Act of speech that is oriented to the theme of conversation. This act of speech is often referred as keigo : 敬語

- **Subject honorifics, called *Sonkeigo*: (尊敬語)**

The speakers elevate or show respect towards the subject of the utterance (appreciative towards the non-speakers).

- **Non-subject honorifics, called Humility, or *Kenjougo*: (謙譲語)**

The speakers humble themselves by showing respect to the non-subject referent, generally the object of the utterance (depreciative towards the speakers).

The honorific system is sometimes viewed as a morpho-syntactic system, with substitution of verb auxiliaries and addition of special suffixes. We aim at recognising honorific forms inside corpora as well as generating them by graphs with output.

The following graph enables the humble form to be extracted.

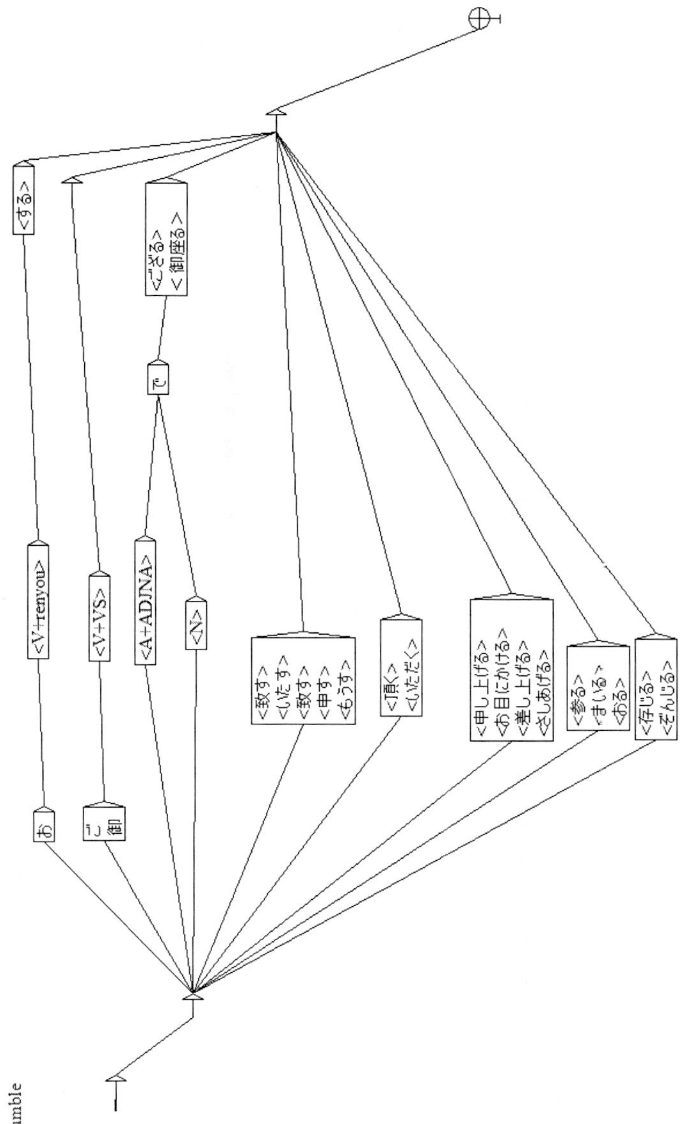
humble
お
ご
御
<V+renyou>
<V+VS>
<A+ADJNA>
<N>
で
<ござる>
<御座る>
<する>
<致す>
<いたす>
<致す>
<申す>
<もうす>
<頂く>
<いただく>
<申し上げる>
<お目にかける>
<差し上げる>
<さしあげる>
<参る>
<まいる>
<おる>
<存じる>
<ぞんじる>

References

Shimamori, R. 2001 *Grammaire japonaise systématique*, volume II - Edition Jean Maisonneuve Paris- 12ème édition, 2001

Siegel M. 2000. *Japanese Honorification in an HPSG Framework,* Proceedings of the 14th Pacific Asia - Conference on Language, Information and Computation. p. 289-300.

Silberztein M. et al. (Ed.). 2007. *Formaliser les langues avec l'ordinateur: de INTEX à NooJ.* Cahiers de la MSH Ledoux, Presses Universitaires de Franche-Comté, Besançon.

Sugimura, R. 1986. *Japanese honorifics and Situation Semantics,* International Conference on Computational Linguistics COLONG. p. 507-510.

Tanaka S. et al. 1983. *Keigo wo totonoeru (Treatment of the honorific form), in «Asakura Nihongo Shin-Kôza», vol. 5,Asakura Shoten, Tokyo..*

Terrya, K. 2007. *Interpersonal grammar of Japanese* in A Systemic functional grammar of Japanese, Vol 2, Ch 4, p135-205.

Tsujimura, N. (ed.) 2005. *Japanese Linguistics Vol II syntax and Semantics Vol III Pragmatics, Sociolinguistics and language contact* Ed Routlege London

Wetzel, P. 2004. *Keigo in modern Japan from Meiji to the present,* University of Hawai press

Wlodarczyk, A. 1988. *Les traits pertinents du système honorifique japonais (une tentative d'implentation en Prolog)* in « European studies in Japanese Linguistics 1988-90», Lone Publications, London, 1991 (pp. 127-150).

—. 1996. *Politesse et Personne – Le japonais face aux langues occidentales*. Editions L'harmattan.

—. 2007. *Towards a Unified Treatment of Linguistic - Person and Respect - Identification* Japanese Linguistics – European Chapter Tokyo.

Zock M. / Lapalme G. 2010 *A Generic Tool for Creating and Using Multilingual Phrasebooks.*

RECOGNITION OF COMMUNICATION VERBS WITH NOOJ

HAJER CHEIKHROUHOU

Abstract

This paper is concerned with French verbs and in particular, the communication verbs. The main resource applied in the analysis is the database of French verbs of Jean Dubois and Françoise Dubois-Charlier (2007). In this study of communication verbs, we basically want to develop methods for automatic recognition of verbs, as well as a French-Arabic automatic translation module using the platform NooJ.

Introduction

Nowadays, computing provides valuable tools for linguistics. On the one hand, computing tools impose on linguists to describe very precisely the morphological, lexical and syntactic phenomena. On the other hand, the computer can automatically apply the resources on large corpora. Therefore, in this article we propose to describe the process of formalisation of communication verbs (class C) based on the database of French verbs created by Jean Dubois and Françoise Dubois-Charlier (LVF). Also, we show the integration of this class in the NooJ software in order to use the formalisation for the purposes of automatic translation from French to Arabic.

Linguistic characteristics of the class C

The French Verbs of Jean Dubois and Françoise Dubois-Charlier (LVF) is a thesaurus of syntactic-semantic classes. The LVF is composed of 25,610 entries for 12,310 different verbs. There are fourteen classes and among them the "C" class, which contains 2039 entries, presents the class of communication verbs. To accomplish this task, we examine the semantic-syntactic classes, operators, syntactic constructions, derivation, the domain and, finally, the usage.

The semantic-syntactic classes

Class C contains four semantic-syntactic classes C1, C2, C3 and C4.

C1	« s'exprimer par cri, paroles, sons » (human, animal)	10 subclasses
C2	« dire ou demander quelque chose » (human)	11 subclasses
C3	« montrer quelque chose » (human)	6 subclasses
C4	« dire ou montrer » (figuré)	4 subclasses

Table.1: Semantic and syntactic classes of the class C

The Syntactic subclasses

The four semantic-syntactic classes are divided into thirty one syntactic subclasses.

Class C1, 1059 entries, « s'exprimer par un son, une parole »			
Syntactic sub-classes	Entries	Operators	Example
C1a	232 entries	« émettre un cri », human ou animal	bavarder, aboyer
C1b	39 entries	« émettre un chant », human	vocaliser
C1c	49 entries	« émettre son, bruit significatif », human	violoner
C1d	24 entries	« parler, écrire à qn »	causer
C1e	144 entries	« s'exprimer d'une certaine manière »	argoter
C1f	166 entries	« émettre un discours pour /contre/sur »	baver
C1g	35 entries	« dire oui ou non à qn, à qc »	pardonner
C1h	63 entries	« parler à/avec qn de qc »	colloquer
C1i	246 entries	« interpeller qn vivement, en bien/en mal »	alerter
C1j	61 entries	« parler bien ou mal de qn, de qc »	flatter

Table.2: The syntactic subclasses of C1

Class C2, 688 entries, « dire ou demander qc »			
Syntactic sub-classes	Entries	Operators	Example
C2a	174 entries	« dire que, dire qc à qn »	annoncer
C2b	55 entries	« dire que, donner un ordre à qn »	imposer
C2c	78 entries	« décrire qc à qn au moyen de »	adresser
C2d	85 entries	« dire qc, que devant qn »	asserter
C2e	57 entries	« dire qc devant/ auprès de qn »	célébrer
C2f	52 entries	« dire qc d'une certaine façon, une suite »	formuler
C2g	33 entries	« dire une décision sur »	arbitrer
C2h	35 entries	« demander à qn de faire »	prier
C2i	24 entries	« interroger qn sur »	consulter
C2j	39 entries	« informer qn de qc »	avertir
C2k	56 entries	« demander qc à qn »	revendiquer

Table.3: The syntactic subclasses of C2

Class C3, 172 entries, « montrer qc »			
Syntactic sub-classes	Entries	Operators	Example
C3a	35 entries	« montrer qc/qn à qn par un signe »	doigter
C3b	19 entries	« montrer qc à qn ou qp »	signaliser
C3c	19 entries	« montrer le sens de qc »	définir
C3d	51 entries	« publier un texte qp »	diffuser
C3e	37 entries	« montrer qc/qn par la parole ou le dessin »	peindre
C3f	11 entries	« montrer, représenter, par soi-même »	représenter

Table.4: The syntactic subclasses of C3

Class C4, 120 entries, « dire ou montrer qc », figuré of C1 and C3			
Syntactic sub-classes	Entries	Operators	Example
C4a	10 entries	« figuré de C1a et C1b, sujet non-animé »	balbutier
C4b	35 entries	« montrer qc », sujet nom de comportement	dessiner
C4c	27 entries	« montrer qc à qn, exprimer qc »	dévoiler
C4d	48 entries	« montrer, indiquer un sentiment »	censurer

Table.5: The syntactic subclasses of C4

The operators

The operators are intended to define the classes and the syntactic analysis of the verb; they represent the basic units of each class. The operators of class C are:

dic= dire	**f.cri**= émettre un cri	**f.chant**= émettre un chant	**f.son**= émettre un son	**f.bruit**= faire bruit pour
loq= parler	**ind**= montrer à qn, publier	**loq.bien**= parler en bien	**loq.mvs**= parler en mal	**mand**= demander

The syntactic constructions

Each verbal entry is identified by a code (const), and this rubric notes the syntactic construction of patterns.

The one appertaining to transitive or intransitive constructions is encoded in a letter. The code of the following letter indicates the nature of the subject and the complements:

-A = 2 codes: subject + supplements

-N = 2 codes: subject + prepositional complement

-T = 4 codes : subject + direct object + prepositional complement + supplements

-P = 4 codes : subject + direct object + prepositional complement + supplements

The nature of the subject and the supplements are indicated by numbers, whereas prepositions are encoded by a small letter. The syntactic constructions which characterise class C consist of ninety constructions:

-Ten intransitive constructions (A)

-Fifty direct transitive constructions (T)

-Ten indirect transitive constructions (N)

-Twenty pronominal constructions (P)

The derivation

In the LVF dictionary, there is a section (DER) regarding nominal and adjectival derivations of the verb. It consists of fourteen codes in four groups.

-The first group indicates the verbal adjectives:

* in -ant (code 1) **Example:** accabler = accablant
* in -e [-i ,-u ,-t,-s] (code 2) **Example:** affecter = affecté
* in -able (code 3) **Example:** abattre = abattable

-The second group shows the nominal derivatives:

* in -age (code 5) **Example:** bavarder = bavardage
* in -ment (code 6) **Example:** raffiner = raffinement

-The third group indicates the nominal derivatives:

* in -ion (coder 8 and 9) **Example:** hésiter = hesitation
* in -eur (code 10 and 11) **Example:** raper= rapeur

-The final group indicates the nominal derivatives:

* in -oir (code 13) **Example:** heurter = heurtoir
* in -ure (code 14) **Example:** lire = lecture

For example, the verb **argumenter01** (to argue) is associated with LVF by the code-1---RBRB – in which code 1 represents the derivation in "é" which gives "argumenté". The codes 8et9 "RB" represent the derivation in "–eur" that is to say "argumentateur" and, finally, the codes 10 and 11 "RB" give the derivation in "-ion" (argumentation).

In Dubois dictionary there is another rubric that may note the derivation. This is the rubric noun "Nom" which concerns basic words or deverbals. Example: the verb alerter 01 is coded by "1 *" which means that the deverbal is alerte.

The flection

Section C of flexion regards flexional patterns and the auxiliary.

Example: The verb "affranchir07" has the code 2AZ which means this verb belongs to the second group and is conjugated like the verb "finir" and the auxiliary is "avoir".

The use

The verbal inputs can have a single entry or two or more, it depends on their difference and their syntactic or semantic variations. The rubric noun **(Mot: M)** indicates the infinitives.

Example: anecdotiser has only one entry so one use in which the meaning is: "conter anecdotes".

The reflexive form

Example: the verb “abandoner 13 (s)” indicates that the verb is reflexive construction in which the meaning is "s’épancher"

Construction with "en"

Example: The verb “appeler12 (en)” requires the use of "en" in its construction.

The negative form

Example: the verb “broncher 02” as a communication verb, it cannot be used only in a negative form to mean “ne pas moufter”.

After carrying out this semantic, syntactic, morphological and derivational analysis of class C of communication verbs, we move on to the second section where we study the formalisation of class C by using the NooJ platform.

The formalisation of verbs of communication with NooJ

For the automatic processing of class C verbs, we have chosen to use the NooJ platform. As any other application, NooJ has its own tools. With regard to that, we have to formalise linguistic data to make the program able to analyse them and process them automatically and to use them in many applications such as automatic translation.

In this section, we will study the derivational formalisation, then we will move on to the creation of an electronic dictionary and finally, we will show the syntactic formalisation.

Derivational formalisation « `paraderivational.nof` »

We have already presented the codes of derivation that can be:

-Adjectival derivatives in -é,-able and-ant.

-Nominal derivatives in -age,-ment,-ion,-eur, oir and ure.

In fact, the codes which are presented in LVF do not take into consideration the spelling characteristics of each verb, that is to say, the same code is valid for all verbs regardless of its ending and its stem and do not take into account the morphological characteristics of each verb. This stage of creation is based on NooJ operators so that it can calculate the various derivatives. All in all, we have been able to create four hundred and nine derivational paradigms.

For the adjectival derivatives, we have created thirty paradigms.

Example:

<table>
<tr><th>-able</th><th>-é,-u,-t,-s</th><th>-ant</th></tr>
<tr><td>#prononcer=prononçable
AV1a=<B3>çable/A;

#diriger=dirigeable
AV1b=<B>able/A;
#convoquer=convocable
AV1d=<B4>cable/A;</td><td>#abonner=abonné
AV2=<B2>é/A;

#approprier=approprié=i
napproprié
AV2a=<B2>é/A|<B2>é
<LW>in/A;

#écrire=écrit
AV2k=<B2>t/A;

#permettre=permis
AV2l=<B5>is/A;

#prétendre=prétendu
AV2m=<B2>u/A;</td><td>#amuser=amusa
nt
AV3=<B2>ant/
A;

#tolérer=toléran
t=intolérant
AV3a=<B2>ant
/A|<B2>ant<L
W>in/A;

#gémir=gémissa
nt
AV3c=<B2>iss
ant/A;</td></tr>
</table>

Regarding the nominal derivatives ending in-age and in -ment we have made thirty-one paradigms.

Example:

-age	-ment

#abattre=abattage
DN1=<B2>age/N;
 	
#poncer=ponçage
DN1a=<B3>çage/N;
 	
#éponger=épongeage
DN1b=<B2>eage/N;
	#abaisser=abaissement
	DN5=<B>ment/N;
	
	#gémir=gémissement
	DN5a=<B>ssement/N;
	
	#achever=achèvement
	DN7=<B2>ement<L6><B>è/N;

For nominal derivatives in –eur and in -ion, we have created one hundred forty paradigms.

Example:

-eur	-ion

#diviser=diviseur
DN14=<B2>eur/N;
#amplifier=amplificateur
DN17=<B2>cateur/N;
#dénoncer=dénonciateur
DN24=<B2>iateur/N;
	#diviser=division
	DN14a=<B2>ion/N;
	#amplifier=amplification
	DN17a=<B2>cation/N;
	#dénoncer=dénonciation
	DN24a=<B2>iation/N;

For the derivatives in -oir and in -ure there are twenty-eight paradigms.

Example:

-oir	-ure

#claquer=claquoir
DN129=<B2>oir/N;
	#fermer=fermeture
	DN135=<B>ture/N;

#baigner=baignoire
DN130=<B2>oire/N;
	#balayer=balayure
	DN136=<B2>ure/N;

In addition to the nominal and adjectival derivatives, we find the deverbals. There is again the Hapax which means linguistically a word or expression of which we have only one example in a given corpus. For the deverbals we have created one hundred forty-two paradigms and for Hapax we have found thirty-eight paradigms.

Concerning the basic words, we note that there are prefixed verbs.

Example: télésignaliser = signal

This type of verb necessitates well-determined paradigms.

Mot de base	Hapax

#comptabiliser=comptable
Dev107=<B6>le/N;
#extérioriser=extérieur
Dev110=<B6>eur/N;
#présignaliser=signal
Dev133=<B4><LW><R3><B3>/N;
	#colorer=couleur
	Hapax5=<BW>couleur/N;
	#fructifier=fruit
	Hapax16=<B7>it/N;
	#nouer=noeud
	Hapax23=<B3>eud/N;

Syntactic formalisation

In this phase of syntactic formalisation we rewrite the syntactic patterns, which are written as code, replacing the codes by the verb and its arguments and while giving them their semantic features.

Direct transitive verb and doubly transitive

***[T1100] = human subject+Verb + direct object human**

+CONS=T1100+N0VN1+N0Hum+V+N1Hum **Example** : alerter 03

***[T11g0] = human subject + Verb + direct object human + preposition + second object abstract**

+CONS=T11g0+N0VN1PREPN2+N0Hum+VT+N1Hum−N2Abst+ PREP="sur" **Example:** affranchir04

Indirect transitive verb

*** [N1b] = human subject + Verb+ preposition+ indirect object**

+CONS=N1b+N0VPREPN1+N0Hum+VN+N1Abst+N1Hum+PREP= "de" **Example:** justifier 05

Intransitive verb

*** [A10]= human subject + Verb**

+CONS=A10+N0V+N0Hum+VA **Example:** abuser 02

Pronominal verb

*** [P1000] = human subject + pronominal verb Example: citer 02**

+CONS=P1000+N0seV+N0Hum+VP

After this phase of derivational and syntactic formalisation of verbal entries of LVF according to the operators of NooJ platform, we move on to the final phase of the implementation of these formal data in NooJ.

The implementation of communication NooJ verbs for automatic translation

In this part of the formalisation of communication verbs, we show how we have integrated the verbal entries in the NooJ platform. This step has two fundamental phases:

-The creation of a French-Arabic bilingual dictionary; and

-The creation of a formal grammar.

The Creation of French-Arabic bilingual dictionary

This phase of the implementation of a French-Arabic bilingual dictionary of communication verbs involves rephrasing the information in LVF by the operators of NooJ, and then applying this dictionary in French-Arabic automatic translation. For this reason for each verb of communication we have added its translation into Arabic.

In this dictionary we have chosen to include only communication verbs which have a human subject because they present the majority of communication verbs and also they are the most frequently used in texts.

The electronic dictionary, called **"dictcommunication.dic"**, has one thousand eight hundred and thirty eight verbal entries. Figure 1 presents an extract from this dictionary.

```
abandonner,V+COM+Emploi=13+Emploi=Vpronominal+AUX=
ETRE+FLX=AIMER+CONS=P1006+N0seV+N0Hum+VP
+DRV=Dev3:CRAYON+DOM=LANt+CLASS=C1a+OPER="loq
confidence"+SENS="s'épancher"+BASE=Dev3:CRAYON+
LEXI=5+AR="أفصح"
Abîmer,V+COM+Emploi=02+AUX=AVOIR+FLX=AIMER+CONS=T1
907+N0VN1+N0Hum+VT+N1Hum+N1Abst+N1Conc+DOM=LIT+CLA
SS=C1i+OPER="loq.mvsqn,qc"+SENS="éreinter,esquinte
r"+LEXI=5+AR="جرّح"
Aboyer,V+COM+Emploi=02+AUX=AVOIR+FLX=BROYER+CONS=A
16+N0V+N0Hum+VA+CONS=T1300+N0VN1+N0Hum+VT+N1Abst+N
1Conc+DOM=LANf+CLASS=C1a+OPER="f.cri
chien"+SENS="hurler,crieraprès"+BASE=Dev33:CRAYON+
+LEXI=5+AR="صرخ"+SENS="hurler,crieraprès"+BASE=Dev
33:CRAYON+LEXI=5+AR="صرخ"
abuser,V+COM+Emploi=02+AUX=AVOIR+FLX=AIMER+CONS=A1
0+N0V+N0Hum+VA+DOM=LANf+CLASS=C1e+OPER="loq
excès"+SENS="exagérer,attiger"+BASE=Dev2:ABUS+LEXI
=5+AR="بالغ"
```

We notice that there is a difference between verbal input of LVF dictionary and those of the NooJ dictionary.

Example:

*** Enter LVF**

annoncer 02 LIT C2c dic événement A qn faire connaître On a~le séisme à tous. La bonne a~P. La cloche a~la fin. 1eZ T13a8 ----D------ 1* 5

*** Enter «dictcommunication.dic»**

annoncer,V+COM+Emploi=02+AUX=AVOIR+FLX=PLACER+CONS=T13a8+N0VN1PREPN2+N0Hum+VT+N1Conc+N2Instr+PREP="à"+DRV=Dev1:TABLE+DOM=LIT+CLASS=C2c+OPER="dic événement Aqn"+SENS="faireconnaître"+BASE=Dev1:TABLE+LEXI=5+AR="أعلن"

This verbal entry represents the verb announce 02, which is a verb of communication. The verb is conjugated according to the model placer (FLX=PLACER)[1] with the auxiliary "avoir". It has the syntactic construction (CONS=T13a8). It admits the nominal derivation "announce" that flexes as the word "TABLE". It belongs to the realm of literature (LIT) which is the semantic class C2c corresponding to the semantic schema « dire un événement à quelqu'un » (OPER="dic événement Aqn"). The meaning of the verb is « faire connaître ». The deverbal is annonce (BASE=Dev1:TABLE). And finally the verb is translated by the Arabic verb « +AR="أعلن" ».

We can see the linguistic richness of verbal inputs that allows a computer system as NooJ to make syntactic, semantic, morphological analysis of verbs ending in a good translation.

If we apply the dictionary "dictcommunication.dic" on the novel «Les liaisons dangereuses de Laclos», we obtain these results.

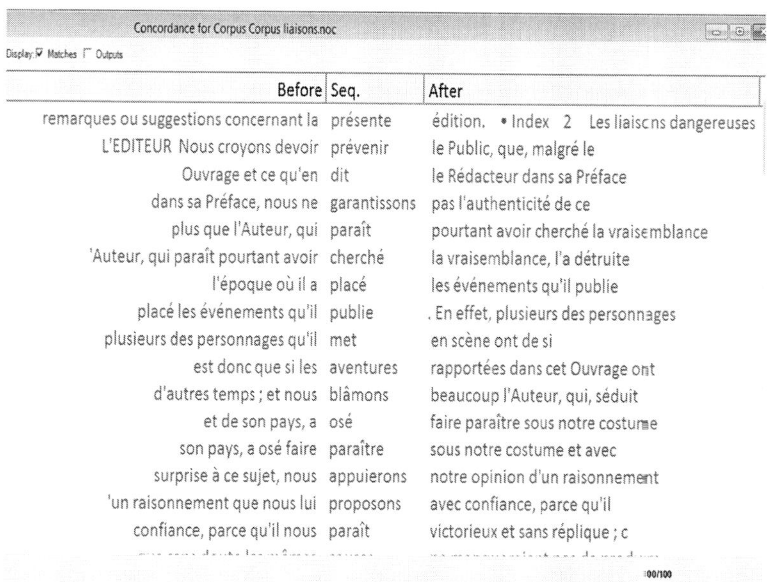

Before	Seq.	After
remarques ou suggestions concernant la	présente	édition. • Index 2 Les liaisons dangereuses
L'EDITEUR Nous croyons devoir	prévenir	le Public, que, malgré le
Ouvrage et ce qu'en	dit	le Rédacteur dans sa Préface
dans sa Préface, nous ne	garantissons	pas l'authenticité de ce
plus que l'Auteur, qui	paraît	pourtant avoir cherché la vraisemblance
'Auteur, qui paraît pourtant avoir	cherché	la vraisemblance, l'a détruite
l'époque où il a	placé	les événements qu'il publie
placé les événements qu'il	publie	. En effet, plusieurs des personnages
plusieurs des personnages qu'il	met	en scène ont de si
est donc que si les	aventures	rapportées dans cet Ouvrage ont
d'autres temps ; et nous	blâmons	beaucoup l'Auteur, qui, séduit
et de son pays, a	osé	faire paraître sous notre costume
son pays, a osé faire	paraître	sous notre costume et avec
surprise à ce sujet, nous	appuierons	notre opinion d'un raisonnement
'un raisonnement que nous lui	proposons	avec confiance, parce qu'il
confiance, parce qu'il nous	paraît	victorieux et sans réplique ; c

Fig.2: The concordance of regular expression <V+COM>

[1] Thanks to Max Silberztein and Mei Wu because they gave me the inflexional paradigms.

We notice that NooJ could automatically analyse the text "Les liaisons dangereuses" from which the verbs of communication are extracted, whether they are in the infinitive, conjugated or even in derivative forms. **Example:** dit, blâmons, ajoute, dévoiler…

The creation of formal grammars for verbs of communication

For a reliable automatic translation of communication verbs, we have tried to create a formal grammar in order to avoid ambiguity in syntactic construction. We have pointed out that the meaning of the verb is related to the type of the subject and the complement (if it is human, concrete, non-animated, etc.).

In this phase we have tried to make a grammar that takes into consideration the type of the object and the complement. For example, the verb ***"accuser"*** has three different syntactic constructions:

T11b0 / T1907 / P10b0 all have a human subject, but the complement is different.

Accuser02: has two constructions

***[T11b0] =N0VN1PREPN2+N0Hum+VT+N1Hum+N2Abst+N2Vinf+PREP= "de"**

***[P10b0] =N0seVPREPN1+N0Hum+VP+N1Hum+N1Abst+N1Vinf+PREP= "de"**

Accuser 03: has the one construction

***[T1907] =N0VN1+N0Hum+VT+N1Hum+N1Abst+N1Conc**

To solve these semantic and syntactic ambiguities, we have created formal grammars that take into consideration the difference between, on the one hand, the types of complements (human, concrete, infinitive) and, on the other hand, the difference in syntactic constructions.

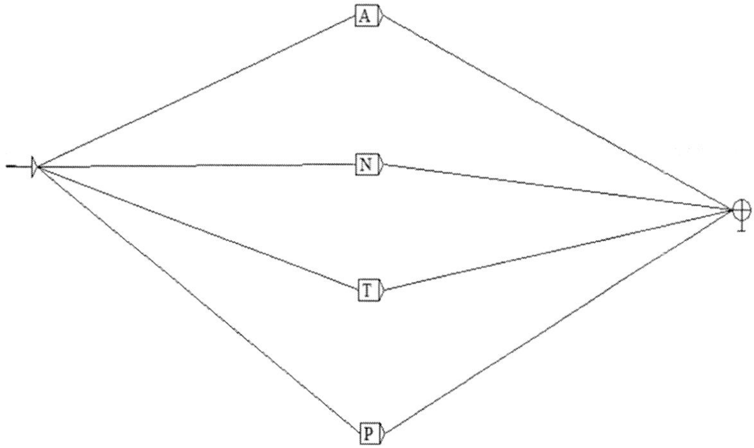

Fig.3: A formal grammar for different syntactic constructions

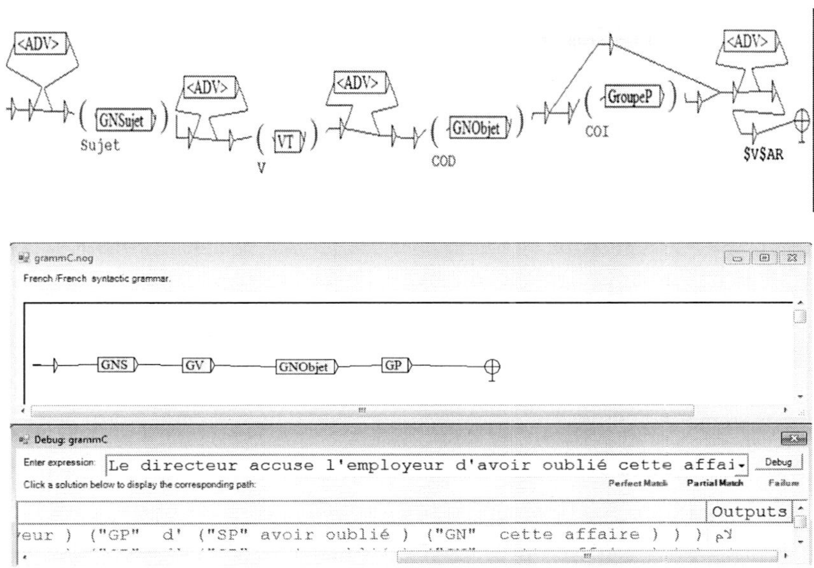

Fig.4: Recognition of the syntactic construction T11b0+meaning=reprocher à qn (to reproach) +AR= "لام"

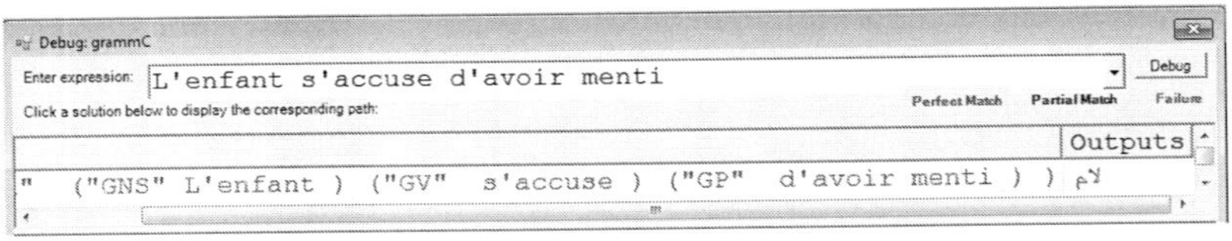

Fig.5: Recognition of the syntactic construction P10b0+meaning=reprocher à qn (to reproach) +AR="لام"

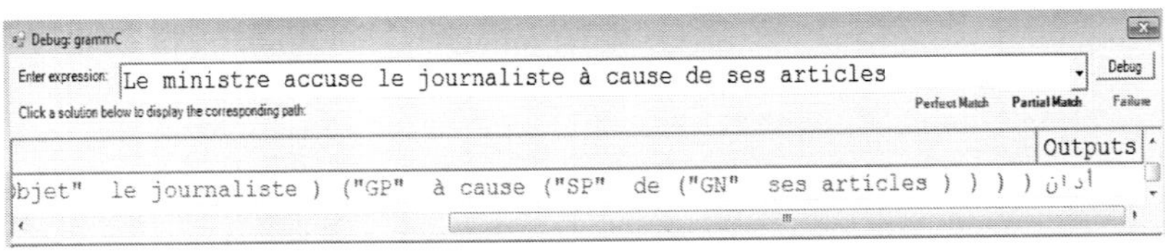

Fig.6: Recognition of the syntactic construction T1907+meaning=critiquer, invectiver (to criticise) +AR="أدان"

Through these grammars, we could make an automatic recognition of syntactic constructions, but also we could start the automatic translation phase.

Conclusion

In this study, we were able to reach, above all, the creation of derivational paradigms and the formalisation of syntactic patterns of communication verbs. Then, we have integrated the communication verbs in a French-Arabic bilingual dictionary entitled **"dictcommunication.dic"**. Finally, to obtain a somewhat reliable automatic translation of verbs, we have tried to create a formal grammar which takes into account the type of the subject and the complement, to avoid all kinds of ambiguities in syntactic construction since the meaning of the verb is related to the type of its subject and its complements.

In conclusion, we can say that this research is not yet complete; there is a lot of work to formalise communication verbs or other classes of LVF. Also, we have to improve our grammar so that it will be able to analyse and essentially to disambiguate syntactically or semantically the different verbs to obtain a reliable French-Arabic automatic translation.

References

Le Pesant D., J. François et D. Leeman. 2007, Présentation de la classification des Verbes Français de Jean Dubois et Françoise Dubois-Charlier, Langue Française 153, Larousse, Armand Colin.

Leeman D. 2010, Description, taxinomie, systémique : un modèle pour les emplois des verbes français, Langages N°179-180, Armand Colin.

Salkoff M. 1973, Une grammaire en chaîne du Français, analyse distributionnelle, Dunod éditeur, Paris.

Silberztein M. 2003a, Finite-State Description of the French Determiner System, Journal of French Language Studies 13(2), Cambridge University Press.

—. 2010, La formalization du dictionnaire LVF avec NooJ et ses applications pour l'analyse automatique de corpus, Langages N°179-180, Armand Colin.

—. 2003, NooJManual, http://WWW.nooj4nlp.net (200pages).

PART III:

NOOJ APPLICATIONS

PROJECT MANAGEMENT IN ECONOMIC INTELLIGENCE: NOOJ AS DIAGNOSTIC TOOL FOR NANOMETROLOGY CLUSTER

SAHBI SIDHOM AND PHILIPPE LAMBERT

Abstract

Economic Intelligence (EI) is a concept that is the subject of multiple definitions. Undoubtedly, these are due to the confusion on the word "intelligence" (i.e. the "intelligence and espionage" in English, but "knowledge and expertise (or know-how)" in Latin meaning the same as in French), (Bachimont B., 1999): "Sometimes equated with economic espionage, sometimes traditional methods of strategy information processing for the benefit of the few companies, (...)". However, most experts in France and Europe seem to agree on the definition of B. Carayon (2003). For this author, doing Economic Intelligence is trying to master, i.e. seek and protect, the critical information necessary to perform an economic activity in a business firm (Bachimont B., 1999). The key verbs of the Economic Intelligence are: inform, anticipate and defend interests. One of the challenges of EI, as described in "The Economic Intelligence: guide for beginners and practitioners-Programme of the European Commission", is "to transform the mass of data available in different forms, from many sources, which is often unorganised, and collected through several channels, into information, and then into knowledge and then into intelligence" (Bachimont B., 2004). The coordinating actions are commonly described by EI practitioners as: "search", "processing" and "distribution" for "exploitation". Starting from both experience and theoretical research in EI, Information systems (IS) and Knowledge Management (KM) domains ((Bachimont B., 2004),(Browne G., 1996)) are joint with the use of Natural Language Processing (NLP). NooJ is employed to add semantic methods to the EI system allowing a gain of performance in information retrieval, in decision problem elicitation towards information monitoring.

The first part of our paper outlines briefly the definitional framework of what EI is and applications of NooJ platform to implement semantic methods for the purposes of our new EI system approach. The second part

presents the case study for the analysis of the cluster structure. Hence, we applied our theoretical schema to the project: specifically dedicated to nanometrology cluster in France, (or "Club nanoMétrologie", club-nanometrologie.fr), which involves both academic labs and industries. Processing with NooJ ((Donabédian A., Khaskarian V., Silberztein M., 2013),(Silberztein M., Anaïd Donabédian., 2013)) includes the following: (i) to study actors linked to information needs in order to get better management of the project; and (ii) to determine interactions between actors in the cluster.
KEYWORDS: *Economic intelligence (EI); information retrieval (IR); decision-problem; nanometrology cluster; "Club nanoMétrologie"; knowledge management (KM), Information Design (ID), NooJ processing, Natural Language Processing (NLP).*

Introduction

On November 26th, 2010, the University of California officially launched its laboratory project on the "Information Design" (ID).

This project aims to develop knowledge exchange between different actors through applications for new media platforms such as "iPad", "iPhone" and similar technologies. Here, we have to think about the catalysts for economic and technological improvement in the responsiveness of the company to face the challenges of tomorrow. Beyond the innovative aspect of this project, we can also note that ID is the projection of an important "Prospective Approach" in the Anglo-Saxon research world.

This point is reinforced by the comparison of the scientific literature on this topic. Since the 70s, research teams have specialised on the study of connections between the graphical representation of information and its interpretation. One of the representation techniques which tends to develop, is the "spatial" information across neural networks.

Especially in France, this approach has been popularised at first and developed by the introduction of mind maps (i.e. Mind Mapping) in education research. In recent years this research focus has been applied to data mining from the Web (i.e. Web Mining and Semantic Web). That helps to develop new knowledge from large corpora (text themes). The techniques cause increasing interest for leaders who have responsibility to detect topics that might have been missed in a linear reading. In the field of "Economic Intelligence" (EI) studies, the implicit properties identified from corpus analysis are called "Weak Signals" (WS) (and respectively, the explicit properties are "strong signals").

The detection of WS allows the watcher in an organisation to take better account of its environment in a dynamic sense and foresight (i.e. "prepare today for tomorrow"). However, the connection between ID and

WS detection requires the development of complex processes in the context of a performance methodology which comprise the topics of this paper.

In section 2 the paper outlines the methodology of EI and its complexity in concepts and processes. Section 3 presents the examination of the theoretical foundation for knowledge representation through noun phrase processing. Section 4 discusses the application framework of nanoscience and nanotechnology in the context of the nanometrology cluster in France. The implementation was carried out on the NooJ platform. The methodology applied includes five phases (data selection, cleaning, linguistic resources development, processing and analysis of results). The aspect of ID is integrated in the methodology to perfect the visual perception for decision making in context and the identification of community manager in the cluster project. Finally, we present the methodology through a specific case study in nanometrology, which allows the evaluation of the internal structure and the creation of links between actors, themes and projects in the innovation process.

What is Economic Intelligence?

Economic Intelligence is a concept that is the subject of multiple definitions. Undoubtedly, these are due to the confusion on the word "intelligence" (i.e. the "intelligence and espionage[1]" in English, but "knowledge and expertise (or know-how)" in Latin meaning the same as in French), [28]: "Sometimes equated with economic espionage, sometimes traditional methods of strategy information processing for the benefit of the few companies, (…)". However, most experts in France and Europe seem to agree on the definition of B. Carayon (2003). For this author, doing Economic Intelligence, is trying to master, i.e. seek and protect, the critical information necessary to perform an economic activity in a business firm [28]. The key verbs of the Economic Intelligence are: inform, anticipate and defend interests.

One of the challenges of EI, as described in "The Economic Intelligence: guide for beginners and practitioners-Programme of the European Commission", is "to transform the mass of data available in different forms, from many sources, which is often unorganised, and

---

[1] THE ETHICAL AND LEGAL FRAMEWORK FOR EI (pp.88-96) in Economic Intelligence: guide for beginners and practitioners. Programme of the European Commission. [visited URL in June 2012]: http://www.madrimasd.org/queesmadrimasd/socios_europeos/descripcionproyectos/documentos/cetisme-eti-guide-english.pdf

collected through several channels, into information, and then into knowledge and then into intelligence"2.

The process steps in EI are as follows:

No. step	Step and aspects
1	Define the information needs: The process of Economic Intelligence must begin with an analysis of information needs of decision-makers, employees and executives within the company.
2	Collect "open" information: We consider that information valuable to the company is published openly (Internet, professional databases and institutional networks).
3	Do not ignore "informal" information: It is possible to collect, in a legal and ethical framework, information from working network (forums, interviews of contacts, professional networks, informal networks) and field (at conferences, trade shows and industry events) and by monitoring new, potentially useful sources of information.
4	Analyse and treat the information gathered.
5	To disseminate information timely: It is needed to disseminate relevant information to the right person at the right time, and in the most appropriate way. To do this, it is essential to build a pattern of information flow and create a culture of sharing within a company.
6	Influence the environment: Measuring the satisfaction of the recipients who will be responsible to undertake strategic actions for the company. The value-added information can also be used as a lever for action to promote company's interests in a legal framework (lobbying, influential communication, etc.).
7	Increasing the support: Raising awareness of the information sharing and networking culture is essential for the company.

Each step can be organised in a process alone or combined with others. For example, (i) steps 2, 3 and 4 can be integrated in a single complete process of information monitoring; (ii) steps 1 and 5 can be integrated in the process of strategic information management; (iii) steps 6 and 7 can be integrated into decision processing based on developed strategies in a legal framework; etc.

---

[2] Introducing Economic Intelligence (pp.14-21) in Economic Intelligence: guide for beginners and practitioners. Programme of the European Commission. [visited URL in June 2012]:
http://www.madrimasd.org/queesmadrimasd/socios_europeos/descripcionproyectos/documentos/cetisme-eti-guide-english.pdf

Furthermore, EI encompasses a holistic approach because it is beyond the scope of the company. Below is the explanation of this process in five clusters3:

No. cluster	cluster and aspects
i	Environment and International Competitiveness: EI is a response to cultural and operational challenges of globalisation and information society.
ii	Economic intelligence and Organisations: We have to understand that Economic Intelligence (i.e. facet of Competitive Intelligence) is a key success factor for all types of organisations. It is a collective intelligence approach. This term, becoming more common, clearly shows that the proper functioning of the company depends heavily on the ability to provide pertinent information in a timely manner.
iii	Information and Knowledge Managements: The monitoring process is at the center of Economic Intelligence (i.e. facet of Business Intelligence). In information management, this includes operations to collect, use and disseminate information (both published and informal). The challenge in knowledge management is to select and build a tool that fits the context of the overall plan (i.e. needs of the company) and encourage employees to share information.
iv	Protection and defense of information assets and knowledge: It is necessary to identify the elements to protect as well as external and internal threats to material and immaterial assets.
v	Influence and cons-impact: Companies must be able to identify and manage the maneuvers and informational processes that may affect their image, behavior and strategy.

Thus, EI has grown from an abstract concept into a "Tool of Management" (i.e. process and methodology) for the control and protection of strategic information for any economic actor. Like PM, it is no longer understood as "Methodologies, metrics, processes and systems used to monitor and manage the business performance" (Donabédian A., Khaskarian V., Silberztein M., 2013).

However, these companies are still waiting for clarification and explanation on how to proceed. This is what our project is built around – the management of data, information and knowledge for the purposes of Economic Intelligence.

[3] Training reference to Economic Intelligence-SGDN Commission. (A. Juillet, 2005). [FR] Les cinq OCDIE du référentiel de formation. [visited in June, 2012] www.intelligence-economique.gouv.fr

Knowledge extraction through Noun Phrases Processing: Fundamental Theory

Our study focuses on discourse moving from its textual materiality towards the organic units that compose both extensional and intensional levels in language description. Here, we do not provide theoretical introduction in (computational) linguistics but a theoretically based outline of this process. We leave to the specialist, the linguist, a large number of decisions that we cannot make and we only give recommendations. Our orientations determine the theoretical basis of the approach, which is described in the work of S. Sidhom ((Sidhom S., Hassoun M., Bouché R., 1999), (Sidhom S., 2002)), about the indexing model vs. the language model. From practical aspects, the second phase of the analysis constitutes real challenge for the transition from model of language (by extracting the morphosyntactic structures) to the indexing model (through its semantic representation structures of NPs and their properties).

The physical holder of a document should provide information about its integrity, indexing and how to find and consult it ((Bachimont B., 1999), (Bachimont B., 2004)). In such environment, professional synthesis on content analysis (documentary, professional or social) is required. Technologies for manipulation and automatic extraction of knowledge take a central role in the information society ((Guimier-Sorbets A-M., 1993), (Régimbeau G., 1998)). It is obvious that a document without any attached indications (like traces of usage) has limited applicability for analysis, indexing and reindexing and cannot be reused ((Maniez J., 1993), (Harbaoui A., Ghenima M., Sidhom S., 2009)).

Sentence Model : organisation of internal structures

Below we present the different morphosyntactic rules (in the French language) which were used in the implementation of the parser based on Sidhom's previous work related to cognitive grammar (Sidhom S., 2002).

A-Prefixed structures in sentence: Introductive Proposal (PI)

PI	Examples
SP, ⊂ S	Pour les 20 ans d'AIRBUS INDUSTRIE, …
EP, ⊂ S	En parallèle, …
EP + SP, ⊂ S	En direct depuis l'observatoire de Meudon, … En compagnie de Marianne GRUNBERG-MANAGO, …
PPas + SP, ⊂ S	Embarqués à bord de l'astrolabe depuis l'extrême sud de l'Australie, …
PPré + SN, ⊂ S	Proposant un voyage à travers les sites industriels de France, …
Prép(en) + SNdat, ⊂ S	En juin 1986,
Prép(en) + PPré + SP, ⊂ S	En passant [par (la littérature)], …
Conj, ⊂ S	Cependant, …
Conj + Adv + SP, ⊂ S	Car contrairement aux Américains, …
« en » + PPrés, ⊂ S	En vaccinant,

B-NP structures in sentence: Noun Phrase or Nominal Syntagma (SN)

SN	Examples
SN (détails sur SN dans (Sidhom S., 2002))	Le lac … ⊃SN le lac dans le nouveau Québec (…)⊃SN
EP ⊂ SN	Une équipe ⊃de tournage … Un avion Hercule ⊃de transport stratégique
SP ⊂ SN	La présence ⊃d'un lac …
{ SN, SP, EP} ⊂ SN	L'utilisation ⊃d'images de synthèse …
REL (relative explicative) ⊂ SN	La présence d'un lac ⊃qui se serait formé suite à la chute d'une météorite …
Exceptions :	
SN^{∇}= SN sans déterminant	Psychologues et physiciens (se penchent sur leurs multiples facettes.)

C-Relative structures in sentence: Relative Sentence (REL)

REL	Examples
/REL = Prel + SN/ ⊂ SN	…, qui + son père, …
/REL = Prel + SV/ ⊂ SN	… qui + se serait formé suite à la chute d'une météorite …
/REL = Prel + S/ ⊂ SN	a) … qu' + il a réalisé sur le même sujet en 1973. b) … dont + le pouvoir suggestif déborde largement le cadre du bâtiment lui-même.

D-Verbal structures in sentence: Verbal Syntagma (SV)

SV	Examples
V + (Prép + V-inf)+ SP	...est (de récupérer) de la matière cosmique
V + (Prép + V-inf)+ SN	...sont montrées (pour comprendre) les difficultés techniques et économiques
V + (V-inf) + SN	...a pu (rencontrer) AIRBUS INDUSTRIE
V + (V-inf) + (Prép + V-inf)+ SN	...devait (permettre) (d'identifier) le sexe
V + (PPrés) + SN	...a suivi (durant) trois semaines les activités d'une équipe
V + SN	...sont le reflet de notre société
V + SP	... est réservée aux avions Hercule
V + {SN, SP, EP, PV}	... essaie d'expliquer le mystère de l'étoile de Bethléem
V + (Adv) + SN	...explique (comment) les pays européens exportent des armes
V + (Adv) + V	...sont intimement liées ...est ainsi développé
V + (Adv) + (Prép + V-inf)+ SN	...s'attache (plus) (à expliquer) la course du côté soviétique
V + /EP/ + SN	...démontre /en particulier/ la polititique de la France à ce sujet
V + /Conj/ + SN	...poursuit /donc/ cette balade à la fois historique, sociologique et architecturale
V	Ce chien mord
V + (Adj) + SP	...furent (découvertes) en 1988
V + {Adv, Adj}	(il) résout scientifiquement...

The sentence construction (S) in our study is based on three fundamental structures, namely:-the structure that precedes the sentence (PI, $\subset$ S),-the subject of S (in the form of complex-NP or SN_max $\subset$ S),-the verbal phrase of S (SV $\subset$ S), and-the relative structure (REL) that can complete SN or SV in option ([REL $\subset$ SN|SV] $\subset$ S). Each of these structures is identified by its unit components and its morphosyntactic organisation:

$$S \rightarrow [PI]+ \quad SN+ \quad [REL_{SN}]+ \quad SV+ \quad [REL_{SV}]$$
$$[x]\text{: } \textit{optional structure}$$

We consider this sentence model of grammatical structures as the "cognitive" model of the sentence. It will serve both as a tool for automatic indexing (SN extraction as index descriptor) or as assisting tool in writing texts and, intrinsically, for reindexing.

Reindexing process oriented to nanoscience and nanotechnology observations

For the purposes of applying in the fields of nanoscience and nanotechnology, a new corpus was: it was made from a public opinion survey which aims to observe members of a new collaborative structure, the Nanometrology Cluster in France, (or "Club nanoMétrologie", club-nanometrologie.fr), set up by the consortium of laboratories in nanoscience and nanotechnology in France (NanoSciences France-C'Nano) and the National Laboratory of Metrology and Testing (LNE). The main hypothesis made about the nature of the text from the opinion survey is the following: it is (i) free text, (ii) carried in open sessions and (iii) there are no stylistic or editorial constraints. The diversity in the contents validates the robustness of the cognitive grammar implemented. In the process, it is a free text to submit for automatic analysis in order to build a knowledge representation: extraction of NPs and their properties (cf. Fig.1).

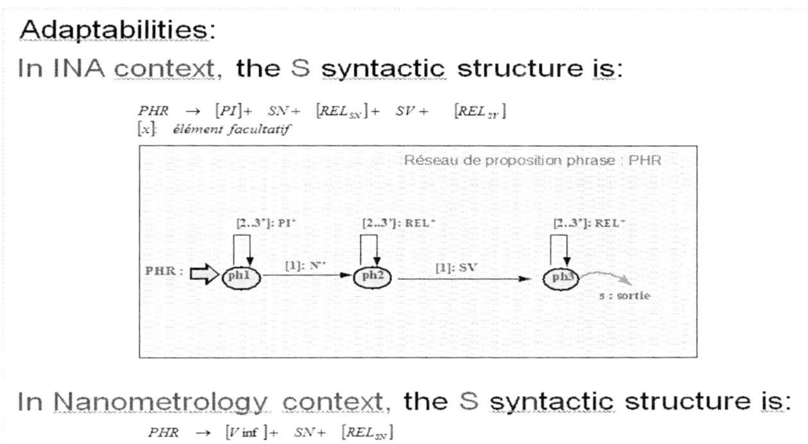

Fig.1: Analogy in the adaptability of cognitive grammar in context.

In Fig. 1 we have demonstrated the reusability of the cognitive grammar model by changing the context of the study corpus while preserving the grammar properties and inherently, the implemented language model.

During the parsing of the survey corpus, the composite morphosyntactic organisation of syntactic structures is identified using the subgrammar (S'):

$$S' \quad \rightarrow \quad [V\inf] + SN + \quad [REL]$$
$$[x]: \ \textit{optional structure}$$

The extension in the language model implemented at the origin (S) requires to simply add a new rule in PI, expressed by: Vinf ⊂ PI. This parsing proposal is not unique as a solution.

Parser implementation in NooJ platform

NooJ is a computational linguistic environment developed by Max Silberztein (2005) from the University of Franche-Comté (France) (Donabédian A., Khaskarian V., Silberztein M., 2013), (Silberztein M., Anaïd Donabédian., 2013). It is based on .NET technology and supports a variety of document formats. Besides this advantage, its use is easy and it is relatively fast to get a grip on. In the context of terminology tracking applied to our bibliographic corpus, NooJ offers the possibility to create a set of local grammars (i.e. finite automata) completely configurable for information extraction and knowledge representation as NPs. NooJ processing of resources includes mainly a set dictionaries (for natural language) and syntactic graphs as finite-state transducers (for NP rules and properties), enabling the identification of complex expressions, extracting lemmas and automatic annotation of text resources (Sidhom S., and Lambert P., 2011).

The survey carried out as part of this research (in nano domain) aimed to identify the reasons for joining theNanometrology Cluster, to seek new collaborative institutions by LNE and C'NANO, to better understand their information needs and what they expected from such a project. Thirty questions were developed in this survey. Its construction was carried out in close collaboration with the various committees of the Cluster.

The survey methodology used to reach the most members and ensure to have a maximum number of responses, was to implement it using the open source software LimeSurvey (www.limesurvey.org) as online survey to collect responses adherent with security requirements. We will focus for this case study on two main open questions that have been automatically processed in NooJ, namely: (i) "What are the reasons for which the respondent has joined the Cluster?", and (ii)" What is specifically expected in such collaborative structure? ". One hundred respondents contributed to the survey and specifically to the open questions.

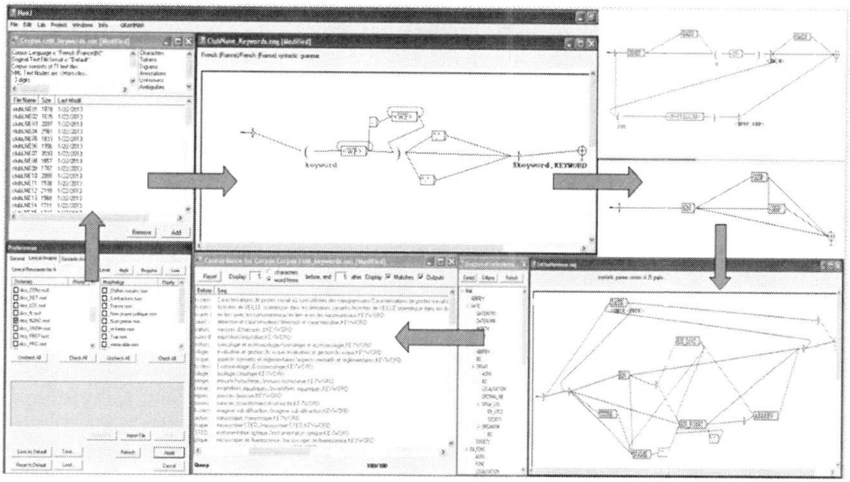

Fig.2: Methodology in the five phases of NooJ processing.

For the response treatments, the methodology used includes five phases: (i) data selection, (ii) data cleaning, (iii) the development of ad-hoc linguistic resources, (iv) data processing, and (v) analysis of results (cf. Fig.2).

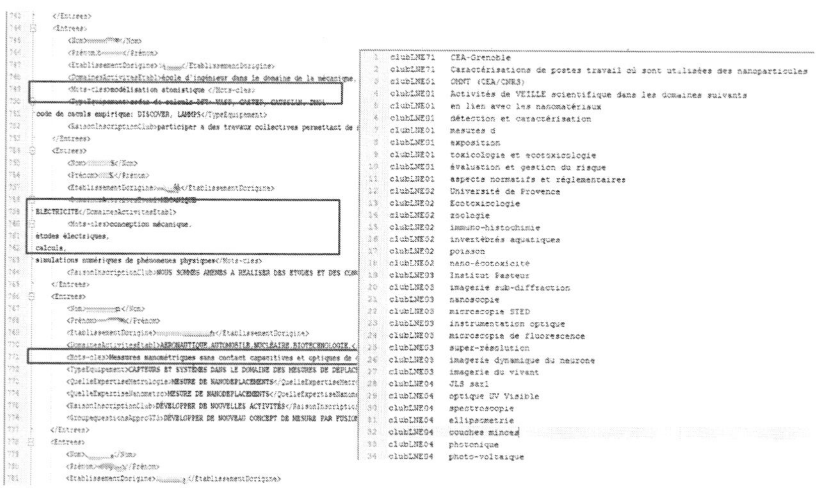

Fig. 3: Instance of XML file answers and NooJ processing of the survey.

The LimeSurvey system allows downloading of responses into csv format. To facilitate the processing of hundreds of responses, we decided to reformat the responses file into XML format. This choice corresponds to two specific treatment criteria: (i) obtaining a better structuring of the source document to find easily the original answers, and (ii) giving the system to iterate over the XML nodes to study their particularities. The source file has also been divided into as many texts as responses, thus constituting a corpus of a hundred xml files. This has allowed to easily find the source document for extracting units or tokens (NPs and structure properties) during NLP with NooJ (cf. Fig.3).

Data cleaning consisted primarily in correcting spelling mistakes and cleaning each node of noise created by system analysis.

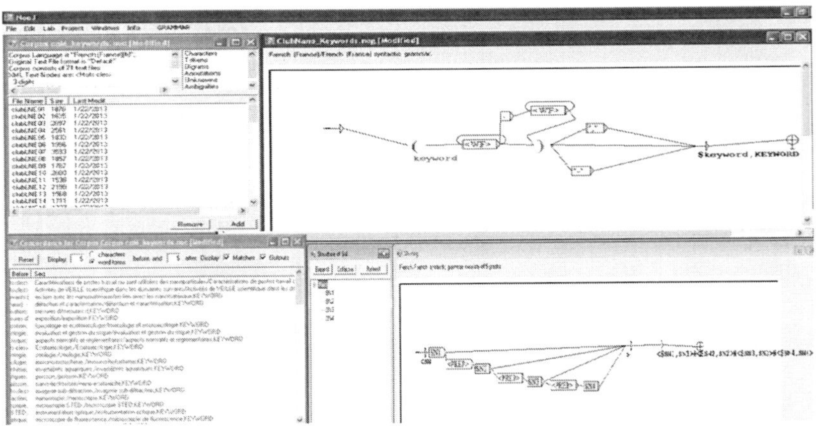

Fig. 4: Instance of finite state automaton for NP extraction in cascade.

The development of linguistic resources was done in two stages: the first stage was to create specific thematic dictionaries in nanosciences and nanotechnologies. NooJ offers useful features for creating automatic dictionary consisting of entries labeled as unknown (<Unknown>), thus giving the opportunity to integrate into the existing dictionary. Thus, a dictionary with hundreds of tokens has been quickly created, bringing together the themes of the nanometrology cluster techniques and specific types of measurement for nanosciences. The second stage concerned the creation of finite state automata to extract specific data and reformatting for further NLP processing (cf. Fig. 4).

In NooJ automata are used in a cascaded manner. Iteration permits labeling of selected structures at several levels.

In the phase of data processing, the work was focused on labeling nodes "What are the reasons for your membership?", and "What do you expect from Nanometrology Cluster?", then the extraction of type structures as: S' :: = <Verb> + <SN emboîtés>. We have obtained twenty significant results showing that the reasons for participation in the cluster are linked in the same semantic field (i.e. networking). The majority of responses are logically related to it: "creating network", "community integration", "identification of community Manager ", etc. NooJ has the functionality of statistical processing, giving it the status of a hybrid system and allowing the ranking of results based on TF-IDF indexes of each extracted NP. The result is a collection of needs expressed by the participants, in order of importance, sorted on the basis of semantic weight calculated by NooJ.

Main results: identification of Community Manager

The main results of this methodology stand on three levels.

The first level was to treat open responses in the nano survey dedicated to the identification of the "information needs of the members" and the reasons to "become member in the Nanometrology Cluster". The hierarchisation of the answers to these questions through a hybrid process on NLP and statistics with NooJ, returns rather good results with little noise. The identification has been made relatively easily.

The second level is more about the diagnostic aspect on our approach, allowing us to obtain a projection at time T of the structuring of the Nanometrology Cluster. For this, a network mapping was performed (cf. Fig. 5). This mapping projection allows firstly to identify the actors' positioning in relation to the general theme of the cluster (or centrality notion) and secondly, to identify weak signals, i.e. themes, completely eccentric but which may prove decisive and determining in the evolution of the cluster.

At the end, the graph of thethird level is also designed in a logic of diagnosis (Sidhom S., Ghenima M., Lambert P., 2010): it will compare the clusters on a time scale T+24 months and observe which themes are ranked highest (number of creation links between actors, themes, etc. (Lambert P., Sidhom S.,2011)) and those in which a specific effort must be made to improve their representation and thus tend to completeness (cf. top right window in Fig. 5).

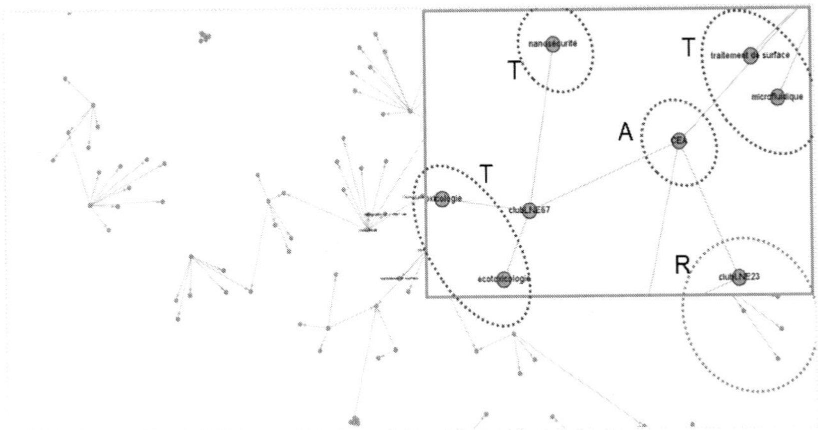

Fig. 5: Mapping graph on actors involved in the thematic of Nanometrology Cluster: trilogic representation (A: actors, T: theme, R: Resources).

Conclusion and perspectives

In conclusion, the objectives of this study were to build an adaptive model using a morphosyntactic parser and develop resources open for social re-indexing. The formalism and implementation in NooJ and automatic processing are much closer to the theoretical concepts and their evolution in practice in line with the nature of the studied object: for opinion surveys and for open web resources in nanosciences and nanotechnologies. The Nanometrology Cluster involving several research organisations in France was used as the subject of our tests and theoretical validations.

In the analysis of results, we demonstrate the relation between "natural language processing" (NLP) and knowledge organisation (KO), and the valuations observed by social reindexing through new concepts. Open questions in nano survey have been the subject of specific automatic processing: (i) "What are the reasons for which the respondent has joined the Cluster?", and (ii) "What specifically is expected in such collaborative structure?" At the end of the processing and analysis of the survey that was undertaken by a hundred respondents, recommendations for decision support have been proposed for the harmonisation of the activities, projects and actors' skills. These results highlight the need for Community Management (CM) work. The advantage of this practice enhances proactive actors ((Lambert P., Sidhom S.,2010), (Sidhom S., Ghenima M.,

Lambert P., 2010)) and their cohesion for the emergence of new offers in nano projects by the combination of activities and skills (Lambert P., Sidhom S.,2011).

The developed methodology also allows the evaluation of the internal structure of the network in Nanometrology Cluster. Detection of the heterogeneous nature of the network can be exploited to carry out the re-balancing around the center of gravity in the structure (or the cohesion network).

On a time scale T+24 months, it is essential to evaluate how to evolve the strongest thematic network, but also to consider the role of secondary network (or associated networks) to enable the creation of links between actors, themes and projects in the innovation process.

In perspectives, other complementary survey will complete the research on identifying Community Manager for direct or indirect project types. We will look at implementing emerging new valuations (as weak signals processing) and new skills against actors and resources.

References

Bachimont B. (1999). La documentation au coeur du processus de production. in Dossier de l'Audiovisuel, Janvier-Février 1999, n°83, INA-Publications, p.38-39.

Bachimont B. (2004). Signes formels et computation numérique : entre intuition et formalisme. In H. Schramm, L. Schwarte & J. Lazardzig (Eds.), Instrumente in Kunst und Wissenschaft-Zur Architektonik kultureller Grenzen im 17. Jahrhundert. Berlin: Walter de Gruyter Verlag.

Browne G. (1996). Automatic indexing and abstracting. in Indexing in Electronic Age Conference, Robertson, NSW 20-21 April 1996, Australian Society of Indexers, 8p.

Carbonell J.G., alii. (1997). Translingual Information Retrieval: a comparative evaluation. in Proceedings IJCAI-97, Nagoya, Japan, Morgan Kaufmann, San Mateo, CA (1997).

Champenier T., Pautet D. (1996). Mise à disposition à travers le réseau Internet de la littérature grise produite à l'INSA. Projet de PFE 1996 , INSA-Lyon, 65p.

Guimier-Sorbets A-M. (1993). Des textes aux images : accès aux informations multimédias par le langage naturel. Documentaliste – Sciences de l'information, 1993, vol.30, n°3, p.127-134.

Régimbeau G. (1998). Accès thématiques aux d'art contemporaines dans les banques de données. in Documentaliste Sciences de l'Information, Volume 35, n°1, janvier 1998, p.15-23.

Lambert P., Sidhom S. (2011). Problématique de la veille informationnelle en contexte interculturel : étude de cas d'un processus d'identification d'experts vietnamiens". in Proceedings : ISKO-Maghreb'11 – Concept and Tools for Knowledge Management (KM). ESCE-University of la Manouba Edition. Hammamet (Tunisia) May. 2011.

Lambert P., Sidhom, S. (2010). Vers le Design d'information pour valoriser les résultats d'une veille sur les maladies chroniques. in Proceedings: Journée d'étude sur la "Mutualisation des ressources documentaires : Hétérogénéité des ressources et accessibilité dans un espace collaboratif." ELICO-Université Jean Moulin Lyon3, 05/11/2010 Lyon (France).

Maniez J. (1993). L'évolution des langages documentaires. Documentaliste et Sciences de l'information, 1993, vol.30, n°4-5, p.254-259.

Harbaoui A., Ghenima M., Sidhom S. (2009). Enrichissement des contenus par la réindexation des usagers : un état de l'art sur la problématique. in 2nd International Conference on Information Systems and Economic Intelligence-SIIE 2009 vol.1 (2009) pp. 932-942 IHE Edition Tunis.

Van Slype G. (1987). Les langages d'indexation : conception, construction et utilisation. in dans les systèmes documentaires Paris : Editions d'organisation, 1987. 277 p.-(Systèmes d'information et de documentation).

Maret P., Pinon J-M., Martin D. (1994). Capitalisation of consultants' experience in document drafting. Conference Proceedings RIAO 1994, Printed by CID Paris France, p.113-118.

Calmet J., Maret P. (2013). Toward a trust model for knowledge-based communities. WIMS 2013: 47.

Vercouter L., Maret P. (2012). Introducing Web Intelligence for communities. Web Intelligence and Agent Systems 10(1): 91-92 (2012).

Stan J., Do V-H., Maret P. (2011). Semantic User Interaction Profiles for Better People Recommendation. ASONAM 2011: 434-437.

Mseddi R., Sidhom S., Ghenima M., Ben Ghezala H. (2011). From information to decision: information management methodology in decisional process. in in Proceedings SIIE'2011 : Information Systems and Economic Intelligence (SIIE'2011) vol.1 (2011) pp.219-226, IGA Edition. Marrakech (Morocco) Feb. 2011.

Pinon J-M. (1996). Projet SEMUSDI : Serveur de documents Multimédia en Sciences de l'Ingénieur. Rapport de Présentation Technique : insa de Lyon, Juillet 1996, 15p.

Bertin B., Scuturici V., Pinon J.M., Risler E.. (2012). CarbonDB : a Semantic Life Cycle Inventory Database. in Conference on Information and Knowledge Management (CIKM) 2012, Maui, Hawaï.2012.

Sidhom S., Hassoun M., Bouché R. (1999). Cognitive grammar for indexing and writing. ISKO-España Conference Proceedings, 22-24 april 1999 Granada, p.11-16.

Sidhom S. (2002). Plateforme d'analyse morpho-syntaxique pour l'indexation automatique et la recherche d'information: de l'écrit vers la gestion des connaissances. Thèse de doctorat de l'Université Claude Bernard Lyon1. France. Mars 2002. p.247.

Sidhom S., Ghenima M., Lambert P. (2010). Systèmes d'information et Intelligence économique : enjeux et perspectives. in Proceedings IEMA-4, 4ème Colloque International sur l'Intelligence Économique et le Knowledge Management-vol.1 (17/05/2010) Alger. (Sidhom S. comme conférencier invité).

Sidhom S., and Lambert P. (2011). "Information Design for Weak Signal detection and processing in Economic Intelligence: case study on Health resources". in Proceedings SIIE'11: Information Systems and Economic Intelligence, IGA Edition. Marrakech (Morocco) Feb. 2011.

Sidhom S. (2013). Conjoncture des processus d'indexation et de gestion des connaissances : vers la réindexation par les usages. in Didactiques et métiers de l'humain et de la relation : nouveaux espaces et dispositifs en question. (direction de Frisch M.), ID Collection L'Harmattan. pp.85-125. Paris, 2013.

Donabédian A., Khaskarian V., Silberztein M. (2013). NooJ Computational Devices. In *Formalising Natural Languages with NooJ.* Eds. Cambridge Scholars Publishing: Cambridge.

Silberztein M., Anaïd Donabédian. (2013). *Formalising Natural Languages with NooJ: selected papers from the NooJ 2012 International Conference*. Cambridge Scholars Publishing: Cambridge.

USING NOOJ AS A SYSTEM FOR (SHALLOW) ONTOLOGY POPULATION FROM ITALIAN TEXTS

EDOARDO SALZA

Abstract

With this paper we propose an original use of the parsing and annotation capability of NooJ software. In our work we started from a domain-specific corpus of e-mail in Italian and we performed the annotation of lexical elements that constitute the basis of a shallow ontology, mapping them into classes, subclasses and properties. We directly generated OWL code while parsing and we put it inside the TAS (Text Annotation Structure) taking advantage of the XML-like format used by NooJ.

Introduction

The availability of corpus processing software such as NooJ, equipped with linguistic resources such as electronic dictionaries for various languages (including Italian), facilitates the implementation of deterministic techniques based on RTNs (Recursive transition networks). Our purpose was to build an ontology-based information extraction system making use of a combination of finite-state parsing techniques and linguistic resources. We tested our system with a domain-specific unannotated corpus of e-mails in Italian sent in an academic context. NooJ recognises lexico-syntactic patterns corresponding to the relevant text elements containing the information to be extracted. Then, the system performs the annotation of all the elements required to build a lightweight ontology constituted by the concepts expressed in the text and by the relations between them.

The Knowledge Representation model

We used a shallow ontology structure as a knowledge representation model. An ontology is defined, according to Gruber (1993), as *"formal, explicit specification of a shared conceptualization representing concepts relevant for a given domain";* such a model can thus efficiently represent knowledge in a delimited universe of discourse. Knowledge is encoded in a formal way using specific languages usually based on either first-order logic (FOL) or description logic (DL) called *ontology languages*. Since we wanted the system to generate a set of logical declarations in ontology language while parsing the text, we chose to dynamically generate language's statements using NooJ's transducers and to store them in an XML output file. For this purpose, we chose OWL2 Web Ontology Language[1] in order to represent the extracted knowledge. OWL2 provides a useful human-readable high-level syntax called *functional syntax* in order to express axioms and assertions (or facts) describing knowledge.

OWL2 is both a representation and authoring language and it is part the DL-based OWL language family. Moreover, it is endorsed by W3C (World Wide Web) organisation and is compliant with Semantic Web standards. We implemented a cascade of empty-string transducers where their output should match the information represented by the parsed text with an appropriate statement. Furthermore, thanks to the Open World Assumption underlying OWL reasoning, we can represent knowledge as we discover it in the text. In this approach, if some assumption about a fact is not held because it (still) does not appear in the text, no inferences or deductions will be made (e.g. by a reasoning agent) until they are explicitly stated[2].

NooJ extracts the relevant chunks of text recognising specific linguistic categories and maps them into their logical counterparts inside the ontology structure. Ontology elements are named according to FOL terminology and they consist in *Classes*, *Subclasses*, *Properties* (or *Roles)* and *Individuals*. A shallow ontology is constituted by a tree-structure of dependent concepts represented by *Classes* and *SubClasses* (taxonomy) and by a set of *Properties* defining the relations between them, while *Individuals* represent the instances of the classes. Properties and classes form the *intensional* part (the so-called terminological box or TBox) of the ontology whereas Individuals constitute the *extensional* part (the so-called assertional box or ABox).

[1] See for details www.w3.org/TR/owl-2-primer/

[2] In a Closed World Assumption approach, such as frame-logic, statements unknown to be true are considered false.

Ontology population

To extract and populate the ontology, we implemented a set of mapping rules for building the taxonomy and detecting relations between its elements.

We first set up a Tbox where the system can insert the elements to be extracted. The starting TBox is consisted of two classes, *Entity* and *Action,* and of two basic properties, *subject* and *object,* as in Figure 1 (Saias and Quaresma, 2003).

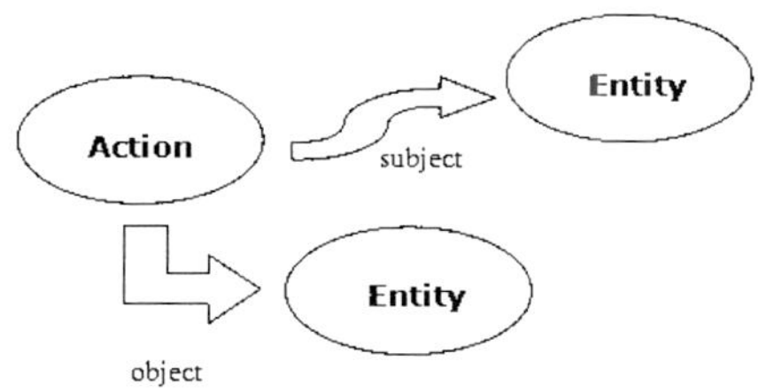

Fig.1: The starting TBox.

More formally, our TBox is defined with the following FOL axiom

$$\exists(a, e) \wedge Entity(e) \wedge Action(a) \wedge subject(a,e) \wedge object(a,e)$$

Equivalent to the set of assertions in OWL2 language listed below:

```
Declaration(Class (a:Entity))
SubClassOf(a:Entity owl:Thing)
Declaration(Class (a:Action))
SubClassOf(a:Action owl:Thing)
ObjectPropertyDomain(a:subject a:Action)
ObjectPropertyDomain(a:object a:Action)
ObjectPropertyRange(a:subject a:Entity)
ObjectPropertyRange(a:object a:Entity)
```

Entity thus forms the superclass of all the extracted concepts while *Action* forms the superclass of all extracted properties.

Taxonomy extraction

The system first extracts the taxonomy by parsing noun phrases and mapping them into *Entity*'s subclasses. Among them, the most relevant are the compound nouns because it is observed that they commonly constitute the kernel of domain knowledge (Gross, 1986). In Italian language the most productive forms of compound nouns are[3]:

- **N+Adj**: ex. *Laurea magistrale, beni culturali*
- **Adj+N**: ex. *urgente delibera, appositi bandi*
- **N+Prep+N**: ex. *corso di laurea, Segreteria di Presidenza*
- **N+N**: ex. *elenco esami, ufficio stage*

In our system heads are mapped to subclasses of *Entity* while modifiers are mapped to subclasses of the corresponding head (Buitelaar et al., 2004). We report below an example where a compound noun such as "*lettera di referenze*" (letter of recommendation) is mapped into their related ontology elements using a set of OWL2 statements.

```
Declaration(Class(a:lettera))
SubClassOf(a:lettera a:Entity)
Declaration(Class(a:lettera di referenze))
SubClassOf(a:lettera di referenze a:lettera)
```

A compound noun can also be a multiword expression, i.e. a linguistic construction constituted by two or more words whose meaning is non-compositional. Generally, in this case, the construction is considered a single lexeme. The same occurs for named entities, where the system treats them as monolithic forms mapping the whole expression into a unique subclass of *Entity*. Moreover, named entities are mapped by the system into abstract classes because they cannot have instances. Multiwords have always been a key problem for NLP systems and we partially overcome this issue by inserting them into a domain dictionary, so that NooJ's parser can match them properly. This can also help to disambiguate them from other similar sequences in which the words occur together exclusively for mere juxtaposition (Vietri, 2004).

The system also identifies and annotates different types of compounds along with their gender, number, head and modifier with respective lemmas.

[3] See (Voghera, 2004)

In order to recognise compound nouns, we implemented a set of local grammars considering that frozen expressions should be treated as single words (Vietri and Elia, 1999).

In Figure 2 we report an example of the grammar extracting all sequences of *noun-preposition-noun*.

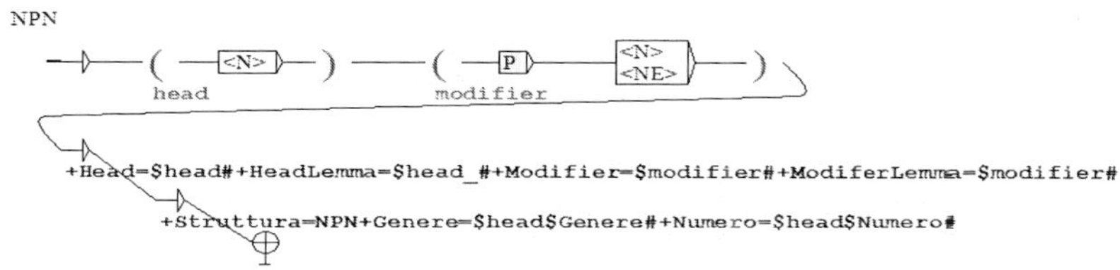

Fig.2: *N+Prep+N* sequences extraction grammar.

The system also recognises more complex noun patterns such as the ones reported below:

- **N+Adj+Adj**: ex. *scuola media superiore*
- **N+Adj+Prep+N:** ex. *laurea magistrale in editoria*
- **N+Adj+N+Adj**: ex. *Scienze Politiche indirizzo storico*
- **N+Prep+N+Prep+N+Prep+N**: ex. *Corso di Laurea in Scienze della Comunicazione*

For a complex compound such as *laurea magistrale in editoria* (master's degree in publishing) NooJ generates the following OWL2 code:

```
Declaration(Class(a:laurea))
SubClassOf(a:laurea a:Entity)
Declaration(Class(a:laurea magistrale))
SubClassOf(a:laurea magistrale a:lettera)
Declaration(Class(a:laurea magistrale in editoria))
SubClassOf(a:laurea magistrale in editoria a:laurea magistrale)
```

In Figure 3 we also show local grammars used for extracting such complex compounds. A set of empty-string transducers generating a *SubClassOf* (Head+Modifier, Head) assertion is shown in Figure 4.

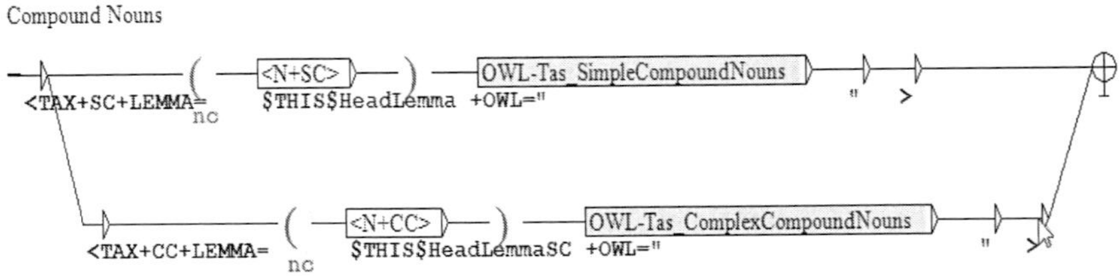

Fig.3: NOOJ grammars for compound nouns' recognition and parsing

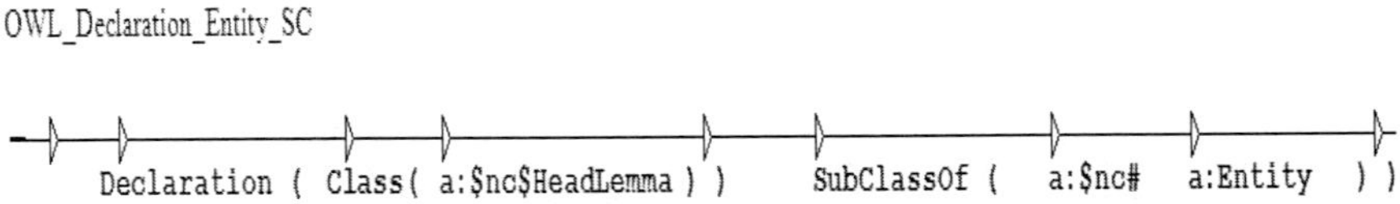

Fig.4: Example of empty-string transducers generating OWL2 code

NooJ stores the code in an OWL2 attribute of the <TAX> tags in the XML TAS file. The system outputs a file as the one in Figure 5.

```
<TAX
    LEMMA="studente "
    OWL="Declaration (Class( a:studente) )
      SubClassOf ( a:studente a:Entity )">
</TAX>
<TAX
    TYPE="CC"
    LEMMA="laurea"
    OWL="Declaration (Class( a:laurea) )
      SubClassOf ( a:laurea a:Entity) )
      SubClassOf ( a:laurea a:Entity)
      Declaration (Class( a:laurea magistrale) )
      SubClassOf ( a:laurea magistrale a:laurea )
      Declaration (Class( a:laurea magistrale in editoria) )
      SubClassOf (a:laurea magistrale a:laurea magistrale )">
</TAX>
```

Fig.5: Example of XML output file containing OWL2 code for taxonomy generation

In Figure 6 we then show an example of the annotation structure generated after parsing the compound noun "*lettera di referenze*".

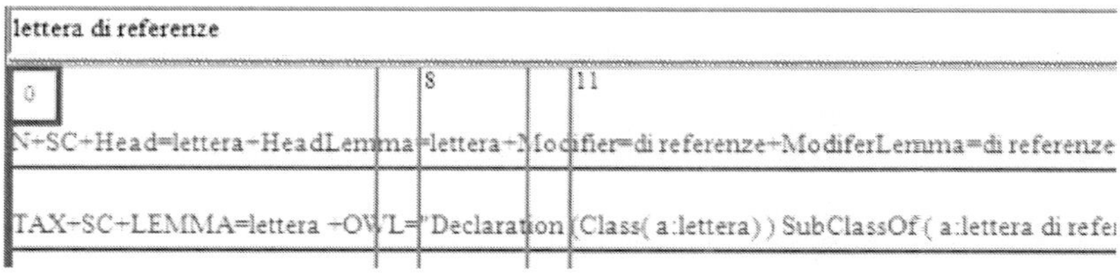

Fig.6: Annotation structure of a compound noun

Sentence mapping

Our system also parses predicate-argument structures consisting of *subject-verb-direct object* triples or *verb-direct object* pairs[4]. In our work we follow the assumption that verbs denote relations among events and participants and that predication involves existential quantification over events (Davidson, 1967). A specific event (expressed by a predicate-argument pair) belongs to the subclass of *Action* both as an individual and as a subclass, being thus present in the TBox, but also in the assertional box. Being present in the ABox, individuals allow to describe relations expressed by transitive verbs via the OWL2's *ObjectPropertyAssertion* statements, using *subject* and *object* properties (already defined in the starting TBox).

As example, a sentence like[5]:

(1) *lo* [*studente*]$_{SUBJ}$ [*consegue*]$_{PRED}$ *la* [*laurea magistrale in editoria*]$_{DOBJ}$

is mapped into the ontology in the following steps:

- SUBJ and DOBJ are mapped into subclasses of *Entity.*
- PRED's lemma is mapped into a subclass of *Action* (here the present infinitive form *conseguire,* to earn).

PRED-DOBJ pair is mapped into a subclass of PRED's lemma.

- Subject and object are linked to their predicate via *subject* and *object* property.
- Predicate is mapped into a subclass of *Action*

It is worth to note that subject and object should not be considered respectively as domain and range of the role expressed by the predicate. This would be correct following a closed-world logic but not using an

[4] Italian is a null-subject language so the first element (the subject) is often omitted.

[5] The [student]$_{SUBJ}$ [earns]$_{PRED}$ a [M.A. in Publishing]$_{OBJ}$

open world approach where it will lead to the erroneous inference by which all elements belonging to a particular domain pertain to the same range (i.e. in the example (1) we will erroneously infer that <u>all</u> *students* implicitly earn a *M.A. in Publishing*). Moreover, assertions concerning SUBJ and OBJ belong to a specific event and thus they need to be done in the ABox. The same occurs for PRED-DOBJ pair. OWL2 overcomes this limitation thanks to *punning*: relaxing the separation between categories, it allows different uses of the same terms, e.g. a term representing an individual can be used also for a class or for a property and vice versa (*Class ↔Individual* or *Class ↔Property* punning)[6].

The next and last step is to link PRED with SUBJ and DOBJ:

- PRED-DOBJ pairs are declared also as an *ObjectProperty* with *Class ↔Property* punning.
- PRED-DOBJ pairs are then linked respectively via *subject* and *object* properties to SUBJ and OBJ, considering the latters as individuals (using *Class ↔Individual* punning).

In Figure 7 we show an excerpt of XML output file generated while parsing the sentence (1):

```
<S AGENT="studente"
   PATIENT="laurea magistrale in editoria"
   OWL="Declaration(Class(a:conseguire ) )
        SubClassOf(a:conseguire a:Action )
        ClassAssertion(a:conseguire laurea magistrale in editoria a:Action)
        SubClassOf(a:conseguire laurea magistrale in editoria a:conseguire)
        Declaration ( NamedIndividual ( studente ) )
        Declaration(NamedIndividual(a:laurea magistrale in editoria ) )
        ObjectPropertyAssertion( a:subject a:conseguire laurea magistrale in
   editoria a:studente )
        ObjectPropertyAssertion( a:object a:conseguire laurea magistrale in
   editoria a:laurea magistrale in editoria )">
</S>
```

Fig.7: Example of generated XML output file parsing a sample sentence

The corresponding example of the NooJ's TAS is reported in Figure 8 while the respective local grammar is shown in Figure 9. Our system can extract the following sentence patterns: N0-V-N1, V-N1 and N1-V-da-N0, where N1 refers to the role of patient and N0 to the role of agent, in order to parse both active and passive forms.

---

[6] See http://www.w3.org/TR/owl2-new-features/#F12:_Punning

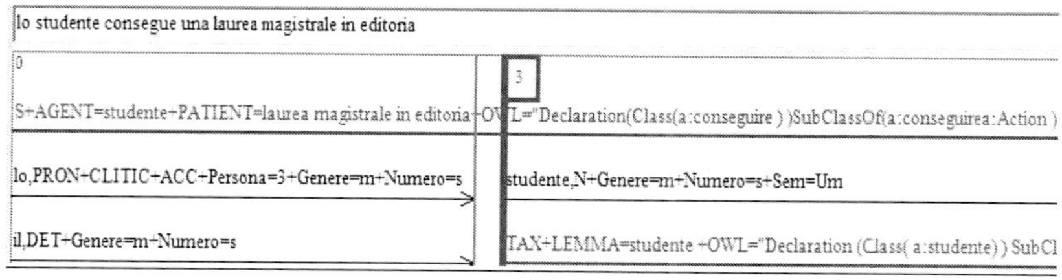

Fig.8: TAS structure of a parsed sentence

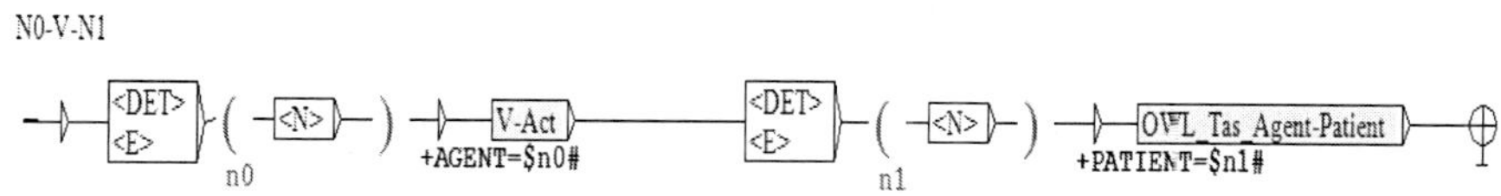

Fig.9: N0-V-N1 sentence extraction grammar

Ontology generation

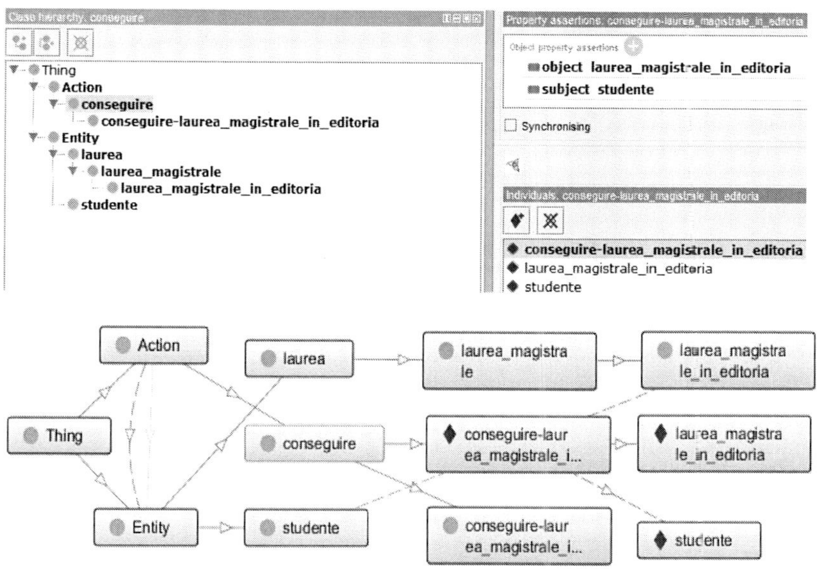

Fig.10: Example of the ontology extracted from a sample sentence (top) with its respective graph (bottom)

Once NooJ has performed the annotation, the system exports the data inside <TAX> and <S> tags of an XML output file, representing respectively taxonomy and sentence mapping. The lines of code are extracted by parsing the resulting file and then they are imported to an ontology browser in order to visualize the extracted ontology as shown in Figure 10[7].

Results

In order to test the system in a specific domain, we used a text corpus of about 15K words pertaining to a set of e-mails sent by students to the Head of Department of their faculty about various kinds of requests like clarifications about taking exams, registration processes, scholarships and so on. Such a corpus of e-mails keeps a halfway position along the diamesic axis because it shares characteristics of both written and spoken language. Moreover, delimiting corpus semantic field makes it well suitable for testing a system aiming to extract a domain ontology. In Figure 11 we report an excerpt of the taxonomy extracted from an example corpus.

[7] We used VBScript to parse XML file and Protégé software as ontology browser

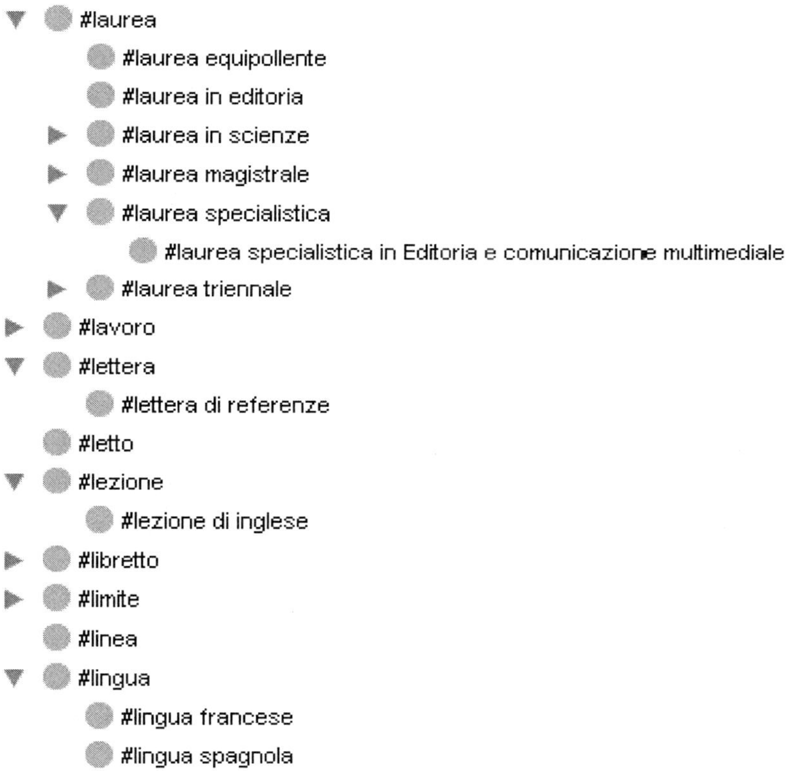

Fig.11: Excerpt of the taxonomy extracted from an example corpus

Conclusions and future works

We presented here an original approach to the use of NooJ, exploiting not only its parsing and annotation modules but also its capability to generate an XML file that can be subsequently elaborated in order to build an NLP pipeline. We also exploited new features of OWL2 language, such as punning, to perform text to ontology mapping. Moreover, we showed how NooJ can be used in an NLP pipeline with an ontology analysis and acquisition software such as Protégé[8]. Further steps can be made, for example, using a more fine-grained set of semantic roles, i.e. relying on

[8] See http://protege.stanford.edu

big semantic resources such as FrameNET (Baker et al., 1998) or on upper ontologies in order to map lexical units into more detailed ontology patterns[9]. It will be also possible to integrate our system in a pipeline to perform tasks that can take advantage of a shallow ontology structure such as automatic document classification or machine translation.

References

Baker C.F., Fillmore C.J., Lowe J.B. (1998). The Berkeley FrameNet Project. In *Proceedings of the 36th Annual Meeting of the Association for Computational Linguistics and 17th International Conference on Computational Linguistics - Volume 1* (ACL '98), Vol. 1. Association for Computational Linguistics, Stroudsburg, PA, USA, 86-90

Buitelaar P., Olejnik D., Hutanu M., Schutz A., Declerck T., Sintek M. (2004). Towards ontology engineering based on linguistic analysis. *LREC, European Language Resources Association, 2004*

Davidson D. (1967). The logical form of action sentences. In Rescher, N.,editor The Logic of decision and action, pages 81-95. University of Pittsburgh Press, Pittsburgh

Gross M. (1986). Lexicon-grammar: the representation of compound words.In Proceedings of the 11th conference on Computational linguistics, COLING '86, pp. 1–6, Stroudsburg, PA, USA.

Gruber T. (1993). Towards principles for the design of ontologies used for knowledge sharing. International Journal of Human and Computer Studies. Originally in N. Guarino & R. Poli, (Eds.), International Workshop on Formal Ontology, Padova, Italy. Revised August 1993.

Saias J., Quaresma P. (2003). A methodology to create ontology based information retrieval system. In Proceedings of the EPIA Conference, pp.424-434, 2003

Vietri (2004). Lessico-grammatica dell'italiano. UTET, Torino.

Vietri S., Elia A. (1999). Electronic Dictionaries And Linguistic Analysis Of Italian Large Corpora. SIGLEX Workshop On Standardizing Lexical Resources

Voghera M. (2004). Polirematiche. In Grossmann M., Rainer F., (acura di) La formazione delle parole in italiano. Tübingen, Niemeyer

[9] As example, the verb to buy will "evokes" the Commerce_scenario frame and it then maps its direct object into a subclass of Goods.

NooJ as Concordancer in Computer-Assisted Textual Analysis: The Case of the German Module

Ralph Müller

Abstract

Computers do not only allow for writing, storing and distributing texts, but also for investigating large corpora of texts with quantitative and empirical tools. In this context, NooJ is a tool for computer-assisted textual analysis which has been recently supplemented with a module for German text. In literary studies, the term "computer-assisted textual analysis" refers to the use of computer programs to gather information about textual regularities, particular expressions or features within a text or a selection of texts (a "corpus" of texts). Rather than a new discipline, computer-assisted textual analysis constitutes a new approach to literary texts. It is part of the larger turn towards "digital humanities" or "humanities computing", and is related to "corpus-stylistics" as it makes use of quantitative data gathered from the analysis of many texts in order to improve the understanding of singular texts (cf. Stubbs 2005). The German Module of NooJ (Silberztein 2003ff.) has been developed with a focus on the high but also the particular demands of literary text analysis. Of course, NooJ can be used for various tasks beyond literary objectives. Nevertheless, the particular demands of literary analysis demonstrate the versatility of NooJ as a concordancer. Therefore, first, this article provides a basic introduction to the use of computer assistance in literary studies, before describing NooJ's German module, and discussing some examples of its application in various tasks of computer-assisted textual analysis.

Computer-assisted textual analysis in literary studies

Despite the fact that "digital humanities" has become a buzzword in academic circles, quantitative and computer-assisted textual analysis have not yet been widely adopted in literary studies. Probably there are many literary scholars who use the computer to look for particular citations or usages of words in electronic texts; however, they remain mostly reluctant to uncover the use of databases and search tools in their fulfilment of daily tasks. In fact, I assume there is a widespread but rather implicit practice of using the computer as some kind of extension of the individual researcher's memory by looking up, electronically, some vaguely remembered passages. Unfortunately, there is little reflection on the possibilities and standards of computer assistance in textual analysis in such tasks. Maybe such attitude is understandable with respect to some more demanding tasks of digital philology such as data mining, corpus annotation and stylometric investigation that go not only beyond the competences of most literary scholars but also beyond their interests, which are traditionally focussed on a small set of canonical texts. However, simple reading is not the only acceptable way of access to a piece of artistic language. In fact, most literary scholars will admit that to know many texts is an essential prerequisite to enable the understanding of single texts. It is important to know more about the typical use of language in particular genres or epochs, in order to understand the individual literary works. This is where the use of electronic corpora comes in. Corpus-stylistics investigates frequent text elements and structures with the aim of describing particularities of literary and rhetoric style. Since corpora of electronic texts have been growing, there is also more and more data available for analyses – and some corpora contain more text than a team of researcher could possibly read in a traditional way (cf. Lieberman Aiden et al. 2010). Franco Moretti created the term "distant reading" for this type of literary analysis that investigates general developments across many texts rather than singular samples:

> *"[If] you want to look beyond the canon [...] close reading will not do it. It's not designed to do it, it's designed to do the opposite. At bottom, it's a theological exercise—very solemn treatment of very few texts taken very seriously—whereas what we really need is a little pact with the devil: we know how to read texts, now let's learn how not to read them. Distant reading: where distance, let me repeat it, is a condition of knowledge: it allows you to focus on units that are much smaller or much larger than the text: devices, themes, tropes—or genres and systems." (Moretti 2000: 57)*

Even if literary scholars are tempted to leave 'distant readings' to a small number of philologically interested computer nerds, it is still important to acknowledge that digital literary studies have an impact on traditional tasks of literary studies such as the digital publishing of scholarly and literary texts but also – and in particular – on the use of electronic devices in the actual study of texts. Human beings are not only notoriously slow in reading but with respect to remembering stylistic details also unreliable. The growing digital corpora of literary texts are now changing the work of literary scholars, at least with respect to the widely used method of comparing "parallel places" respectively concordances: the comparison of the uses of similar words in different contexts. This type of comparison of concordances is an old and established philological technique which has now been revolutionised by electronic concordancing programs such as *NooJ,* without philologists even taking notice of it.

Concordances in literary studies

The use of concordances in order to understand biblical texts has already been described by the Lutheran theologian Matthew Flacius Illyricus in the 16th century (Flacius Illyricus 1968). In German philology Friedrich Daniel Schleiermacher's lectures on the use of concordances in biblical and literary texts (that was published posthumously in 1838, cf. Schleiermacher 1977) have been particularly influential (cf. Szondi 1967). Schleiermacher suggested that the meaning of an unclear expression may, on the one hand, be determined with respect to its contemporary language system (as it is described in dictionaries). On the other hand, Schleiermacher proposed a procedure which essentially considers (1) the actual co-text of the word in question and (2) so-called parallel places (in Latin "loca parallela", in German "Parallelstelle") which are the same expression in similar co-texts, or – for want of a more contemporary and technical term – Key Words In Context (KWIC).

In summary, producing concordances in order to improve the understanding of literary (but also sacral) texts has been part of philological work for centuries. Compiling these concordances used to be an arduous job. Moreover, printed books with concordances were not actually user-friendly, as concordances used to provide nothing more than a key term and relevant page numbers in a renowned edition of the text in question. Evidently, computers and electronic corpora have changed this situation by making available electronically sortable lists of keywords, usually with a direct link to the full text. Nevertheless, most electronic collections of literary texts come with rather limited search and sort functions. Therefore, anybody interested in the understanding of texts should also be interested in the performance of advanced concordancing programs such as *NooJ.*

NooJ is a free concordancer that runs on a regular Windows system and is capable of syntactic and semantic analyses (cf. Silberztein 2003ff.). Moreover, *NooJ* fulfils the various basic requirements of suitable concordancing software in literary studies. In the practice of electronic literary concordancing there are several challenges to overcome. First of all, there is the issue related to the construction of suitable literary corpora which will not be elaborated here (cf. Semino/Short 2004). Secondly, there is a need for a flexible and versatile concordancer. Baßler and Karczewski – two literary scholars – have developed a list of requirements that a literary concordancer should fulfil: Apart from (1) calling for a digital full text archive (cf. Baßler/Karczewski 2007) the authors ask for a software that does (2) not alter the original texts (e.g., by adding tags), but provides (3) context sensitive search functions which could (4) produce lists of occurrences with a minimal co-text that might be saved (5) together with the query. Moreover, Baßler and Karczewski wish that concordancers would take into account (6) alternative spellings. And, finally, concordancing software should come (7) with an intuitive graphical interface.

Clearly, *NooJ* does not come with a digital text archive. It only operates on texts that have been collected by the user. Nevertheless, *NooJ* provides (apart from regular statistical information such as digrams, number of tokens etc.) various concordancing functions that fulfil the requirements mentioned by Baßler and Karczewski with the exception of (5): *NooJ* exports the lists of concordances without a report of the underlying query. However, *NooJ* does not alter the original files, but creates its own searchable, and by a new analysis, renewable annotation layer ("TAS", Text Annotation Structure). *NooJ*'s Text Annotation Structure allows (depending on the information stored in a dictionary) to search for word classes, word paradigms, semantic features, syntactic structures, and alternative spellings. More specifically, *NooJ* provides various concordancing functions, and apart from locating strings of characters or processing perl-queries, *NooJ* makes its analysis available in the following, *NooJ*-specific, forms:

- Search for lexemes: each entry in the dictionary is available for lemma search.
- Search for word classes: all paradigms that have been defined within the German module of the dictionary (e.g., <V> for verbs, <N> for nouns, etc.) are available for search; the paradigms might be further specified by inflectional information.
- Search for semantic features (at the moment this option has not yet been developed in the dictionary of the German module).
- Search by *NooJ*-grammar: *NooJ* offers the possibility of writing complex search grammars by the use of a graphical interface.

Finally, *NooJ* does not eliminate ambiguity (unlike *Treetagger,* cf. Schmid 1994ff.), unless it is explicitly told to do so by the grammar. In the context of the high demands of literary concordancing this is an important advantage, as there is less danger of losing interesting cases because of a decision towards the most probable analysis.

NooJ's German Module V2

NooJ, in itself, needs a language and task specific module in order to be fully operative on texts. The German module for *NooJ* was first published in October 2010. It has been continuously developed and consists, at present, of a regular dictionary database with 23,000 lexical entries. This dictionary needs to be compiled with the help of inflectional and derivational grammars before it can be used in *NooJ.* The compilation turns the .dic file into a database that recognises more than 3,000,000 individual word forms which may subsequently be used by the linguistic analysis engine of *NooJ.*

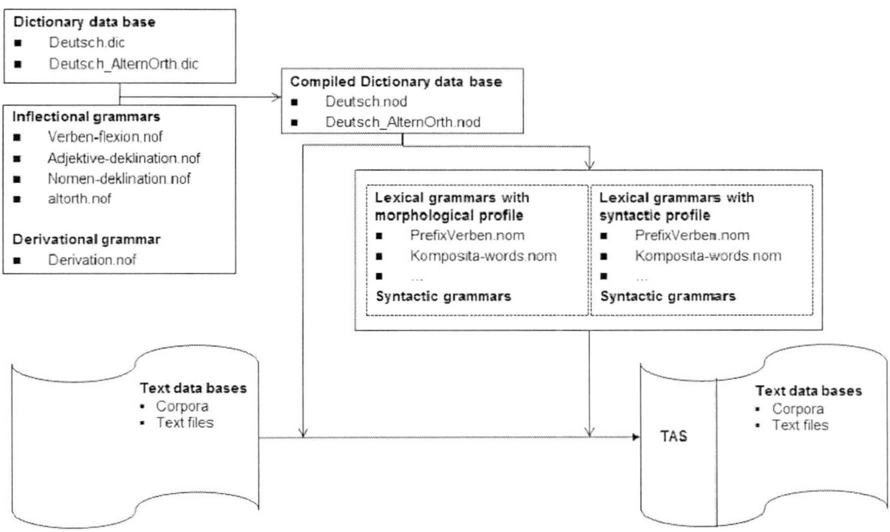

In the process of adding a Text Annotation Structure (TAS) to a text, *NooJ* makes use of the compiled dictionary database. Moreover, the same database is also used by a series of so-called lexical grammars that are able to detect word forms in various combinations, the most important of which are compound nouns and split verbs. More specifically, the German module can analyse compounds of up to four words which is sufficient for most cases. The grammar is, however, susceptible to extremely large compounds such as “Zärtlichstinnigstbrünstigstsehnlichstschmachtender” (Wezel 1997). The analysis of (over)large compounds may overstrain the current capacity of regular computers. Nevertheless, within the limits of the local lexical grammar (and processing power) *NooJ*-grammars allow for a study of compound expressions in German language, and we built a version of the lexical grammars that retains the morphological information of the initial analysis (profile “Preferences_MORPH”). Using this profile, a search for the lexeme <haus> (‘house’) would also provide the compounds in which the lemma (or a derivation of it) has been used. However, this profile is not suitable for large corpora as it increases file size and processing time.

Typically, a corpus would be analysed with a profile that discards the information on the morphological elements of the composite words (profile “Preferences_SYNT”). This profile is also more reliable in the syntactic analysis of sentences in which complex compounds occur; however, a search for lexemes will not list compound nouns in which the lexeme (or derivations of it) occurs.

The current version of the German module has been particularly designed for the high demands of literary concordancing. One of the major challenges is the orthographic diversity of a historical diachronic corpus. As a consequence, we created an additional dictionary (“Deutsch_AlternOrth.nod”) and lexical grammars that can detect different orthographic versions of the same word. For instance, in German there are two major orthographic reforms (e.g., the elimination of the letter “h” after “t” in most Germanic words in 1901). At the current stage, this dictionary contains approximately 1,500 entries and recognises 170,000 word forms, allowing, for instance, to search for the colour “rötlich” (‘reddish’) and also the obsolete form “röthlich”. Of course, if one does not need this additional capacity of analysis, it is necessary to turn this dictionary off at the “info” > “preferences” menu.

The German dictionaries have been written with the particular aim of not developing too many word categories. Whereas the frequently used Stuttgart-Tübingen-Tag set STTS proposes a dozen of tags for verb forms and many general classes, the German module of *NooJ* uses only 9 general word classes (<N>, nouns; <V>, verbs; <PP>, prepositions; <PN> pronouns; <AV>, adverbials; <AJ>, adjectives; <KJ>, conjunctions; <PT>, particles; <IJ>, interjections). Various word classes can be further differentiated by inflectional information such as <V+PT+s+3> for a verb in past tense third person singular. Such inflectional information, but also context may be used to disambiguate the word forms in targeted queries. Of course, users are free to edit the content and the structure of the dictionary for their own purposes. This openness is probably the most important feature of *NooJ*.

Applications

A description of three literary concordancing tasks may provide an impression of the functionality and performance of *NooJ*.

First of all, *NooJ*'s capability of searching compound words was used for finding metaphorically used expressions in a corpus consisting of 1670 speeches (2,5 Million tokens) on European Policy (cf. Müller 2012). As this corpus was analysed with the MORPH-profile, a search for the lemma <haus> ("house") found occurrences such as "das neue europäische Haus" ('the new European house'), but also compound metaphors (e.g., "zu einem Armenhaus degradieren", 'to degrade to a poorhouse') including plural forms with German 'umlaut' (e.g. "Idealhäusern von Europa"; 'ideal houses of Europe'). As it can be seen from these examples, *NooJ* is – due to its dictionary – able to look for words beyond identity of spelling which is a considerable advantage over regular concordancers in which the user needs to think of possible alternative spellings. Of course, *NooJ* can also process words written with "ß" and "ss".

Metaphors are a typical case for which the search for particular expressions is important. Nevertheless, metaphors are also syntactic phenomena, as the co-textual surroundings of metaphorically used expressions are of interest. In this context, *NooJ* proved to be versatile in terms of searching syntactic combinations such as compound nouns and genitive constructions which can subsequently be checked manually for possible metaphorical usage. The following graph shows *NooJ*'s graphical representation of the query.

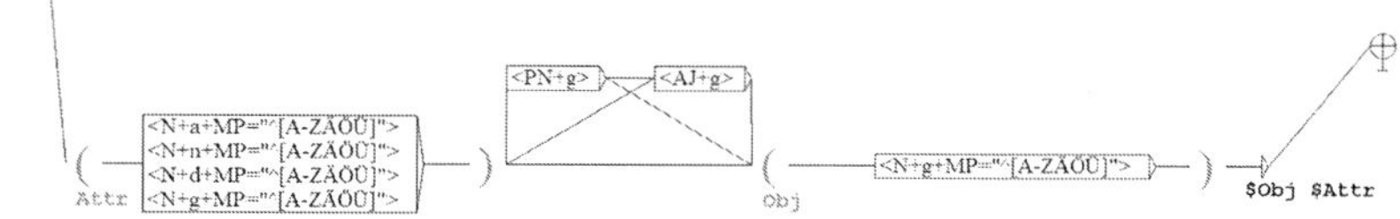

The grammatical structure above looks for nouns (beginning with a capital letter) that are eventually followed by a pronoun and/or an adjective plus a final genitive object. In addition, the information about the match is, at the same time, re-written in such a way that, apart from displaying the "Matches", one can also sort the concordances according to the "Outputs" ($Obj $Attr) with the genitive object first.

As can be seen in the grammatical structure above, an additional criterion (that nouns should start with an uppercase letter) was introduced in this grammar. The explanation is that (by default) all entries in the *NooJ* dictionary – including nouns, which in German are written with an initial capital letter – are written in lowercase. In *NooJ,* only lowercase letters may fit both upper- and lowercase letters; whereas uppercase letters will only fit uppercase letters; thus, writing some dictionary entries with initial capital letters would produce problems with the recognition of compound words. For instance, the dictionary entries "Haupt" and "Bahnhof" would only recognize "HauptBahnhof", but not "Hauptbahnhof".

Grammars can also be used to store complex queries consisting of several search routines. The following grammar represents a rather simple search routine which we used in another study to find different forms of "as if"-descriptions (cf. Müller/Lambrecht 2013).

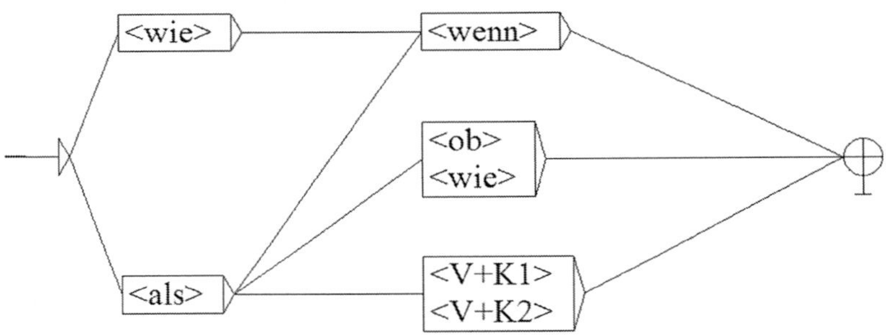

This grammar recognises the word sequences "wie wenn", "als wenn", "als ob", "als wie" and in particular "als" followed by a verb in the subjunctive mood such as "als sei" or "als hätte". Due to systematic ambiguities in the linguistic analysis, this grammar also finds "als" plus the possessive pronoun "meine" or the indefinite article "eine", since these forms are identical with verb forms of "einen" ('unify') and "meinen" ('assume'). Unless particularly programmed, *NooJ* retains ambiguous interpretations of word forms. As a consequence, the word sequence "als meine" can be found by <als> <V>, but also by <als> <PN>.

Further challenges

The German module has made *NooJ* available as a functional concordancer, and it has already proven itself in various analytical tasks. Nevertheless, it also needs further development in many respects.

First of all, the extension of the dictionaries is an issue. *NooJ* as a concordancer can only find information that it is added by its dictionaries and grammars. In addition, increasing the dictionary will not only improve *NooJ's* applicability but also processing speed if less words in a text need subsequent parsing with lexical grammars. Therefore, the main objective is to double the size of the existing basic dictionary Deutsch.dic to a number of approximately 50,000 entries. There is also a need for a full compound noun dictionary with approximately 100,000 entries, in order to speed up corpus analysis. This lexical information should be stored in an additional dictionary in such a way that this information can be 'turned off' if a more detailed morphological analysis is required. In addition, a new differentiation between nouns and names will be introduced.

As mentioned above, the German module of *NooJ* has also been designed to cope with different orthographies (e.g., changes of spellings between "ß" and"ss"), in particular with older orthographies ("rot" and "roth", both 'red'). However, *NooJ*'s capability of recognising texts that have been written with earlier German orthography still depends, to a large extent, on lexical grammars which systematically look for words that may potentially be parsed in terms of an obsolete spelling. In order to improve *NooJ*'s performance on older texts, Deutsch_AlternOrth.dic should also be extended with respect to its actual size. Moreover, this dictionary should also be extended to cover words that are spelled according to earlier stages of German orthography. For instance, in the 17th century, German words were not only spelled in a distinctively different way from today's spelling, orthography was generally less uniform, which poses an additional challenge to any form of literary concordancing. A project on the Austrian Baroque Corpus is currently exploring *NooJ*'s applicability on texts from the 17th and early 18th century (cf. Declerck/Resch 2013).

There is also a potential for further development concerning the lexical and syntactical grammars of the module. At the moment, the local lexical grammars are focussed on recognising the different parts of compound nouns and split verbs (e.g., recognise "hervortreten" and "heraustreten"). However, we need to develop grammars that are able to identify truncated nouns such as "Staats- und Parteichef" that should be analysed in terms of two complete nouns. In addition, it would also be interesting to develop grammars that detect detached particles of split verbs as a semantic unity (e.g., "sie treten hervor").

Computer-assisted textual analysis of literary texts is a particularly complex task, as literary studies are primarily concerned with investigating textual complexity. Nevertheless, for more practical uses *NooJ* should be equipped with grammars that recognise basic sentence structures without embedded clauses. At the same time *NooJ* should provide grammars that are able to discover more practical information such as time and date indications or expressions of measurements. Hence, searching for useful information is not only the task of literary studies.

References

Baßler, M. and Karczewski, R.. 2007. "Computergestützte Literaturwissenschaft als Kulturwissenschaft. Eine Wunschliste." *Computerphilologie* 9.

Declerck, T. and Resch, C., ABaC:us – Austrian Baroque Corpus. Aufbau, Annotationen und Anwendungen." Vortrag am Historische Textkorpora für die Geistes- und Sozialwissenschaften. Fragestellungen und Nutzungsperspektiven in BBAW, Berlin (18.2.2013).

Flacius I., M. 1968. *De Ratione Cognoscendi Sacras Literas. Über den Erkenntnisgrund der Heiligen Schrift. Lateinisch-deutsche Parallelausgabe.* Lutz Geldsetzer (ed.). Düsseldorf: Stern-Verlag Janssen & Co.

Lieberman A., Erez, M., Jean-Baptiste, Shen, Yuan Kui, Presser Aiden, Aviva, Veres, Adrian, Gray, Matthew K., The Google Books Team, Pickett, Joseph P., Hoiberg, Dale, Clancy, Dan, Norvig, Peter, Orwant, Jon, Pinker, Steven and Nowak, Martin A. 2010. "Quantitative Analysis of Culture Using Millions of Digitized Books." *Scienceexpress.*

Moretti, F.. 2000. "Conjectures on World Literature." *New Left Review* 1: 54–68.

Müller, R.. 2012. *Die Metapher. Kognition, Korpusstilistik und Kreativität.* Paderborn: mentis.

Müller, R. and Lambrecht, T.. 2013. "'As if': Mapping the empathic eloquent narrator through literary history." *Language and Literature* 22:3: 175–190.

Schleiermacher, F. D. E. 1977. *Hermeneutik und Kritik. Mit einem Anhang sprachphilosophischer Texte Schleiermachers*. Frankfurt, Suhrkamp.

Schmid, H. *TreeTagger*. 1994ff.

Semino, E. and Short, M.. 2004. *Corpus Stylistics. Speech, Writing and Thought Presentation in a Corpus of English Writing.* London, New York: Routledge.

Silberztein, M., 2003.: *NooJ Manual*. available at

http://www.nooj4nlp.net.

Stubbs, M.. 2005. "Conrad in the Computer. Examples of Quantitative Stylistic Methods." *Language and Literature* 5,1: 5–24.

Szondi, P.. 1967. "Über philologische Erkenntnis." In Peter Szondi. *Hölderlin-Studien. Mit einem Traktat über philologische Erkenntnis.* 9–30. Frankfurt: Insel.

Wezel, J. K. 1997. *Herrmann und Ulrike.* Bernd Auerochs (ed.). Heidelberg: Matthes.

INTRODUCING MUSIC TO NOOJ

KRISTINA KOCIJAN, SARA LIBRENJAK AND ZDRAVKO DOVEDAN HAN

Abstract

NooJ has so far been used in various analyses of textual data in a wide variety of natural languages. In this project, we intend to explore the possibility of using NooJ for the analysis of sheet music notation which can be turned into textual notation with LilyPond software. Selection of two pieces chosen from a large database of classical music available online will serve us as test corpus for this stage of our project. Description of a dictionary of terms used in sheet music notation together with the description and examples of 20 syntactic grammars used for processing sheet music are given in detail. This introduction of music to NooJ opens up the doors for different analysis such as stylistic analysis of authors, composer comparison or musical genre detection to name a few.

Introduction

Many will agree that music is a language (Simões et.al., 2007), and that as such it can be analysed just as easily (or difficultly) (Nettl, 1958). If we can say that words of a language are coded using letters, numbers and symbols (like: *3-year old boy*), and language is something that we venture to analyse, than, if we code notes using the same set, we should be able to analyse it as well.

NooJ has so far been successfully used in various analyses of textual data in a wide variety of languages[1]. But, could NooJ read musical notes? If not, how could we make NooJ read musical notes? And even if we make NooJ read music, what can we do with that data?

This is just what our project is about. We intend to explore the possibility of using NooJ for the analysis of sheet music in order to find out, among other possible answers, what notes a composer uses the most,

[1] Acadian, Arabic, Armenian, Belarusian, Bulgarian, Catalan, Croatian, French, English, German, Greek, Hebrew, Hungarian, Italian, Latin, Polish, Portuguese, Russian, Serbian, Slovene, Spanish, Turkish, Vietnamese.

what octave does s/he prefer, what are the similarities among compositions from the same musical period, etc.

Since NooJ does not understand notes[2], we need to translate them into text before starting any kind of analysis. For this purpose we are using the *LilyPond* program's notation for musical notes and a free online library of classical music, as a courtesy of *Mutopia* project (Mutopia, 2013). Using this raw data, we created a NooJ environment that is able to read and process sheet music. Upon creating a dictionary of terms used in sheet music notation, 20 syntactic grammars for processing sheet music were created to get us started with the analyses of music.

Although some similar experiments were conducted using for example Cunningham-Grout-Bergen model (Cunningham et.al, 2005) or Weka open-source data mining toolkit (Simões et.al., 2007), this is, to our knowledge, the first attempt to describe the language of notes with the help of NooJ.

The Scope of our Research

If we observe musical notes as letters of an alphabet different from the Latin alphabet, one approach could be to convert that 'foreign' alphabet into the Latin one to make it easier to analyse. This is the road we choose to follow in order to introduce music to NooJ development environment. We explain the conversion in more details in sections on building the musical dictionary and syntactic grammars.

There are numerous linguistic-like procedures that can be undertaken after building the musical dictionary (Nettl, 1958). These can include stylistic analysis of respective authors, composer comparison or musical genre detection. At this stage of the project, we have decided on the following: counting the number of single tones, chords, beams and slurs (see Figure 1).

Single note Chord Beam Slur

Fig.4: Types of notes recognised by the syntactic grammars

[2] NooJ „only" understands the variants of DOS, EBCDIC, ISCII, ISO, OEM, Windows, MAC, UNICODE, Arabic ASMO, Japanese EUC and JIS varians, Korean EUC and Johab, character encodings (Silberztein, 2003:64).

In the following sections we will explain each step in more details.

Sample Compositions

Selecting a Sample

As a demonstration and a mind opener about what can be done with NooJ considering the musical sheets, we selected two compositions for the preliminary analysis. The selection includes two sonatas written during the classical musical era. The first one is written by W.A. Mozart in 1777 and the second one by L.van Beethoven in 1794/95.

Our source of musical material is a library of free content sheet music placed on the Mutopia Project web site. And, while Simões et.al. (2007) analysed the monophonic scores for violin, cello, flute, recorder and clarinet, at this stage of our research we will only analyse the scores for piano.

As our selection of scores shows, we used several criteria when choosing the works: the composers to be from the same musical era (we decided on classical musical period), the same form of music (sonata), they are played with only one instrument (piano) without vocal sections, they are prepared for the Mutopia by the same person[3] and are of approximately the same size.

Out of 1736 pieces of music available at the time when we started the research, there were 367 that were written for the piano. From that number we excluded 57 Traditional Swedish Folk Dances, 2 Anonymous pieces, 15 single representatives of a musical era and 175 pieces that were prepared for Mutopia by the author that has less than 2 pieces in his/her collection. From the remaining files, we excluded all the pieces that were shorter than 6 pages or longer than 10 pages which left us with 25 compositions (and three composers: Schubert, Beethoven and Mozart). However, since we needed to satisfy one more criteria (that the compositions were prepared by the same person), we were left with only one Mozart's Sonata (*Piano Sonata in C Major – KV 309 – 1st Part*) and 11 Beethoven's Sonatas (we chose *Sonata No.1 – 1st Movement: Allegro* since it is of similar length as Mozart's Sonata).

Our sample compositions have 8966 tokens (2519 of which are notes) and 6472 tokens (1886 of which are notes), respectively. The two pieces

---

[3] LilyPond software allows certain amount of freedom when describing notes, so with this restriction, we wanted to make sure to have unified notations in both compositions at this time of our research.

seem to be of quite different sizes, but the numbers are a bit misleading due to the value of notes used in each piece. In fact, they both have the same time signatures (4/4) and the number of bars is by only 6 larger in Beethoven's sonata[4]. Thus, we can conclude that the two pieces are of similar length.

Sample Text Modifications

We cleaned up both compositions by removing some forms of notations that were added to each piece either as as additional instructions for the layout design (paper-height, paper-width, line-width, padding, font-size, colour, etc.) or information about the person preparing the notation for the Mutopia site that were placed under the header section marked as *\header{}* like mutopiatitle, mutopiapoet, mutopiacomposer, etc., and the information that was placed inside the footer section marked as *footer ="Mutopia-yyyy/mm/dd-number"*. The data we deleted from the sample text was not considered to be of any relevance[5] for our research and since it produced lots of noise, we decided to erase it at this stage of the project development, so we can concentrate more on the notes themselves. However, we have left the trail to the original data by replacing the text with self-explanatory tags.

The following modifications were thus made in order to keep the reference to the original: everything marked as *footer = "...."* in the original LilyPond file was replaced with the notation **<footer>**, *\midi {...}* was replaced with **<midi>**, *\paper {...}* was replaced with **<paper>**, *\layout {...}* was replaced with **<layout>**, *tagline = \markup ...* was replaced with **<tagline>**, all the comments were replaced with a tag **<comment>.**

Building the musical dictionary

We started our musical NooJ journey with the construction of musical dictionary. Its content can be divided into two main parts (see Table 1 for examples):

1. the elements that describe the music:
    a. note,
    b. pause,

[4] Beethoven's Sonata has 153 bars, and Mozart's has 147.

[5] The purpose of our reasearch is not to parse the LilyPond notation but only to parse the musical notes presented by the LilyPond notation.

    c. ornament,
    d. grace note,
    e. dynamics,
    f. global information;
2. the elements that describe everything else on the page:
    a. description of composition (placed inside the header section of the document),
    b. note blocks (places where to put notes),
    c. page layout information,
    d. reference to deleted page descriptions/printer instructions.

With the help of LilyPond manual we described and manually added to the NooJ dictionary various musical terms. For the purpose of this research, we assigned to each of the musical terms one of the five categories: *N, PA, DYN, ORN* and *GN.*

Elements that describe the music	**Elements that describe everything else**
#use muzicke_note.nof **# N= notes** c,N+Octave=0+FLX=TRAJANJENE+LANG=Nederlands d,N+Octave=0+FLX=TRAJANJENE+LANG=Nederlands **#PA =pause** r,PA+Length=U **# ORN = ornaments** staccato,ORN **# GN = grace notes** grace,GN acciaccatura,GN **# DYN=changes in dynamics** cr,DYN+Value=crescendo f,DYN+Value=forte	**#inside the header** header,HEADER title,HEAD+Value=Title+DRV=HEADER composer,HEAD+Value=Composer+DRV=HEADER **#NB=note blocks-place where to put notes** score,NB+Level=0 new GrandStaff,NB+Level=1+UNAMB new StaffGroup,NB+Level=2+UNAMB new Staff,NB+Level=3+UNAMB **#PL= page layout** <comment>,PL+comment+UNAMB <footer>,PL+footer+UNAMB markup,MARK large,FONT+Value=markup

Table.2: Examples from musical NooJ dictionary

N stands for **note** and, at the dictionary level, describes only the name of the musical note (c, d, e, f, g, a, b). This is the only category in the dictionary that has FLX property (see next section for the details). **Pause** is marked as PA to distinguish it from other notes on the sheet.

DYN marks the changes in **dynamics** or the volume of the note (e.g. *pp, pppp, ffff, fp, sf, sfz*) and has an additional attribute Value (e.g. *piano, forte*).

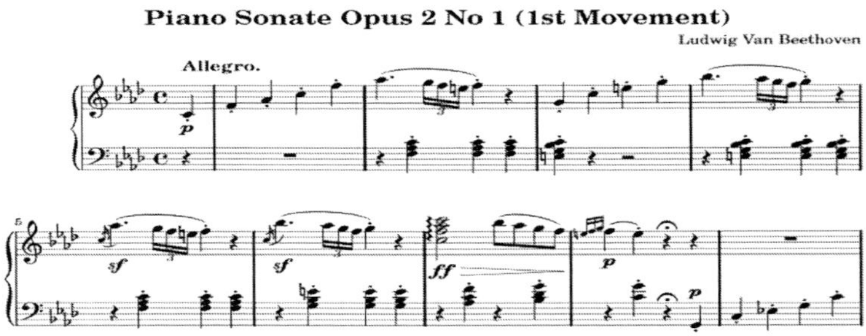

Fig.5: Musical notation

Different types of **ornaments** (e.g. *staccato, arpeggio, trill, prall*) are marked as ORN while **grace notes** (e.g. *grace, acciaccatura*, and *appoggiatura*) are marked as GN.

Now, instead of making NooJ read musical sheet as shown in Figure 2, it reads the notes' descriptions as presented in Figure 3.

```
\header {
 title = "Piano Sonate Opus 2 No 1 (1st Movement)"
 composer = "Ludwig Van Beethoven" ...}
\score {
 \new GrandStaff <<
 \new Staff = "up" {
 \clef treble
 \key f \minor
 \time 4/4
 \tempo 4 = 190
 \repeat volta 2 { \partial 4 c'4\p\staccato^\markup { \large \bold "Allegro."
} f'\staccato aes'\staccato c''\staccato f''\staccato aes''4.( \times 2/3 { g''16[ f''
e''] } f''4\staccato) r4 g'\staccato c''\staccato e''\staccato g''\staccato bes''4.(
\times 2/3 { aes''16[ g'' f''] } g''4\staccato) r4 \acciaccatura c''16 aes''4.\sf(
\times 2/3 { g''16[ f'' e''] } f''4\staccato) r4 \acciaccatura c''16 bes''4. ...}
```

Fig.6: Musical sheet – LilyPond notation

Inflectional Grammar

As already mentioned, there is only one category in the dictionary that uses the FLX property and that is the note category – **N**. In addition to the category, the note has 3 more properties defined: ***octave, language*** and ***FLX***.

All the notes from the main dictionary are described as belonging to the primary octave marked as <**Octave=0**>**.** The octave, together with the information about the length, changes after applying syntactic grammar for defining the complete[6] note.

Each note has accidental suffixes (**sharp**-sharp, **flat**-flat, **dblsharp**-double sharp, and **dblflat**-double flat notes) which were the main reason for building inflectional grammar. Since LilyPond supports 11 different sets (languages[7]) of note names, which differ not only in the note names but accidental suffixes as well, we decided to describe these changes using FLX property. So, depending on the language, the paradigms were marked as TRAJANJExy – where xy stands for the first two letters of the language it represents.

For example, the suffixes for accidentals in Netherland's notation are described as:

TRAJANJENE = **<E>/main + is/sharp + es/flat + isis/dblsharp + eses/dblflat;**

This way, the concordance for **<c>** will find all the forms of note 'c': ***c***, ***cis***, ***ces***, ***cisis*** and ***ceses.*** We can compare this to the results of a search for the forms of a verb **<play>** which would include: ***play, plays, playing*** and ***played***.

Syntactic Grammars

We build 20 syntactic grammars to complete our goal in finding all the single notes, chords, beams and slurs. We can divide them in the following manner:

- **disambiguating f** – 'f' is a name of a note, but it is also used for *forte* i.e. as dynamics in the case it is proceeded with a backslash;

[6] The complete note consists of a note name, octave, length and ornament if available (see the next section for details).

[7] Nederlands, Catalan, Deutsch, English, Espanol, Italiano, Norsk, Portugues, Suomi, Svenska and Vlaams.

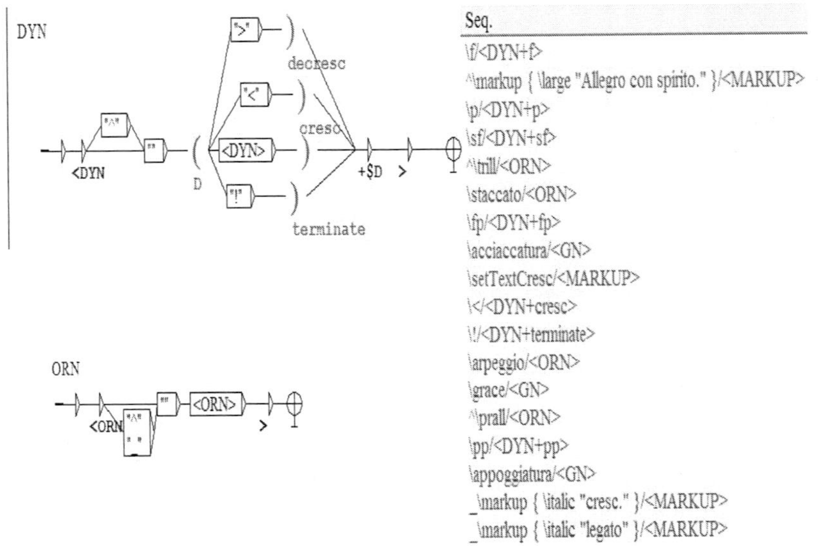

Fig.7: Description of dynamics and ornaments with an extract of related concordances

- **markers** – all the words that are not part of a note but are written inside the note blocks (style information) are tagged as <MARKUP>, while ornaments, grace notes and dynamics that come with obligatory backslash (\) and optional position markers (^, _) before the ornament itself are tagged as <ORN>, <GN> and <DYN>, respectively (Figure 4);
- **brackets** – 4 types of brackets are used in the text: '( )' for slurs, '[ ]' for beams, '< >' for chords and curly brackets'{ }' that have several uses (check LilyPond Music Glossary for details); each bracket has been marked as <BRA+Open+S|B|C|V> or <BRA+Close +SC|BC|CC|VC> (Figure 5);
- **octaves** – in LilyPond notation, octaves above the primary octave are marked with 1, 2, 3 or 4 apostrophes, while the octaves below the primary one are marked with 1, 2, 3 or 4 commas if found immediately after a note or pause; in NooJ we annotated the first set as <OC+Octave=1|2|3|4> and the second one as <OC+Octave=m1|m2|m3|m4> where 'm' stands for 'minus' (Figure 5);

Seq.	Seq.
(/<BRA+Open+S>	a,,/<OC+Octave=m2>
)/<BRA+Close+SC>	a,/<OC+Octave=m1>
[/<BRA+Open+B>	a'/<OC+Octave=1>
]/<BRA+Close+BC>	a''/<OC+Octave=2>
{/<BRA+Open+V>	aes'/<OC+Octave=1>
}/<BRA+Close+CV>	aes''/<OC+Octave=2>
</<BRA+Open+C>	ais''/<OC+Octave=2>
>/<BRA+Close+CC>	b,,/<OC+Octave=m2>

Fig.8: Excerpt of concordances for Brackets <BRA> and Octaves <CC> grammars

- **single notes** – 11 grammars that given below describe the complete notes (including pauses) taking into account the name of the note (c, d, fis, ces etc.), octave (-4 ... 4), length (1, 2, 4, 8, 16, 32, 64, 128) and additional ornamentation (staccato, arpeggio, trill, prall, fermata) that the note may or may not have. If there is a notation indicating grace note[8] prior to the note name, this notation is also considered to be part of the note it proceeds. The first grammar from this set recognises single notes (Figure 6), including pauses, with all the information given next to the note name.
-

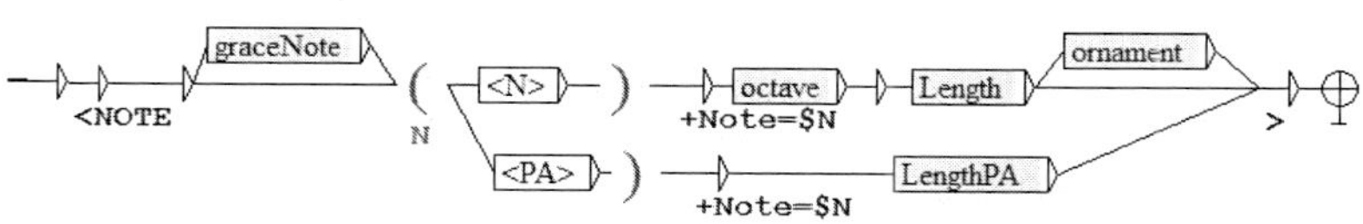

Fig.9: Grammar recognising single notes with all the information immediately after the note name

Entire recognised string is marked as **<NOTE, Note=note name +Octave=*Octave*+Length=*Length*+Ornament=*Ornament*>[9].**
Of course, it is quite natural for a note to appear without ornament, but this cannot be said for *Length* since all notes must have this attribute.

---

[8] Small ornamental notes whose length is not included in the total lentgh of the bar.
[9] Note name =c|d|e|f|g|a|b|their alternations (cis, ces, dis, des etc.);
Octave= 1|2|3|4|m1|m2|m3|m4; Length =1|2|4|8|16|32|64|128;
Ornament = trill|staccato|arpeggio|prall.

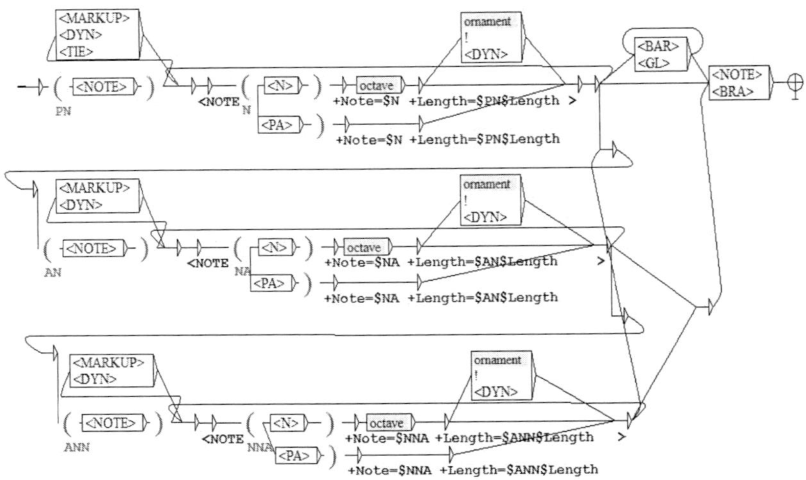

Fig.10: Recognising lengthless notes positioned between two complete notes

However, LilyPond's notation allows this value to be inherited from either the last note that has this information and is positioned any number of places before the note we are analysing, or from the first note that has this information and is positioned after the first closed chord bracket that can be any number of places after the note we are analysing.

For this reason, we had to introduce 10 more syntactic grammars that search for those notes placed between two complete <NOTE>s and, depending on the context, inherit the Length property either from the complete note that is before it (Figure 7) or after it.

- **set of notes** – the last 5 grammars are recognising chords, beams and slurs found as separate instances, or when in combination with one another. Only after all the notes are annotated with their complete information, we apply the chords/beams/slurs grammars so that their annotations can inherit all the information about the <NOTE>s they consist of. At this time, we are only adding information about the note name (Figure 8), but this can be augmented with the information about each note's octave, length and/or ornament.

```
Seq.
a''^\prall([ g''\staccato])/<SLUR+Notes=a<BEAM+Notes=a g> g>
g''8([ e''])/<SLUR+Notes=g<BEAM+Notes=g e> e>
g''8.^\trill([ fis''32 g''] d'''4 e''')/<SLUR+Notes=g<BEAM+Notes=g fis g> fis gd e>
<c''! fis'' c'''!>4\fp\arpeggio/<CHORD+Notes=c fis c>
<fis a d'>/<CHORD+Notes=fis a d>
<g, g>\staccato/<CHORD+Notes=g g>
<g,, g,>2/<CHORD+Notes=g g>
dis''\staccato[ a'\staccato c''\staccato fis'\staccato]/<BEAM+Notes=dis a c fis>
e'8.[ d'16 c'8. b16]/<BEAM+Notes=e d c b>
g32[ bes d']/<BEAM+Notes=g bes d>
a8( c' a c' f c' f c' e c' e c' c c' c c' f a f d')/<SLUR+Notes=a c a c f c f c e c e c c c c c f a f d>
b,16\f( g fis g a g fis g b,4)/<SLUR+Notes=b g fis g a g fis g b>
f''( c''' aes'' g'' fis'')/<SLUR+Notes=f c aes g fis>
f''^\prall( e''\staccato)/<SLUR+Notes=f e>
```

Fig.11: Excerpt of concordances for chords, beams, slurs and their combinations

After applying all of the grammars to the composition, we are able to determine the number and type of single notes used, note values, intervals, chords, beams and slurs. The results (see section on Results for more details) we get from our sample compositions look as a good start for any further analysis of musical sheets transcribed using LilyPond notation.

Results

After applying the linguistic analysis, we were able to check the distribution of single notes in each Sonata. The results show that Beethoven (Table 2) used the most note C among natural notes, sharp F among sharp notes and flat A among flat notes. There are no sharp C, sharp D, sharp E, sharp G, sharp A or sharp B in his Sonata.

	c	D	e	f	g	a	b	R
natural	356	52	93	242	193	19	42	194
flat	6	148	161	11	20	179	168	/
sharp	0	0	0	2	0	0	0	/
1886	362	200	254	255	213	198	210	194

Table.3: Distribution of notes in Beethoven

Mozart (Table 3) also used the note C among the natural notes and sharp F among sharp notes the most, but used flat B among flat notes and did not use sharp B, or flat C, F and G at all.

	C	D	e	f	g	a	b	r
natural	399	379	271	157	391	246	243	146
flat	0	5	16	0	0	13	37	/
sharp	40	18	2	124	30	2	0	/
2519	439	402	289	281	421	261	280	146

Table.4: Distribution of notes in Mozart

We can go even further in our analyses and see more detailed distribution for each note (see Table 4 for an example), depending on the octave and length as well.

Note	Oct.	Len.	#
		1	2
		2	4
		4	18
	1	8	90
a		8.	4
		16	41
		32	2
	2	1	1
		2	4
		4	9
	2	8	23
a		16	31
		32	3
	m1	2	2
		4	6
a		8	3
	m1	16	2
	m2	2	1
aes	1	8	8
		16	2
	2	8	3
ais	2	8	2

Table.5: Detailed distribution of Mozart's note 'a' with all its variants

The distribution of top 5 chords, beams and slurs for both compositions is given in Table 5. At this time, we only considered the note names inside the chords, beams and slurs without taking into account the octave or the length properties.

Mozart			Beethoven		
<CHORD>	<BEAM>	<SLUR>	<CHORD>	<BEAM>	<SLUR>
25 <c c>	4 [c e g]	10 (e f d c)	7 <f aes c>	6 [g f e]	5 (aes g f e f)
18 <g g>	3 [a d a d]	8 (f e)	5 <c f aes c>	4 [aes g f]	4 (a c bes)
13 <c g>	3 [b d b d]	7 (a g)	4 <c c>	3 [c bes a]	4 (bes aes g f g)
10 <a a>	3 [e d c b]	6 (b a)	4 <des des>	3 [des c b]	4 (f f e e)
7 <c e>	3 [f e]	6 (c b)	4 <e g bes c>	3 [ees des c]	4 (fes ees des bes g)

Table.6: Distribution of top 5 chords, beams and slurs

If it is true that an individual (even brief) composition carries stylistic tendencies and structural rules as Nettl (1958) argues, then our results could be used to prove that other works of our test authors would show similar results. Well, at least now we have a way to prove or disprove this.

References

Cunningham, S., Grout, V., Bergen, H. 2005, *Mozart to Metallica: A Comparison of Musical Sequences and Similarities* in Proceedings of the ISCA 18th International Conference on Computer Applications in Industry and Engineering, Honolulu, Hawaii, USA, pp. 332-339.

LilyPond Music Glossary, http://tinyurl.com/q8jz49w (visited on July, 1st 2013).

Mutopia, http://www.mutopiaproject.org/ (visited on July, 1st 2013).

Nettl, B. 1958, *Some Linguistic Approaches to Musical Analysis* in Journal of the International Folk Music Council Vol.10, International Council for Traditional Music, pp 37-41.

Silberztein, M. 2003, NooJ manual. http://www.nooj4nlp.net (223 pages)

Simões, A., Lourenço, A., Almeida J.J. 2007, *Using Text Mining Techniques for Classical Music Scores Analysis* in New Trends in Artifical Intelligence (eds. J. Neves, M.F. Santos, J.M.Mahado), pp 791-799.

STORM PROJECT: TOWARDS A NOOJ MODULE WITHIN ARMADILLO DATABASE TO MANAGE MUSEUM COLLECTION

RANIA SOUSSI, SLIM MESFAR AND MATHIEU FAGET

Abstract

The STORM project aims to gather museum data collections, especially about Arabic culture and art. Then, it also allows to enrich them with the existing information in the open linked data, and to offer to the user the possibility to perform multilingual queries on them. STORM uses semantic web technologies to defeat the different challenges related to these tasks.
The main contribution of this work is to propose a generic architecture that stores all the museum collection (potentially from heterogeneous data sources) with a uniform model using Armadillo database. Firstly, the data will be analysed using NooJ linguistic engine integrated with the Armadillo indexing process and based on a museum entities ontology (built in the project's context). Secondly, the stored data will be enriched in the Armadillo database using the available linked open data. Finally, the Armadillo querying module will use the concordance indexes from NooJ analysis step to process user queries.

Introduction

The increasing publication of linked data makes the vision of the semantic web a probable reality and these data an important information resource which can be used to complete the data sources in enterprises, newspapers, museums and so on.

At the same time, cultural institutions such as museums, archives or libraries typically have large databases of metadata records describing the objects they curate as well as thesauri and other authority files used for these metadata fields.

However, these databases are proprietary databases. Recently, museums have been trying to make these data available to be connected with open linked data. However, the experience so far shows that publishing museum data on the linked data cloud is difficult: the databases are large and complex, the information is richly structured and varies from museum to museum, and data can be multilingual.

In this context, the STORM project proposes to design a new tool to manage and disseminate museum data collections in French, English and Arabic as cultural open data.

The STORM project has three main purposes: (1) Collect the vocabulary used in different museums to describe the same objects and make it available through an open portal to be enriched by experts, (2) Store all the museum collections (from heterogeneous data sources) with a uniform model using Armadillo database, and enrich them with the existing information in the open linked data, (3) Perform multilingual queries on the collections.

The rest of the paper is organised as follows. We first depict our general architecture and then detail the various processes involved: lexicon construction and enhancement, corpus treatment and query processing.

General Architecture

The general architecture is depicted in figure 1. The main components are summarised as follows:

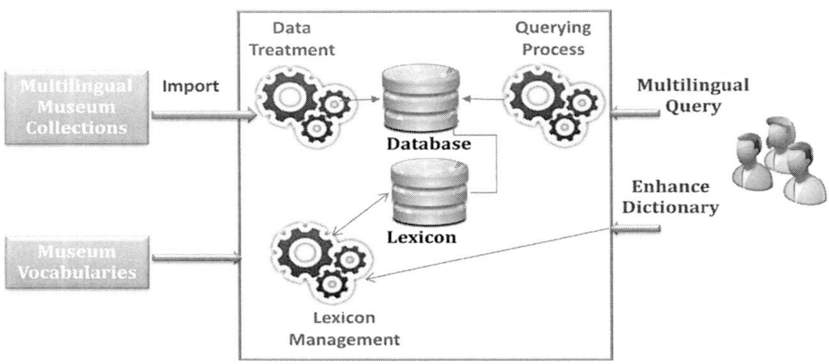

Fig.1: STORM general architecture

1. **Lexicon Management**: as a first step lexicon is collected from the different museums and culture institutions. Then, the lexicon is enriched by different experts.
2. **Data treatment**: this module allows analysing museum collections using the common vocabulary and storing them in Armadillo database and a uniform model.
3. **Querying process**: this module allows querying the stored collections with multilingual queries.

Each component will be described in detail in the next sections.

Lexicon Management

As a main step of the project, it is mandatory to regroup the lexicon and vocabulary of the different museums in order to use it in the treatment of the museum collections corpus. In order to easily manage the lexicon, we use the linguistic development environment NooJ. It includes tools for constructing, testing and maintaining large-coverage lexical resources. These lexical resources will be applied to historical texts in order to locate morphological, lexicological and syntactic patterns, remove ambiguities, and tag simple and compound words.

The initial lexical entries are provided by our partner INVISU from the French National Institute of Art History (INHA – Institut National d'Histoire de l'Art). Our first mission is to build three trilingual dictionaries (Arabic, English and French).

Furthermore, these dictionaries will be enriched by experts using web interface that will be deployed at the last step of the project.

Building trilingual dictionaries: Arabic culture lexicon

In this paper we describe the building process of the French lexical entries. Since the dictionary has to be trilingual, each French lexical entry is associated with, at least, its English and Arabic translations or set of translations.

Our main dictionary includes lexical entries representing historical monuments. For each monument we provide:

- The part-of-speech: Noun, Adjective, …
- The inflectional description (in case of a declinable entry)
- The monument type: mosque, mausoleum, citadel, church, …
- The style or period: Tulunid, Abbassid, Ottoman, …
- The localisation / the city

- The founder (a historical person)
- Founding dates : anno hegirae and anno domini
- The list of orthographical variants
- The list of synonyms
- Arabic translation
- English translation

Obviously, we added more general lexical entries to integrate monument types or styles. These lexical entries are detailed and associated with sufficient properties in order to be able to recognise inflected and derived forms. In the following section, we show the equivalent entries from the three trilingual dictionaries:

A sample French lexical entry:

ʿAmr ibn al-ʿĀṣ,N+FLX=Neutre
+Categorie="Monument"
+Type="mosquée"
+Style="xxx"
+Localisation="miṣr al-qadīma"
+Fondateur="ʿAmr ibn al-ʿĀṣ"
+AnnoHegire="21"+AnnoDomini="641"
+Ar="عمرو بن العاص"
+En="Amr ibn el-As"

The corresponding English lexical entry

Amr ibn el-As,N+FLX=Neutre
+Categorie="monument"
+Type="mosque"
+Style="xxx"
+Localisation="miṣr al-qadīma"
+Fondateur="ʿAmr ibn al-ʿĀṣ"
+AnnoHegire="21"+AnnoDomini="641"
+Ar="عمرو بن العاص"
+Fr="ʿAmr ibn al-ʿĀṣ"

The corresponding Arabic lexical entry :

عمرو بن العاص,N+FLX=Neutre
+Categorie="Monument"
+Type="mosquée"
+Style="xxx"
+Localisation="miṣr al-qadīma"
+Fondateur="ʿAmr ibn al-ʿĀṣ"

+AnnoHegire="21"+AnnoDomini="641"
+Fr="ʿAmr ibn al-ʿĀṣ"
+En="Amr ibn el-As"

Since we formalised a link between the three trilingual dictionaries, it will be possible to detect all synonyms and related terms starting from a simple monolingual query. Using some easy routines, it is also possible to identify all associated translations as well as their inflected forms, derived forms and synonyms.

Furthermore, we developed a set of morphological grammars to deal with contractions and agglutination, especially for Arabic texts. In fact, the Arabic agglutination phenomena cause serious problems for the automatic analysis of Arabic since an Arabic word can have several possible analyses: proclitic(s), inflected form and enclitic. We start our analysis with the application of a decomposition system, implemented via a NooJ morphological grammar, to each word of the text to identify its radical and affixes. In the second step, grammars (finite-state transducers) produce lexical constraints checking the validity of segmentation thanks to a dictionary lookup. So, these grammars associate the recognition of a word to lexical constraints, working only with valid combinations of the various components of the form [Mesfar, 2010].

Lexicon Enhancement

In order to enrich the dictionaries, we have created a web interface that allows Arabic culture experts to add new concepts.

The concepts are defined as follow:

$c = (l, \lg, d, \sum_{1}^{n} sy_i, \sum_{1}^{n} sr_i)$, where:

- l: the concept label
- lg: the concept language
- d: the concept definition
- $\sum_{1}^{n} sy_i$: is the set of synonyms, which can be multilingual; each sy_i is defined by the pair $(w_i, \lg_i)$, where w_i is the synonym of the concept c and $\lg_i$ is the corresponding language.

- $\sum_{1}^{n} sr_i$: is the set of semantic relations which can have the concept c with other concepts in the vocabularies database; sr_i is defined by (r_i, c_i), where r_i is the relation name and c_i is the concept name.

  We take the example of the concept 'vase':
- l: 'vase'
- lg: 'english'
- d: a vessel used as an ornament or for holding cut flowers
- $\sum_{1}^{n} sy_i$: ('vase','fr');('مزهرية','ar')
- $\sum_{1}^{n} sr_i$:(skos:broader,pottery)

An expert validates the new added concept in the database.

However, to use the collected vocabulary in other existing ontology or to link it to open linked data schema, it is mandatory to model it with standard language. In this context, we have chosen to use SKOS [Miles et al., 2007] which is a W3C recommendation designed for representation of thesauri and vocabulary by using RDF and RDFS triple [Klyne et al., 2004]. A triple consists of three parts: the subject, the predicate and the object.

Each dictionary concept is modelled using SKOS as follow:

<c> rdf:type skos:concept
  skos:prefLabel l@lng
  skos :altLabel w_i @ $\lg_i$
 ri ci

For the example above, the corresponding SKOS triples are the following:

<vase> rdf:type skos:concept
  skos:prefLabel vase@en
  skos :altLabel vase@fr
  skos :altLabel مزهرية @ar
  skos:broader <pottery>

Then finally, we have built an Arabic culture museum ontology using SKOS.

Data treatment using the Arabic culture lexicon

Having the corresponding lexicon, we can analyse and annotate the domain corpus. The domain corpus is treated as follow (see Figure 2):

1. Firstly, the corpus is semantically analysed and predefined vocabulary is detected in each document.
2. Finally, the annotated corpus is indexed and stored in the Armadillo database.

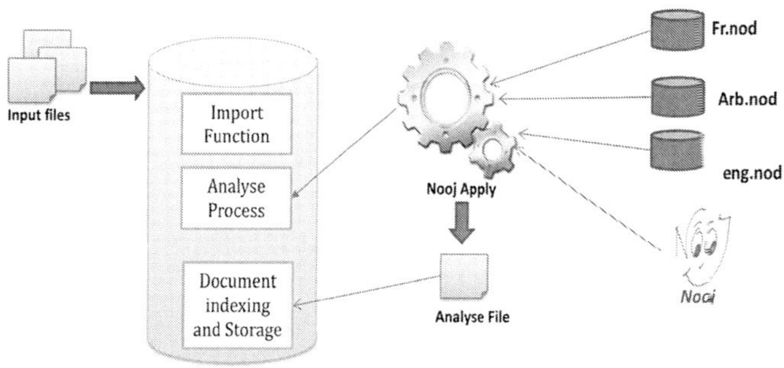

Fig.2: The data treatment process

Linguistic analysis

The goal of this step is to identify relevant information in the corpus. In our context, the indexing process aims to detect the lexicon concepts in the documents.

As a first step, the corpus is annotated using NooJApply. NooJApply is a command-line program allowing us to use NooJ functionalities in external programs.

NooJApply provides specific annotation and is executed with the following command:

NooJApply lng outputFile resourceFiles inputFiles,
where :

- lng: is the input files languages, which can be Ar, Fr or En
- outputFile: the annotation file
- resourceFiles: list of resources which can be a NooJ dictionary, grammar, …
- inputFiles: is the set of files to process

Using the command above, NooJ builds a Text Annotation Structure (TAS) in which each linguistic unit is represented by a corresponding annotation.

An annotation stores the position in the text of the text unit to be represented, its length, linguistic information and the translation in the other languages.

The resulting annotation is then stored in the Armadillo database in order to create specific index.

For instance, from the text depicted in Figure 3, NooJApply extracts the annotation presented in Figure 4.

Un pichet est un petit récipient à col légèrement resserré et disposant d'un bec verseur, avec ou sans poignée, permettant le service des boissons à table.
Les pichets peuvent être en verre, céramique ou métal.
Un grand pichet à anse peut également être appelé broc à eau.
Une Jarre (de l'arabe djara « vase d'argile à large bouche ») est un grand vase de terre cuite, de forme ovoïde et de différentes dimensions, où l'on conserve l'eau, l'huile, les olives.
De son nom ont dérivé différentes appellations.

Fig.3: French text sample.

```
3,9,<pichet,N+EN="jug"+AR="إبْريق|قبْنج"+Genre=m+Nb=s>
149,154,<table,N+EN="table"+AR="طَاوِلَة"+Genre=f+Nb=s>
161,168,<pichet,N+EN="jug"+AR="إبْريق|قبْنج"+Genre=m+Nb=p>
222,228,<pichet,N+EN="jug"+AR="إبْريق|قبْنج"+Genre=m+Nb=s>
284,289,<jarre,N+EN="jar"+AR="جَرَّة"+Genre=f+Nb=s>
310,314,<vase,N+EN="vase"+AR="إنَاء"+Genre=f+Nb=s>
355,359,<vase,N+EN="vase"+AR="إنَاء"+Genre=f+Nb=s>
```

Fig.4: NooJApply annotation result

Document indexing and storage process

After analysing the corpus with NooJApply, we obtain a set of analysis files which annotate each document separately. The document indexing and storage process aims to use these annotations to index the corpus documents in the Armadillo database and then store it within a uniform model. In this section, we start by presenting Armadillo indexes and the process of the semantic indexes based on NooJ annotation. Finally, we discuss the storage model.

Armadillo database Indexes

A database index [LU et al,2000] is a data structure that improves the speed of data retrieval operations on a database table. Indexes can be created using one or more columns of a database table. Armadillo has devised new indexes which are the result of a function (trigger) applied on the columns of the original table. These indexes are also based on virtual columns which can be used as standard columns for querying in the 'where' clause.

Let us build a case insensitive index on the column 'state' of our example table Person.

id	name	state
1	Mark Twain	Mississipi
2	Jack London	California

Fig.5: Table example.

A standard index on this table column is created as follows:

create index ix_Person_state on Person (state)

And the index entries are: {California, Mississipi}. A trigger index is a program specifying the function to perform, in our case the UPPER function. The trigger is: IndexPersonState = UPPER(state)

Then we can use it to create the case insensitive index:

create index ix_Person_state on Person (state) index_trigger IndexPersonState

The index entries are transformed to {CALIFORNIA, MISSOURI}.

In this context, any function can be devised and any column combination can be used. For example, the full text index can be written like that:

IndexPersonText=WORDS(concat(name,state,city,...)),

where WORDS function passes to the index an array with all the distinct words found in the specified columns.

One can see that there is no column name available to use the index in a standard SQL query. Therefore, the notion of a virtual column has been added to use the desired index.

The creation order becomes: create index ix_Person_text on Person (virtual text lchr) index_trigger IndexPersonText

and a typical query can be:

select * from Person where text='Twain' and text='California'

There is no limit to the indexes which can be built on the same column or group of columns to create virtual columns used like ordinary columns to perform sophisticated searches.

We can define three main classes of indexes in Armadillo

- The programmable indexes we have seen above.
- The paragraph indexes, which are based on programmable indexes. These indexes, intended for long texts, can split a document in paragraphs and perform searches in the context of each paragraph.
- The proximity indexes, which are used to query all pairs of words found close together in the document.
- The associative indexes, which have been devised to index automatically xml documents and transform tags in virtual columns and tag attributes in virtual columns content.

Armadillo NooJ indexes

As we have seen in the previous section, Armadillo index is a function or a trigger posed on a table: Index(index_name) = function(table column_list). An index is built after a real table, but the function which gives birth to it can be any procedure. Then, it is perfectly suited to NooJ principles.

NooJ performs dynamic text analysis. This analysis can be completely embedded in an Armadillo index trigger. The result of the analysis can be used by an Armadillo programmable index to populate automatically virtual columns of the database.

The first index can be the index built after the vocabulary in all the languages.

For the result annotation presented in Figure 4, pichet and pichets are indexed as PICHET, JUG and قِدْح|إبْرِيق. Then, when a user is looking for قِدْح|إبْرِيق, they obtain all the records containing either Arabic, English or French terms with all their forms.

Other programmable indexes can be added at will, such as Genre, Number, Tense, and so on.

Storing Data

The corpus documents are imported in the database and stored with their annotations using four tables:

- Database (*id,tbname,datatype)*: this table describes the source corpus, where the *id* is the corpus unique identifier in the database, *tbname* is the corpus name and *datatype* is the data type which can be a set of documents, images, etc.

- Columns *(colno,tbname, name,coltype)*: this table describes the metadada of each corpus, where *colno* is column number, *tbname* is the related corpus name, *name* is the column name, *coltype* is the column type
- Document *(docid, tbname, fields, content)*: this table contains the set of documents, where *docid* is the document identifier, *tbname* is the corpus name, *fields* is the value of the metadata in this document and *content* is the document content.
- Concept *(docid, concept, metadata)*: this table describes the lexicon concepts contained in each document, where *docid* is the document that contains the concept, *concept* is the concept value and *metadata* is the set of information provided from NooJ.

The stored documents are then indexed using the Armadillo-NooJ indexes described above. These data can be exported to RDF forma in order to be linked or exploited with open linked data.

Querying process

This module allows the STORM project users to query the resources using natural or SPARQL query.

In the case of a natural query, it is analysed with NooJ to obtain the list of terms derived from the query terms. Then, the query is transformed into a sql query adapted to find a multilingual result in the stored document.

In the case of the SPARQL query, it will directly retrieve the SKOS files using a research index.

Conclusion

This paper presents a software application developed within the STORM Project. This application allows users to retrieve information from a corpus of museum text collection, using queries in Arabic, English or French. NooJ is ensuring the whole linguistic analysis layer (lexical and morphological) and querying steps. The generated analysis and querying indexes are used within the Aramadillo indexing engine.

Acknowledgements

This work is supported by STORM (**S**émantisation et triples**tor**e **M**ultilingue) research project.

References

Klyne, G., Carroll, J., and Mcbride, B. "*Resource description framework (RDF): Concepts and abstract syntax*". W3C recommendation, 2004, vol. 10.

Lu, H., NG, Y. Y., and Tian, Z. "*T-tree or b-tree: Main memory database index structure revisited*". In: Database Conference, 2000. ADC 2000. Proceedings. 11th Australasian. IEEE, 2000. p. 65-73.

Mesfar, S. "*Towards a Cascade of Morpho-syntactic Tools for Arabic Natural Language Processing*". Proceedings of the International Conference CICLing 2010, LNCS Springer Verlag, p. 150-162.

Miles, A. and Perez-Aguera, J. R. "*SKOS: Simple knowledge organisation for the web. Cataloging & Classification Quarterly*", 2007, vol. 43, no 3-4, p. 69-83.

Silberztein M., 2003. *NooJ Manual*. Available at: www.nooj4nlp.net.